Because He Could

Also by Dick Morris

Rewriting History
Off with Their Heads
Power Plays
Behind the Oval Office
Bum Rap on America's Cities

Because He Could

Dick Morris

and Eileen McGann

10 ReganBooks
Celebrating Ten Bestselling Years
An Imprint of HarperCollins*Publishers*

HarperCollins books may be purchased for educational, business, or sales promotional use. For information please write: Special Markets Department, HarperCollins Publishers Inc., 10 East 53rd Street, New York, NY 10022.

FIRST EDITION

Designed by: Publications Development Company of Texas

Printed on acid-free paper

Library of Congress Cataloging-in-Publication Data has been applied for.

ISBN 0-06-078415-6

04 05 06 07 08 PDC/RRD 10 9 8 7 6 5 4 3 2 1

A Note on the Authors

This is the fourth book my wife, Eileen, and I have written together. But it's the first time she has let me add her name to the cover.

For the purposes of clarity and style, we generally use my voice to describe my conversations with President Clinton; in a few places we use the first person plural to describe events in which we both participated. The book as a whole, however, is jointly written. And both Eileen and I have a lot to write about. During the twenty years I worked with Clinton she served as my political consultant and adviser, guiding me with her insights through the maze of the president's peculiar mind. Now, her observations of this complex man animate our joint work.

—Dick Morris

*To the two genies: Gene Morris, Dick's father,
and Jeanne McGann, Eileen's mother*

Contents

Acknowledgments

We would like to thank Joni Evans for her support, advice, and encouragement. Judith Regan made this book possible with her sharp instincts and quick mind. Cal Morgan's editing hand was, as always, deft and skilled. Katie Maxwell's research was timely and accurate. We thank Tom Gallagher for helping to pull it all together.

Thanks also to Jennifer Suitor, an incredible publicist, who develops a promotional schedule that makes running for president seem like part-time work. And thanks also to Cassie Jones, Anna Bliss, Paul Brown, Katie Vecchio, and Nancy Land.

1

Cracking the Clinton Code

A riddle wrapped in a mystery inside an enigma": Sir Winston Churchill's famous phrase has become familiar shorthand for almost anything we cannot easily understand. And in modern politics no figure embodies this phenomenon better than our forty-second president, William Jefferson Clinton. So much about him is still a puzzle. Even after eight years of watching his extraordinarily visible presidency and twelve years of listening to the endless scrutiny of his personality by pundits from every segment of the political spectrum, we still can't really say that we truly understand this complex, contradictory man.

Bill Clinton is a study in opposites. Consider the facts: He was one of the most popular and successful presidents in modern history. At the same time, he was disgraced by his transgressions in office, becoming only the second president to be impeached by the House of Representatives since the creation of our republic. As the first post-modern president, he was revered as a cultural icon by his supporters, while at the same time loathed and reviled by his opponents as "illegitimate." His charisma, intellect, and charm are the core of his attractiveness, and captivate even the most skeptical observers. But his dark side—his moodiness, temper, self-absorption, and lack of discipline—are unappealing and make him an easy target for his critics. Even reaction to the story of his life, as he has now told it in book form, has been widely split. When he appears on television to hype its publication, the ratings go through the roof. And yet, when reviewed in print, the book has been panned, even ridiculed. This polarity itself—in his personality and in his image—only adds to his mystery and his celebrity. Whether they love him or hate him, the public wants to know all they can about him.

So curious are Americans about who Bill Clinton really is that his memoir, *My Life,* sold more than a million copies in its first weeks. In fact, among politicians, Clinton's only serious rival in the nonfiction best-seller lists has been his equally opaque wife, Hillary Rodham Clinton, and her autobiography, *Living History.*

But the two memoirs are as different as Bill and Hillary themselves. In *Living History,* a thoroughly self-disciplined woman carefully masks who she really is. In *My Life,* a very complicated and sometimes dysfunctional man inadvertently and unwittingly reveals his actual character—at least to readers diligent enough to find him in its almost one thousand pages.

My Life is a metaphor for Bill Clinton himself. Like him, it is sometimes interesting, sometimes refreshingly open, sometimes fascinating. Just as often, however, it is incomplete, misleading, chaotic, overly detailed, superficial, and inconsistent. Still, hidden among the disorder is the remarkable story of who Bill Clinton is. And that story is very different from the one he tries to tell, and to sell. Despite the 957 pages he has exhaustively written about himself, the Bill Clinton in *My Life,* remains impenetrable, lurking somewhere behind the mind-numbing litany of trips, meetings, campaign stops, meals, and scandals. At first glance, his book seems to reveal little about his thinking, his motivations, or his emotions. He even manages to avoid telling us about the obvious pain and humiliation he must have suffered when he was impeached; instead he merely expresses contempt and rage.

Yet, once we begin judging the text of *My Life* against the available evidence—by piecing together what he says, what he doesn't say, what others have said, and what the public record shows actually happened—a clearer, more accurate picture of the man emerges. In fact, in order to find the real Bill Clinton within the pages of *My Life*, it's important to understand what I think of as the Clinton Code—correlating what Clinton says (or doesn't say) with other data and experience, and reconciling the obvious differences. Without that Code, we cannot grasp all of the former president's assets and failings, his unique abilities, and his countervailing limitations, as they are exposed in the book.

As a twenty-year veteran of Bill Clinton's campaigns and administrations, I have long and rich experience with his politics, his thinking, and his personality. For years I observed him at close range; I watched him think and act, make decisions, delay decisions, and avoid decisions. Eventually I grew confident that I understood his mind and motivations. And yet, despite all my experience with Clinton, not until I read *My Life* did I fully crack the Clinton Code. There, like a patient who has spent too long talking on his psychiatrist's couch, Clinton provided the missing pieces that permitted me—for the first time since we met in 1977—to understand this man fully.

Once decoded, despite its obvious omissions and limitations, *My Life* offers a guided tour through the labyrinths of the brilliant but cluttered, disorganized, and often raging mind of Bill Clinton. As a historical guide to the Clinton presidency, *My Life* is disappointing. There are no surprises, no nuances, and no compelling lessons. Page after page provide a diary-style summary of notable events, without any organized or logical theme. State dinners, foreign trips, and meetings with cabinet members are given the same weight as golf outings, appearances before the grand jury, and letters from children of friends. We learn what he ate for lunch every day in college, but not why he pardoned the drug dealer client of Hillary's brother. He describes in detail the floor plan of the small apartment he and Hillary shared in New Haven, but is silent about their solicitation of expensive Spode china, silver, and other gifts from donors while still in the White House. Did he really think readers would care that the bedroom in New Haven was between the dining room and the kitchen? Did he think we wouldn't notice his decision to ignore the gift fiasco?

For centuries, Egyptian hieroglyphics remained mere inscrutable markings to scholars and archaeologists—until finally a soldier in Napoleon's army happened upon the Rosetta stone, where the same text was written in hieroglyphics, Egyptian, and Greek. Comparing the three texts allowed scholars to decode the hieroglyphics and make them comprehensible for all to read. Deciphering *My Life* is a similar exercise in cryptography. Just as the translation of the Rosetta stone led to an understanding of the history and culture of the ancient Egyptians, the unraveling we'll undertake here offers a new way of looking at and comprehending the convoluted world of Bill Clinton. By comparing Clinton's version of reality with what actually happened, we'll be able to understand not only the gaps and errors in his account—but the broader reasons behind the disparity.

But this book has a larger mission. *My Life,* after all, is no ordinary volume, but the memoirs of a controversial and highly image-conscious president. *Because He Could* offers a needed corrective: an attempt to correct, explain, elaborate upon, contextualize, and rebut the spin in the former president's memoirs. This mission is compelling, even urgent, lest Clinton's sometimes distorted and always self-indulgent version of events harden into accepted historical "fact." The telling of stories has always been important to both Hillary and Bill Clinton. Together, they have cleverly used such tales as a tool to establish their brand, convey their message, and shape their public image. Only days after the first Clinton inauguration, Hillary told the president's top aides that one of the reasons for her husband's failure in his first term as governor of Arkansas was that they did not have a "clear story line." Both Clintons were determined that would never happen again. From then on, the stories were always complete. Not always true, but always clear. Bill Clinton's memoirs are just another installment in their continuing efforts to mold their images and rewrite their histories.

In its bid to persuade posterity to view his administration through the same lens as its author, *My Life* has its heroes: Hillary, Boris Yeltsin, Al Gore, the Democratic Party, and, mainly, Clinton himself. It also, of course, has its villains: Newt Gingrich, Kenneth Starr, and the right wing. And it has its missing persons—those who played key roles (even if they were cameos) in his life or administration, yet who simply go unmentioned, like the inconvenient figures airbrushed out of a Stalinist propaganda photo. These ghosts may not exist in Bill Clinton's world anymore, yet their stories remain on the historical record, and they give us important clues about Clinton himself. Why did he choose to obliterate certain people? Why make them disappear?

Because he could.

Not surprisingly, throughout the book Bill Clinton bends and twists the facts to suit his uniquely personal version of events. On nearly every page, we can almost see him straining to create the illusions he wants us to share, to accept his justifications and rationalizations. *My Life* represents Clinton's last stab at making things come out right.

To aid his reelection in 1996, Clinton—with great assistance from his speechwriter Don Baer—wrote a book he entitled *Between Hope and History*. In *Because He Could*, we probe the gap between Clinton's hopes of how history will remember his presidency . . . and what its history actually was.

Why should we bother? Why is it important to revisit the tortured paths of Clinton's story, to parse out the slender threads of reality from the wishful worldview expressed in *My Life*? Is it really worth the effort, merely to correct the former president's latest batch of tall tales?

The demands of history, on their own, make this journey necessary. However, the spectacle of *My Life* also provides an intrinsically fascinating window into how one man has accessed, altered, and articulated his own reality. Like a latter-day Alice, we enter into the Clintonian world on the other side of the looking glass, always comparing and contrasting it with what really happened.

What do we see through that looking glass? For one thing, we see a president who was buffeted constantly by other people—who was seemingly paralyzed by contradictory advice, yet hypnotized by consensus. Time and again, Clinton contends that the actions he took in a given situation were against his better judgment, as though he had no choice in the matter. Yet, of course, he had options. He *could* have led. He *needn't* have taken the path of least resistance.

Those who know Clinton and worked for him find an eerie echo of his real character in the pages of *My Life*. While historians traditionally see activist presidents as initiators—men who grab history by the horns and wrestle it to the ground, twisting it to their own purposes—Bill Clinton was, above all else, responsive and passive, guided and goaded by the stimuli around him. Rapid response, Clinton's enduring contribution to the lexicon of political tactics, emerges from the pages of his memoir as a metaphor for his entire incumbency.

This was not always a liability. When motivated by the pain he saw in the world around him, Clinton was at his empathetic best, grasping the emotions of others and internalizing them, making them his own. His universe is populated by the stories of other people, anecdotes that impel him to act—in his words, to "give people a chance to have better stories." Over and over again, the book describes how one needy person or another motivated Bill Clinton to try to change government programs to protect the disadvantaged.

When he was vexed by political opposition, however, Clinton would lash out in self-protective rages and slashing attempts to apportion blame to others—revealing, in the process, his own essential weakness and curious passivity. In *My Life,* Bill Clinton depicts himself as the victimized president, pushed and pulled by events he cannot control, advised by inept aides, and swept along by the frothing white water of partisan scandal.

Despite its Herculean efforts at self-justification, *My Life* actually provides a wealth of evidence to explain both how he achieved his successes, and how his failures came to bedevil us.

His words are revealing. Through his persistent emphases in *My Life*, we come to see how Clinton's highly tuned antenna amplified all risk to a screeching volume, making the political dangers of each course of action glaringly apparent. So he never ordered the raids that might have killed Osama bin Laden and stopped 9/11. So he never made the critical disclosures that might have nipped many of his most debilitating scandals in the bud. So he never negotiated the political compromises that might have left America with a good health care system or a secure Social Security.

The hero of *My Life*, in fact, often appears frozen in place, torn by his warring desires to please everybody, to minimize conflict, to appease Hillary, to respond to the tales of woe in hundreds of pained stories. The man who held the most powerful post on the planet spends page after page lamenting his inability to take action. The word "can't" looms around every corner; obstacles seem to leave him helpless to carve out his own direction or even policy. Yet most of these inhibitions were fictions, invented to cover Clinton's real motivations or pumped up into major obstacles to protect his inactivity from criticism.

Throughout the second half of the book, which covers the White House years, we see a man in a perpetual eight-year bad mood, brooding over insults, impotently protesting his innocence as his hard-hearted adversaries roast him over a slow fire. But somehow he manages to see himself as a sunny optimist, rattled only occasionally by the evil forces scheming to transform innocent actions by him and Hillary into undeserved scandals.

The scandals march through the pages of *My Life*—each blamed on the fevered imaginations of his partisan pursuers and prosecutors. According to his memoirs, the one common denominator that marked all his scandals—his draft evasion, the Gennifer Flowers affair, the Travel Office firings, Vince Foster's suicide, the missing billing records,

Whitewater, the "consulting fees" to Webb Hubbell after the Rose Law Firm scandal, the FBI file scandal, Hillary's commodities market trading, the Paula Jones lawsuit, the groping of Kathleen Willey, the crisis that led from Monica Lewinsky to impeachment, the campaign finance scandal, the export of satellite technology to China, the pardons for the FALN terrorists, and, in the final hours of his presidency, the pardons for the clients of Hillary's brothers and fugitive Marc Rich, the theft of White House gifts, and Hillary's gift registry—was his own innocence.

We are told that each scandal stems from some misunderstanding exploited and exacerbated by Republicans and right-wing prosecutors. Bill and Hillary Clinton's own missteps are portrayed as almost inconsequential, when they're addressed at all. But the reality is quite different. The real common denominator of the Clinton scandals was the Clintons' propensity to treat the truth as an inconvenience, and to grasp at anything that purports to prove their alleged innocence. By unraveling the threads of deception with which Clinton treats each scandal in *My Life,* we can come to grasp the former president's pathology in a way that was not possible when he was in office. There, protected by spin-doctors, defense lawyers, speechwriters, image-makers, and detectives, we could only dimly grasp the man—and the woman—these scandals revealed. But now, denuded of protection, the angry, raw, ravings of an embattled former president and his uncensored, unedited, and uncorrected self-justifications reveal the truth about the couple that caused all these scandals.

On the other side of the looking glass, of course, stands Saint Hillary alongside her man, as free as he of selfishness and mendacity, but, unlike him, incapable of error. Given the Clintons' prickly relationship with the truth, it may not be surprising that the pages of *My Life* and *Living History* fail to match up in their accounts of the first lady's accomplishments, or even her role in her husband's administration. What *is* surprising is that in his memoirs Clinton generally mentions Hillary only when paired with Chelsea, accompanying him on one state voyage or another. Where, one wonders, are Mrs. Clinton's great policy initiatives and proposals, which the New York senator trumpeted so loudly when she ran for office on her own?

Much of the task of this book is not just to debunk Bill Clinton's claims, but also to explore them more completely than he has. How did this man balance the budget, reduce the national debt, reform welfare, lower the child poverty rate, preside over a cut in crime, expand foreign trade, avert an era of global protectionism, rescue the Mexican currency, cut unemployment to historic lows, narrow the gap between the rich and the poor, and block the cuts envisioned by the Republican Contract with America? *My Life,* curiously, offers no clues. We find ourselves marveling that so many achievements could pile up with no human agency behind them. In *My Life,* legislation magically appears on the president's desk, awaiting only his signature. Good economic news comes rolling in without any accounting of how it came to be. Political opponents bite the dust with no explanation of the combat—or skulduggery—that laid them low.

There is much more to the story. None of Clinton's achievements was the product of virgin birth. Each emerged from a welter of maneuver, negotiation, compromise—often, indeed, from games of political chicken. As much as we need to hear the truth about Clinton's failures, it's equally important that we understand how his successes really came about.

Instead, *My Life* graphically demonstrates Bill Clinton's characteristic inability to rise above the level of the mundane detail or to perceive the broad patterns of his own presidency. Events flow through its pages in a torrent of minutiae—an executive order here, a policy pronouncement there, and a new program elsewhere, with nary a moment wasted on context or theme. Pearls in search of a necklace, they glitter attractively as unrelated accomplishments, no more connected in the pages of *My Life* than they are in the folds of Bill Clinton's mind. In *Because He Could,* we seek to put these initiatives in context, and show how they connect into paradigms and patterns.

Clinton is a master at using his photographic memory to assimilate a massive amount of data and information. His formidable verbal skills and ubiquitous charm empower him to communicate with ease and insinuate his ideas into our psyche. But, like an hourglass, the funnel narrows between the massive accumulation of information above and the effortless—and endless—communication below. His capacity for input and voluble output are not matched by an ability to analyze and conceptualize. This narrow funnel between input and output often becomes sclerotic and clogged, by an overload of information awaiting analysis, inviting a paralysis that often gripped his presidency.

Much of *My Life* concerns events beyond our shores, as the peripatetic first couple trotted the globe in search of problems to solve and photo opportunities to exploit. On the other side of his treasured looking glass Bill Clinton acts the global statesman, intently and determinedly focusing on international events even as his critics try to distract him with petty scandals. In real life, the president was so easily distracted, aloof, and removed from world events that he was only dragged into action when his back was to the wall.

In many ways, as others have observed, the Clinton administration often suggested a kind of living embodiment of chaos theory, unleashed within the walls of the White House. Chaos theory postulates that what seem to be random, unconnected, chaotic events actually connect into an organizing principle, impossible to perceive as they unfold, but visible (with effort) in retrospect. Like the postmodern X and Y Generations, the Clinton administration took as its working paradigm that *there was no paradigm*. Each day was entirely new. There were no absolutes—certainly not when it came to truth—and no constants. In *My Life,* events, days, actions, appointments, policies, programs, and presidential schedules emerged randomly, rapidly, episodically, without ideology, plan, context, or even philosophy.

And yet, as in chaos theory, patterns actually emerge from the whirlwind of directionless activity. Only in retrospect—as in reading between the lines of *My Life*—can we can study inductively what chaos has wrought.

Clinton's writing in *My Life* is certainly disordered. Organized only by chronology, the book jumps from one subject to another and back again with each new page. That itself offers the reader a taste of the inability to prioritize, organize, and systematize that plagued Clinton's presidency. There are no discrete-subject chapters; nor does the reader have the pleasure of watching Clinton pursue any grand, recurring design—either political or narrative. Instead the president flits from issue to issue, guided only by the vagaries of his daily calendar. Echoing his verbal style, the Clintonian monologue of *My Life* seems never to end. Chapter after chapter covers a part, and only a part, of his story: his legislative achievements, his fitful attempts to cope with terrorist threats, his trips with Hillary and Chelsea, his parrying with the Whitewater investigation, his fury at Ken Starr, his campaign stops, his promotion of AIDS research, his balanced budget fight, and on and on and on.

It is maddening. And yet it is vintage Clinton.

Bill Clinton's is no ordinary mind. On the positive side, it is an exceptional tool that permits him to think big, to innovate, to jump-start ideas. But, on the negative side, it is capable of spinning such elaborate and convincing deceptions that it fools not only us but him, too. In *My Life,* it is painfully apparent that Bill Clinton has genuinely convinced himself of his complete innocence in every scandal that touched him and his administration. It's equally apparent that, in the process, he sold himself on his adversaries' own guilt. In the relationship between those classic adversaries, Bill Clinton and Kenneth Starr, the defendant and the prosecutor have switched sides of the looking glass. In the mind of the former president it is Starr, not Clinton, who will be condemned by history.

Somehow, of course, all of Clinton's shortcomings—his failure to contextualize or analyze, his passivity and lack of initiative, his excess of caution, his self-righteous inability to feel guilt—combined to create a man who was one of the most successful modern presidents, a man whose accomplishments should be celebrated by history.

Unlike Lyndon Johnson, George H. W. Bush, and Jimmy Carter, he was reelected. Unlike Richard Nixon, he survived his scandals. Unlike Harry Truman, Gerald Ford, and the post-Iran-Contra Ronald Reagan, he left office more popular than when he entered it.

How did Bill Clinton do it? How did he function?

And more fundamentally, why did he develop these lifelong habits? Why did he evolve these patterns of thinking? Why was he content to be so passive and reactive? Why did he access the world through the stories of strangers he met, the advice of his friends and staff, and the reactions forced upon him by events? Why?

Because he could.

In an interview on the eve of the publication of *My Life*, Dan Rather asked Bill Clinton why he got involved with Monica Lewinsky. "I think that I did something for the worst possible reason," he said: "Just because I could." It was an odd response: Clinton had had every reason to anticipate the question—even in Rather's exceptionally softball interview—and prepare a better answer. It seems unlikely that Clinton was speaking impulsively, even though the line was certainly off-message, not in sync with the generally humble demeanor that Clinton was trying to project.

And yet the line was classic Clinton: ambiguous, unclear, distracting, masochistic. In a split second, he shifted attention from his achievements to his failures. "Because He Could" became the screaming headline. What did he mean by it? Did it simply mean that an opportunity presented itself and he responded to it? Or was there more? He continued: "I think that's about the most morally indefensible reason anybody could have for doing anything. . . . When you do something just because you could."

My Life offers at least one clue as to what Clinton may have had in mind. Shortly after the 1996 election, he writes, Newt Gingrich told White House Chief of Staff Erskine Bowles that the House Republicans would proceed with impeachment despite Clinton's resounding reelection and despite the opposition of moderate Republicans.

When Bowles asked why they would do such a thing instead of choosing some less severe option, Gingrich responded: "Because we can."

Now, eight years later, the onetime most powerful man in the world was telling us that he got involved with Monica Lewinsky because he was in a position to do whatever he wanted, because no one could stop him. "Because I could": It was the ultimate statement of unbridled power.

What liberties can a president take in his personal life? Whom can he bed? Whom can he exploit? From the moment he took office as governor of Arkansas at the age of thirty-one, Bill Clinton lived a life of droit du seigneur—a king's ancient right to do with his subjects what he will. When he ascended to the White House, he presumed that this fringe benefit would follow him . . . until Ken Starr made him pay the consequences.

For a normal person, the thought "I could" represents a passing opportunity, a fortuitous circumstance, a moment's convenience. For Bill Clinton, "I could" was an entitlement of office, a way of life. That is what is truly morally indefensible about his conduct—and what is so revealing about his choice of words.

In *Because He Could*, we'll witness how—despite his best efforts—the words indeed reveal the man.

2

Running on Empathy

Bill Clinton thrives only in the presence of other people. Like a solar battery, he comes alive only when shined on by an external force. When no one is around, it's as though the sun has gone from the sky, and the battery is nothing but a cold, dark lump of metal.

This was Clinton's consistent pattern through all the years I worked with him. When he was alone, or with an aide so symbiotic that he could regard him as an extension of himself, he was cold, lethargic, apathetic, withdrawn, and sullen. But contact with other people energized him almost magically. When he got out and met people or became involved with reading what they said in a newspaper or magazine, he became animated, energetic, and loquacious. It was only in response to stimuli that Clinton began to respond. Nothing came from within. Everything came from the outside.

Whenever he had someone to charm, a voter to meet, a donor to stimulate, a foreign leader to persuade, or a politician to placate, all of Clinton's energy and charisma became focused (yes, like a laser) on the task at hand. It was the mission of winning them over that triggered his animation. But it was his incredible ability to empathize with his object that made it work. Relatively devoid of emotion himself, Clinton made empathy his main way of accessing reality. He was always able to put himself in the other person's position and to see things from his vantage point. No doubt a coping mechanism learned in early childhood, when he spent years learning to anticipate the angry mood swings of his grandmother and stepfather, what has carried Bill Clinton through life is an extraordinary sensitivity to the most nuanced signs of emotion. Whether signaling approval, danger, or anger, Bill Clinton could read the sentiment; this became a trademark of his personality.

In Helen Palmer's illuminating study of personality, she describes a Mediator type who "becomes absorbed with what other people are thinking." For them, she writes, "life is overlaid with other people's ideas."

Clinton's capacity for empathy is ubiquitous, extending not only to the feelings of friends or possible supporters, but to those of his enemies, too. He has always been able to articulate the views of the other side, sometimes with more skill than he showed in explaining his own. As Palmer points out, Mediators "can see all sides of a question, which overwhelms [their] own agenda. Decisions are difficult. Conflicting opinions appear to have equal merit."

Would Clinton consider military action to slay Osama bin Laden? He could hear the anguished howls of global public opinion if we missed him and killed innocent bystanders instead. If we lost men in the process, he could visualize vividly the recriminations against a president who never served in the military and ducked the draft to avoid doing so.

Clinton's uncanny capacity for empathy is the key to understanding him—both his strengths and his weaknesses.

His empathy impelled his accomplishments. Each achievement has a story and a face behind it. He truly felt people's pain, and it catalyzed him to action.

But empathy also led him astray as he tried to satisfy the wrong people—often including his wife, Hillary.

And that same empathy caused so many of his failures, as the vivid imagination with which he anticipated negative reactions forced him into passivity.

On the positive side, the ability to see the world through others' eyes made him a master politician who appealed to a wide range of voters who knew he understood them.

On the negative side, his acute understanding of his opponents' likely reaction led him to procrastinate, delay, and avoid decisions.

These are the flip sides of the Clinton presidency.

The common denominator is empathy.

H ow does a politician learn about the problems of his compatriots? And what tools does he use to formulate ways to improve their lives and mitigate their hardships?

Most political leaders draw on the reservoir of their own life experience to shape their understanding of problems and their ideas for solutions. Harry Truman commanded an artillery company in World War I in Europe, but was a failure in business on the home front. Eisenhower climbed up the military ladder rung by rung. Johnson and Nixon were born into deprived lower middle-class families in isolated hamlets, and clawed their way out. Jimmy Carter experienced real life in the navy, and as a businessman raising peanuts in Georgia.

Bill Clinton, in contrast, was hardly exposed to the challenges of real life. He entered politics as soon as he left school. From the ages of thirty to fifty-four, with only a two-year hiatus, he held statewide or national elective office. For twenty of twenty-two years between 1978 and 2000, he lived in two successive cocoons of publicly funded privilege: the Arkansas Governor's Mansion and then the White House. As he points out in *My Life,* the year 1975, which he spent as a law school professor, was the only time in his career when he did not work in politics.

Bill Clinton's life has not been one of challenges and character-building lessons. Which isn't to say that Clinton was insensitive to the challenges most people faced. Never snobbish, he became intoxicated by his luxurious surroundings only late into his presidency. Throughout his political career, he showed a constant hunger to know what people felt and thought.

But one of the things he must have realized early, in soaking up the stories of these everyday people, is that Americans love a rags-to-riches tale. And, in the absence of such experiences in his own life, as he grew up and began considering a political career Clinton used a combination of stories and data to simulate one.

Bill Clinton has always portrayed himself as a poor Southern boy who overcame his underprivileged background in rural Arkansas to become the youngest governor in the state's history. That was his story. It was an uplifting tale, about a brilliant young man who still believed in a place called Hope—a metaphor for an idealized but very modest rural lifestyle in the small town where he was born. He was the son of a struggling single mother; his father, a truck driver, had died months before his birth.

Clinton was fond of describing the hardships he endured growing up. He once told me he had lived on a farm with no indoor plumbing. As a native of Manhattan who grew up on the ninth floor of an apartment house, I listened in awe: The story of how he would run to the outhouse in the cold night, taking care to dodge the snake that lived there, seemed to come from another planet.

Young Bill Clinton did face certain kinds of challenges—largely emotional ones. Forced to protect his mother and younger brother from his alcoholic stepfather's violent rages, he led a childhood filled with chaos and conflict. As he overcame these hardships, through hard work and his inherent intellect, to become governor and president, he objectified the American dream.

But the famous campaign legend bears only a passing resemblance to the actual events of Bill Clinton's upbringing, which are revealed—almost inadvertently—in his memoirs. This was not a poor boy who lived in a log cabin. This was a middle-class son who grew up being driven around in his parents' Buick.

Young Bill Clinton led a very comfortable life. He lived in the lively, city-like atmosphere of Hot Springs, Arkansas, where legal horse racing and illegal gambling houses mixed in with large old hotels, their clientele attracted by the natural warm water that gushes in the baths for which the city was named. He appears to have suffered no more during his typical small-city American childhood than during his years in the Governor's Mansion or the White House.

To gain a real understanding of Bill Clinton's childhood, you need to decode his memoirs. If you pay attention to the details, they sketch a life very different from the famous campaign biography. As always with Clinton, if you want the truth you have to parse the language, to read between the lines.

Until he was four years old, young Bill's life was, indeed, the struggle he has always described. When he was only a year old, his mother, Virginia, left him in the care of his grandparents while she attended school in New Orleans, studying to become a nurse anesthetist. Already a nurse, she sought the additional credential and the financial rewards she hoped it would bring. For the next two years or more, the young Bill Clinton saw his mother only on occasional visits.

Being deprived of his only living parent this way must have engendered in young Bill a primitive sense of loss, vulnerability, and anger. Child psychologists agree on the importance of bonding between mother and child in the first two years of life and the negative effects of premature separation.

Although Clinton's bonding was brutally interrupted by his mother's move, he never complains about it, or seems to feel sorry for himself. Instead, he writes of how difficult it must have been for his mother to have left *him*!

While Bill's grandmother made sure he was properly cared for, she was not his mother; the boy must have felt the absence of that young, charismatic, and attractive woman acutely. Even while living with his grandparents, though, he had to adjust to separation: They both worked hard running a country store, and Bill was often left in the care of an African-American housekeeper/babysitter. One of the fortunate legacies of that early relationship appears to have been his total lack of racism.

The simple life Bill led in his grandparents' modest home ended when he was four, after his mother returned and remarried. Roger Clinton, Bill's stepfather, was part of a solidly middle-class family that owned Buick dealerships in both Hope and Hot Springs. The lean years were over.

After little more than a year in Hope, the Clinton family moved to a 400-acre farm outside of Hot Springs. This was the home without indoor plumbing the president had described for me. Knowing its advantages in building his political myth, he concedes in My Life, that living on a farm with an outhouse made for a "great story," possibly as good as having been "born in a log cabin."

After they left the farm, the family moved into a large, two-story hilltop house in Hot Springs with, as Clinton recalls, terraced lawns, five bedrooms, a four-car garage, and a large "ballroom" where he entertained friends—hardly the modest house of a disadvantaged family. Clinton lived there until he was fifteen. In My Life, he describes his mother's rose gardens and the large yard with a swing set. The family had a housekeeper/nanny, who cared for him while his mother worked. Every three years, the family got a new Buick. The city of Hot Springs was quite a contrast with the sleepy little hamlet of Hope in northern Arkansas. A lively gambling center, it drew thousands of fans to its horse races, and its warm springs, billed as having curative powers, attracted visits by Theodore and Franklin Roosevelt, Herbert Hoover, Harry Truman, John F. Kennedy, and Lyndon Johnson.

We visited Hot Springs in 1978, and saw a reminder of one of these presidential visits. We stopped in a bar to watch a rock band rehearsing for the night's gig. In the men's room I found a piece of graffiti, which epitomized the old-school flavor of the town: "Eleanor Roosevelt Sucks!"

Clinton's family gave him opportunities for travel. At about the age of eleven, he recalls, he visited an aunt in Dallas (traveling on a "luxurious bus" with an attendant serving sandwiches), attended the Cotton Bowl, and went to the movies alone. Bill, a saxophonist, attended summer band camps, and even had his own set of golf clubs. This was no poverty-stricken kid.

Even when his mother divorced Roger Clinton, Bill's standard of living was not significantly reduced. In 1961, for $30,000, Bill's mother bought what he describes as a modern house with a living and dining room, eat-in kitchen, den, screened porch, three bedrooms, two baths, and central air conditioning.

Bill does not seem to have worked in high school. In fact, he rarely mentions work at all, except for a short summer-camp experience, a gig driving a car cross-country for his uncle, and his work in college on campaigns and for the Senate Foreign Relations Committee. He attended the prestigious—and expensive—Georgetown University School of Foreign Service, where the tuition, room, and board cost about $2,000 per year in 1964. When he left for school, he and his mother flew to Washington and spent a week sightseeing before school started. As a sophomore at Georgetown, he drove a three-year-old Buick convertible from school to Capitol Hill. And in his senior year, he lived with several other students in a large house with numerous decks overlooking the Potomac. His was not a deprived existence at all.

Clinton's relatives were so well off that when he ran for Congress in 1974 his Uncle Raymond lent him $10,000—a huge sum for a rural Arkansas district in those days—to begin his race.

From the age of four, then, Bill Clinton actually lived a rather privileged life, attending an elite college and graduate schools, traveling extensively, and rarely working. Apart from his earliest years, Bill Clinton enjoyed a lifestyle embodied by financial security and tremendous opportunities provided by his family.

He certainly had no taste of the hard, tough lives he would later witness as he campaigned around the country, lives that impelled him to his generous liberalism. But it was through empathy, not personal experience, that he accessed this reality.

Nor did Clinton's adult years give him the remotest opportunity to experience any lifestyle beyond one of pampered luxury.

During his time at Oxford, he traveled all over England and the rest of Europe, visiting Ireland, Spain, France, Sweden, Norway, Finland, Germany, Czechoslovakia, and Russia, while also exploring rural England and London. At Yale Law School, he had a part-time job teaching at a community college and did some work in a lawyer's office. But he recounts how he used his own money to pay for a phone and office for the McGovern campaign in Connecticut.

Three years after he graduated from law school, Clinton was already the Arkansas attorney general; Hillary was working at the most prestigious law firm in Arkansas. Two years later, at the age of thirty-one, he was elected as the youngest governor in the history of Arkansas.

Members of Congress—whether in the House or the Senate—live very different lives from the nation's governors. While senators and congressmen must ante up funds for two homes—one in Washington and another in the district—governors get to live in splendor and luxury in their states' executive mansions.

During his twelve years as governor of Arkansas, the Clintons lived in the beautiful Governor's Mansion in Little Rock, with servants, cooks, maids, housekeepers, chauffeurs, nannies for Chelsea, and personal assistants paid for by the taxpayers. The house had been built and furnished by Winthrop Rockefeller, one of the sons of the legendary John D. Rockefeller Jr.

While Bill and Hillary frequently refer to his meager gubernatorial salary of $35,000 per year, they omit any mention of the lavish perks that came with the job. In addition to the large personal and household staff, they had a substantial entertainment budget, and traveled all over the world at state expense. They didn't have to pay for rent, heat, air conditioning, electricity, homeowners' or health insurance, babysitters, or transportation. They never had to buy a car, pay a mortgage, send a check to the electric company, pay a phone bill, or live like real people.

Their stunning house was furnished with antiques, china, silver, artwork, and oriental rugs. When they wanted an outdoor pool at the residence, they arranged for their friends to donate money to build one. All they really had to pay for was their clothes, dry cleaning, and toys and books for Chelsea.

The lifestyle of the president of the United States is the most privileged existence anyone can lead. No amount of personal income or private wealth could possibly compare with the perks of the presidency. Of course, the super-rich can decorate their house with the same kind of priceless contemporary and traditional art, historic antiques, and gorgeous flowers that typify the White House. They may be able to afford comparable chefs, landscapers, and security facilities. They might even have a jet at their personal disposal for any purpose at any time. But even the incredibly wealthy cannot stop traffic wherever they want, for example, or borrow any piece of art from the National Gallery, or organize overseas trips that cost over $100 million for friends and family, or have the best-trained security guards in the world, or summon any celebrity, entertainer, or intellectual at his whim.

Among modern presidents, most must have arrived at the White House in awe of the unique luxuries of the office. JFK and the Bushes inherited wealth, but they were the exceptions. FDR, too, lived a life of wealth and privilege, but his battle with polio gave him a visceral appreciation for human suffering. Truman, Eisenhower, Johnson, Nixon, Ford, Carter, and Reagan had all lived very real and often harsh lives before they dug their way out and emerged into a life of plenty.

Bill Clinton, on the other hand, despite his everyman affect, had no real experience with which to understand the struggles of average hard-working Americans.

To fill this void—fatal in a politician—Clinton used his amazing ability to empathize emotionally, and to incorporate data intellectually, to understand the world around him.

Clinton's powers of empathy are incredible. I have watched him give speeches and marveled at his ability to study the faces of the audience and react to them while he is speaking. He reads them, and they understand that he does. This extraordinary responsiveness sometimes seems to sharpen his thinking, allowing him to conceive and express ideas he had never really fixed on before the speech.

Whenever he walks into a room, Clinton can instantly tell who likes him and who doesn't. Like a heat-seeking missile, he homes in— not on his friends, but on those who think ill of him—and sets about charming them. He can read from their silent faces what they think, why they believe it, and how to approach them to get them to change.

How did Clinton come by this sixth sense?

For his entire early life, Bill Clinton must have felt like an out-sider—the perennial "other," a visitor in other people's homes. With no father and an absent mother during his most important develop-mental years, he had to accommodate the households of his benefac-tors. Although he loved his grandmother, in *My Life,* he describes her as moody and mean, "full of anger and disappointment and obses-sions she only dimly understood." She raged against her husband and Bill's mother, filling the house with wrath. To a young child, it must have been terrifying, never knowing when he would be the ob-ject, the victim of her fury. While Clinton writes that she spared him "most" of the time, his language suggests that there must have been times that he bore the brunt of her temper himself. The very fact that Clinton remembers these fits of fury, even though he was less than four years old at the time, reflects the psychological damage they must have caused.

When his mother returned, her new husband's alcoholic rages were so violent that Roger Clinton was once jailed after he aimed a gun over Bill's mother's head and fired. Clinton notes, movingly, that the truly "disturbing" part of life with an alcoholic is that "it isn't al-ways bad." Why would that be disturbing? Because Bill would never know when his father might explode into violence. Every moment had to be scrutinized to determine when a rage was likely to come.

Bill Clinton's early life, then, depended on his ability to read people, and to get out of the way when their looks portended danger. Blessed with this ability to put himself in the shoes of others, as an adult he became an anthologist of other peoples' stories, tending to see a single, often troubled, person, with a name, a face, an address, and a voice, behind every political issue. Early in his memoir, he writes, "perhaps most important, I learned that everyone has a story. . . . All my life I've been interested in other people's stories."

Clinton's book is filled with stories. But they are not just illustrative anecdotes, they are integral to his policy formation. He stores his ideas in these stories. In *My Life,* with scant transition from one to another, he gives an endless list of his policy achievements, most of them accompanied with an anecdote recalling just whom he had heard from that made him focus on the problem in the first place.

For example, as he rightly heralds his signature on the Family and Medical Leave Act as one of the landmarks of his presidency, he swings right into the story of a wheelchair-bound teenage girl he met while he was jogging. Her father confided to the president that his daughter was probably going to die, but told him that the three weeks the Family Leave Law permitted him to spend with her were the most important in his life.

Now, Clinton isn't the only president who has recognized the importance of such stories in communicating with the public. (Ronald Reagan—also raised, perhaps tellingly, by an alcoholic father figure—was similarly inclined.) But for Bill Clinton the story *was* the issue, not merely an example of it. The stories lived, fully assembled, in his mind. When he would debate the issue in private, speak about it in public, or recall it in his memoirs, the story would predominate . . .

. . . along with the data.

Where Bill Clinton's left brain tells stories, his right brain memorizes and regurgitates data. Information is Bill Clinton's other gateway to reality. Numbers, for him, are the entry point to policy; throughout his time in office, they provided the foundation on which he based his thinking, and became his rationale for action.

Between his numbers and his stories, Bill Clinton could simulate what it felt like to live in the real world. The personal tales of woe would focus his attention on an issue. The data would give it a policy context, and serve to ratify and underscore the import of the story.

In Clinton's world, the data had to fit together, into a coherent whole. Otherwise the dissonance would drive him crazy.

One day in 1997, I called him at the White House. Before I could even say hello, he erupted. "Dick, I'm so glad you called," he said, beginning a rapid-fire stream of statistical consciousness. As I listened to the numbing catalogue of data, I couldn't escape the feeling that I was peering directly into his mind, witnessing how his grey cells stored reality.

"I was up all night last night thinking about this," he continued. "There were fourteen million people on welfare when I came in but that reduces to about four million households. One million are headed by a mother who can't work. She's disabled or something. She can't hold a job. But that leaves three million who could work."

Continuing without pause for air, he poured it on: "I've gotten one million of them jobs. That's reduced the welfare caseload to about eleven million. They have about three people per household. And I've had to create seven million jobs to do it. One out of seven jobs went to welfare mothers. But I've got to create another two million jobs to get them all off of welfare. But to do that, I'd have to create another fourteen million jobs nationally, if the same ratio prevails—and I don't know if I can do that."

He stopped as suddenly as he had begun. I reminded him that he had passed a lot of incentives to create jobs for welfare mothers—the federal government would pay half of the first year's salary and two-thirds of the second year up to $10,000—and suggested that he continue his focus on getting corporations to hire welfare mothers.

"And who says you can't create fourteen million jobs?" I added for good measure. (He did.)

As Helen Palmer writes, personalities of Clinton's type are "over-whelmed with input, seeing the many sides of a situation and the different contexts in which the same situation could be played out."

In *My Life,* all of Clinton's policy initiatives are couched in peo-ple's stories and economic or other data. The humanity of the for-mer, and the analytic quality of the latter, combine to define him, his thinking, and his presidency.

Such a worldview gave Clinton tremendous qualities as a politi-cian and policymaker. Among other things, they prevented him from losing touch with the needs and aspirations of his constituents, on one hand, and objective reality on the other. Not every president has been so lucky.

But Bill Clinton's way of thinking also saddled him with a key shortcoming—a kind of improvisational, almost haphazard approach to governing the country. For the truth is that the stories and even the data Clinton collected didn't always form a clear policy picture, or a coherent political strategy. They existed only as a list of propos-als, not always related or even compatible. That is why, as president, Clinton never had a clear philosophy. He had only an inexhaustible fount of stories and data, and the ideas and intentions he hit upon to address them.

Most political leaders will first think in generic terms, and then move to the specific. "We need to fix the health care system," they might begin by saying. "And to do that we need to expand insurance coverage," they would continue. "One reason a lot of people don't have coverage," they observe, "is that they've changed jobs, and their pre-existing conditions are not covered by their new employer." Then they would conclude by declaring that we need a new law to require coverage of preexisting conditions when a person changes jobs. (That's what the 1996 Kennedy-Kassebaum bill did.)

But Clinton's mind doesn't work that way. He would begin by telling the story of Ron and Rhoda Machos, of New Hampshire, who were expecting their second child but were burdened by $100,000 in medical bills from their son Ronnie's open-heart surgery. Or he would recall a man he met as he campaigned around the nation who was afraid to change jobs because he needed his health insurance to treat a chronic condition. If this man switched to a new employer, Clinton would point out, the insurance company could exclude the coverage he needed, because the condition was preexisting. Then he'd note that 25 million people are in the same boat. And, voila: the Kennedy-Kassebaum Bill.

This failure to set his specific issues in a broader context often left people wondering what Clinton really stood for. In response, he could only repeat his list of proposals, tell another story, or spout more data. When these approaches failed to convey his message, he would resort to platitudes about opportunity and responsibility, which often were drained of meaning.

Throughout his presidency, I often wondered if Clinton's thinking could really be as episodic, as devoted to the events of the day, as it seemed. Like many who worked for him, though, I hoped that some guiding philosophy was steering his hand—a context overshadowed, perhaps, by the press of daily business, but still a silent influence on his thinking. In the arena of the White House, the crucible of conflict, I assumed he didn't have time to explain the historical or economic context for his actions. But surely, I felt, this supremely intelligent man was aware of how his ideas fit together, and acutely conscious of their place in history. He just couldn't squander his day letting me in on his thinking.

When the news broke that he was writing his memoirs, I thought: *Perhaps now he will bring it all into focus.* No longer harried by the pressure of events, with nothing but time on his hands, I assumed that Clinton would take the opportunity to make a grand case for his deeper purposes, to express the ideological underpinnings of the choices he'd made. Now the proposals would knit together into themes, the ideas form patterns that would find their place in history.

I was disappointed.

My Life reflects nothing more than a catalogue of his proposals, a list of his achievements. For the days he spent in Washington, the book reads like a desk diary; for those he spent elsewhere, it reads like a travelogue. There is so little conceptual order in his memoirs that he does not even designate his chapters by names or subjects, just numbers. Clinton's *My Life*, like his political life, has no organizational motif beyond simple chronology: It is, simply, one darn thing after another.

This editorial failure reflects the chaos of his presidency, the disorganization of his tenure. Without context and often lacking strategy, his presidency was a succession of developments that followed hard on one another, each always receiving just enough attention to prevent an eruption that day.

Clinton lived in chaos; on his best days, he seemed to thrive on it. He was always at the center of a swirl of activity that had no pattern. Interruption was the norm. Meetings would reel from one topic to the next with no conclusion. Order seemed anathema. The events of the day shaped Clinton's presidency; only in passing, and on the fly, was he able to shape them. Not for nothing did the concept of "rapid response" come to define his campaigns and his presidency.

Eventually, when a given situation matured into crisis, Clinton would confront it and finally react. But many such actions seemed only to get him through that moment. Before long, he'd usually have to react again. Clinton even had a name for this process of delay and procrastination, as his limited attention span carried him along giddily from one topic to the next. He called it "kicking the can down the road." In moments of self-awareness, he would gripe, "We can't just keep kicking the can down the road on this issue. Where are we going with it? Where are we headed?"

While we were working together, I tried constantly to frame the specifics we had at hand into helpful contexts, to translate our political tactics into broader strategies. But often the president was reluctant to buy into my formulations. It was as if I were staring up at the stars with Clinton, trying to get him to pick out the constellation

Orion among the many glittering stars. "Over there," I'd point. "You see the three stars? That's his belt. And that's his arm and that's his leg."

"No way," he might say. "The belt isn't straight, and the leg is too far out, and that couldn't be his arm. The stars aren't lined up like that."

Clinton was too much of a perfectionist to see patterns, and he resisted the inclination to think in terms of long-term strategy. Everything was fixed in the here and now. Each new bill we evaluated stood on its own. Each political move had its own purpose, its own justification.

Sometimes, it was hard to imagine a president handling the job any other way. In the White House, events come in rapid-fire bursts, each with its own bolt of kinetic energy or danger to mobilize the chief executive into action. Bill Clinton's political success stemmed, in part, from his native ability to thrive in just this kind of environment.

But amid the chaos, a conceptualizing president will struggle to impose his own order on the rush of developments, and structure them into coherent initiatives he pursues. The great presidents have *directed* the ebb and flow of events, leveraging them to move the country in what he sees as a more positive direction. Franklin Roosevelt used the stimulus of the Depression to fashion a host of new government programs into an enduring social safety net. John F. Kennedy was inspired by the space race with the USSR to reach for the transcendent goal of sending a man to the moon. Ronald Reagan transformed the malaise of the Carter years into a new wave of confidence in our country—and then channeled that momentum into his long-desired victory over the Soviet Union.

But that isn't how Clinton worked, and it isn't how he tells his story in *My Life*. Each event for him was a stimulus that triggered a separate response. He neither approached the day's developments deductively, with a substantive or strategic hypothesis, nor did he look back inductively on random developments to discern patterns.

He merely reacted, and if the reactions were successful, they would coalesce into accomplishments. But never into true philosophical achievement.

This lack of conceptual thinking, especially evident in the pages of *My Life,* redounds to Clinton's detriment. For all the places where he claims undue credit or avoids deserved blame, or stretches our credulity with his claims of innocence, the core weakness of the book is his total failure to make a case for his broader agenda as a politician. It's ironic that this president, who rarified spin to an art form, should fall short in this ultimate test of his ability to shape perceptions of his administration. Unlike JFK, who kept historian Arthur Schlesinger Jr. on his staff to help him retain historical perspective—or Reagan, who seemed to see his presidency as his greatest historical drama—Clinton hands down to posterity no more than a laundry list of what he did and when he did it.

Without this historical context to illuminate their impact, many journalists have assumed that Clinton's achievements are no more than footnotes in history. If Clinton himself won't even bother to frame the case for his time in office, after all, why should they? Instead they paste his list into their mental scrapbooks and file it away without further analysis. Clinton's defenders and apologists, for their part, are so busy explaining away his failures that they, too, have expended little effort trying to elaborate his successes.

And this is a shame, for as a result several significant breakthroughs made during Clinton's time in office are at risk of being ignored by history.

For example, in *My Life,* Clinton hails his decision to sign the GOP's final draft of a welfare reform proposal, correctly defending its key requirements—that recipients take jobs and limit their period of dependency to five years.

But the broader achievement of the Clinton years is that he lowered the percentage of children living in poverty by about one third, while reducing the national welfare population by more than one half. Even in the recession that followed his presidency, the child poverty rate stayed down, and the welfare rolls did too. This magnificent and seemingly lasting accomplishment was the fruit of a mélange of policies and programs that Clinton lists episodically. But he fails to link them together into the coherent structure they actually formed—a structure that protected millions of children from deprivation.

Clinton's welfare reform strategy began in 1993, when he used the Democratic Congress to double the Earned Income Tax Credit (EITC)—the only form of tax cut the left would allow. The EITC, started under the Republicans, grants an income supplement to anyone who works full-time but whose resulting income falls below the poverty line. Depending on how many children the working person has to support, the supplement can range quite high. Clinton extended the EITC until it reached well into the lower middle class, and it did not expire until it had boosted the incomes of large families up to a high of $30,000.

The EITC made work pay, even in low wage jobs. (The repeated cries of liberals that the poor are stuck in low-paying dead end jobs do not take into account public benefits like the EITC, which raise their income to the point where it is worth working.)

It would be tempting to say that the expansion of the EITC was part one of a carefully conceived strategy to make welfare reform work by rewarding low-wage employment. In fact, it was a crisis response to the hue and cry Clinton triggered when he abandoned his campaign plans to cut taxes for the middle class. For the rest of his presidency, he would always cite the EITC as his middle class tax cut.

When the Gingrich Congress tried to repeal or cut the tax credit, Clinton refused to go along. This battle was one of the key issues at stake in the government shutdowns of late 1995 and early 1996; for Clinton it was a total victory, as he repeatedly accused the Republicans of wanting to raise taxes on the poor by cutting back the Earned Income Tax Credit.

The second part of his welfare reform mosaic was an increase of ninety cents per hour in the minimum wage. This traditional

Democratic proposal was especially aimed at single working mothers, who disproportionately held minimum wage jobs.

But the genius of Clinton's strategy was only apparent after the passage of both welfare reform, which required work, and the minimum wage, which raised pay. With both measures safely on the books, he issued an executive order applying the newly raised minimum wage to the jobs welfare recipients had to take in order to satisfy the requirements of the new law. Even if they worked for the government, as an employer of last resort, Clinton mandated that they must receive the minimum wage.

At a stroke, he moved hundreds of thousands of people from dependence on welfare checks of $5,000 or $6,000 per year to forty-hour-a-week jobs paying twice that. Add in the EITC, and their incomes reached into the mid-teens—tax free.

It would have been understandable for Clinton to present the minimum wage increase in *My Life,* as a critical pillar in his successful welfare reform strategy. But Clinton does no such thing. Instead he gives it only a twelve-word mention. And he doesn't even allude to his historic order requiring that welfare mothers benefit from this wage hike.

Similarly, Clinton also took care to flatten out the eligibility for a variety of government benefits like food stamps, housing assistance, and the like, so that welfare recipients wouldn't lose them as they moved from the dole to low-paying jobs.

And, finally, as I had reminded him in our phone call, he had passed incentives to persuade businesses to give jobs to those who were on welfare. To make sure businesses took advantage of these incentives, he devoted considerable effort to reaching out to private employers to encourage them to commit to hiring certain numbers of welfare mothers.

Individually, each of these was a small policy victory. Put together, this mosaic of programs constituted systematic and meaningful welfare reform, and the first major reduction in the poverty rate since the Great Society days of Lyndon Johnson.

But you'd never know it from reading *My Life.* Nowhere does Clinton connect the dots or explain how these measures worked together to bring their historic changes to America.

Were they connected in his own mind? Did he see them in advance as elements of a plan to lift millions off welfare and out of poverty? Failing that, does he recognize these initiatives, at least in retrospect, as pieces of the puzzle, as part of the grand reformation of the broken welfare state that stands as one of his true achievements? And if so, why not crow about it in his memoirs? Why leave it to others to connect the dots?

One is driven to the conclusion, sadly, that Bill Clinton *just doesn't see the pattern.* The ultimate creature of events seems to have no ability to connect them into coherent pictures—or at least no apparent interest in doing so.

Another example of Clinton's episodic approach to achievements and failure to see them conceptually is his list, in *My Life,* of each trade agreement of his presidency. He faithfully records his initiatives, from concluding and passing the NAFTA deal with Mexico and Canada, to the lowering of tariffs in the Pacific Rim initiative, to the conclusion of a new world trade framework in the negotiations leading to the formation of the World Trade Organization, with its global rules for free commerce.

But Clinton doesn't fit these pieces together, or explain how they overlapped. Whether by design or by coincidence, Clinton's approach to trade issues was truly brilliant. He reversed a decade-long trend toward protectionism, and helped usher in the global prosperity of the 1990s by reducing trade barriers. Here in the United States, exports doubled between 1992 and the end of his second term, a crucial boost to the economic expansion.

When Clinton was elected, tariff barriers were on the rise again—and Congress had refused to renew the presidential authority to fast-track trade agreements—that is, to allow them to be considered by Congress strictly as yes-no propositions, with no amendments.

While the former president describes his efforts at expanding trade and lowering barriers, in *My Life,* once again, he fails to connect the dots.

What really happened was a triple play.

First Clinton signed (and persuaded a reluctant Congress to ratify) the NAFTA treaty, establishing a free trade area in North America. It wasn't an easy battle; most of Clinton's labor/left supporters deserted him on this crucial vote. Indeed, the lasting union animosity toward Clinton over NAFTA may have been partly responsible for his loss of Congress in 1994.

But NAFTA was the cornerstone of what emerged as a coherent new free-trade strategy during the Clinton years. By cementing a treaty with a reliable source of cheap products produced by low-paid workers, Clinton was essentially declaring our independence from the Asian economies that had formerly taken the lead in supplying these needs. Shortly after NAFTA was ratified, Clinton went to Seattle for the Asia-Pacific Economic Cooperation organization (APEC), where he laid the basis for lowering the economic barriers to Pacific trade.

What he really did in Seattle was to use the implicit threat in NAFTA—that the United States would stop buying cheap Asian products because it had a plentiful supply coming from Mexico—to pry open Asian markets to American trade. Clinton couldn't say so publicly, because he couldn't admit to American unions that he saw Mexico as a low-cost alternative. But he knew that our businesses needed access to cheap products to create American jobs, and he knew that playing Mexico off against Asia would help get a better deal from both nations.

Then, having moved toward more open Pacific and Mexican trade, Clinton began serious negotiations with Europe. The French, in particular, were driving a hard bargain in the new round of world trade talks, while growing more and more worried about Clinton's tendency to downplay the European relationship and pay more attention to Japan and China. Today, compared with Bush's unilateralism,

Europeans fall all over themselves reciting Clinton's virtues. But at the start of his administration, the new president's Pacific orientation loomed as a potent concern. Was Clinton turning his back on Europe, they wondered?

Realizing that the best way to bring the Europeans to heel is to ignore them, Clinton found the European trade negotiators willing to ratchet back their demands to accommodate American concerns. While Clinton writes that the new General Agreement on Tariffs and Trade (GATT) opened markets to American products, he doesn't discuss how this was the culmination of a triple play—Mexico, Asia, and then Europe—that pried open global markets and laid the basis for much of the prosperity of the 1990s. Instead, in *My Life,* Clinton again treats these negotiations as three different events, unconnected by strategy, context, or bargaining leverage.

Years ago, after their passage, I congratulated Clinton on this "triple play," marveling at the interrelationship of its parts. In return I got only a blank stare; Clinton seemed to be pondering their intersection for the first time. "We'll never get credit for it," was the only response he could manage.

A key pivot in the Clinton presidency was the 1995–1996 transition from economics to values issues as the focus of the administration. Our polling was beginning to reflect a crucial shift among voters, away from bread-and-butter issues to quality-of-life concerns. Worries about jobs, imports, wages, and the like were sublimated; concerns about drugs, pollution, education, health care, crime, media violence, and retirement began to predominate. Particularly among swing voters, many in their twenties and thirties, there was more interest in practical measures to raise their families than in the financial issues that had been a central concern during the recession.

At the time many felt that this shift to values issues was cyclical, and that bad economic times would bring the pendulum back. But Bush's ability to gain seats in Congress in 2002 despite a recession, and Gore's defeat (sort of) despite prosperity, seem to indicate that a more fundamental shift is occurring. Voters are coming to realize that the management of the economic cycle is more the job of the Federal Reserve Board and of international banks and market forces than of the president. In other words, if you want your photo taken in Washington, you should go pose in front of the White House. But if you want to talk to somebody about the economy, you should go to Alan Greenspan's office.

Throughout Europe, candidates who run on economic platforms are losing, while those who focus on values issues are emerging victorious. In Germany, Schroeder won by talking about Iraq while his opponent dwelt on the economy. In France, Socialist candidate Lionel Jospin finished third, not even making the runoff; he was bested by President Jacques Chirac, whose major issue was crime, and the racist Jean-Marie Le Pen, who opposed immigration. In Britain, Tony Blair, of the traditionally economy-oriented Labor Party, campaigns mainly on health care, education, crime, and terrorism.

At the time, the shift in the White House's agenda sparked great controversy. Getting the administration to discuss values issues and not economics was like persuading the Democratic donkey to switch from eating hay to gobbling peanuts out of the elephant's feeding trough.

But nowhere in *My Life,* does Clinton discuss this basic shift in his political agenda—despite the fact that it was a transition we discussed endlessly in our meetings. Instead, the items in his daily-diary litany just begin to change to these social issues and away from economic concerns, like a datebook reflecting new appointments.

This gap between conceptualization and episodic action looms large as Clinton recounts one of the most difficult decisions of his presidency—the deployment of 25,000 American troops in Bosnia to enforce the Dayton Peace Accords. I polled public opinion on this issue, and repeatedly found almost 2:1 majorities opposed to sending in our ground forces. I warned the president of the potentially disastrous consequences of flying in the face of such a determined public opinion, one short year before the 1996 elections.

"Don't tell me it's unpopular. I know it's unpopular," Clinton said, throwing my data back in my face. "I have to do it. Tell me how I can."

As I studied the issue in more detail, it became evident that the voters' bad reaction to sending troops to Bosnia was the result of their unfamiliarity with the mission: They didn't understand the limited tasks our troops would be asked to execute. When I polled a sample of voters, and read them a list of the things our troops were actually going to do in Bosnia—guard ballot boxes, separate enemy forces, and enforce the weapons embargo—voters were quite willing to send troops. What they had feared was that our soldiers would be asked to patrol the mountains looking for war criminals, or intervene to help Muslims get back the homes from which the Serbs had ousted them. When we told them their sons and daughters would not have to perform such dangerous tasks, support for the deployment rose dramatically.

Embracing the polling data, Clinton went on national television for only the third time in 1995 to explain what he would be asking our troops to do. In *My Life,* he dutifully records that he promised America our troops would have a limited mission. But he neglects the more basic function of his speech—that he explained to a skeptical American public what peacekeeping was all about. Lacking the history of such missions that many countries like Canada and the Scandinavian nations had, Americans didn't understand the difference between warmaking and peacekeeping. Clinton explained it to them, and laid the basis for public acceptance of a broad new type of American military involvement. *My Life* doesn't even hint at the importance of his public education on television that night.

Curiously, Clinton also downplays his anti-tobacco policies in *My Life,* giving this historic initiative only a cursory discussion. But what other public policy initiative by a modern American president led to saving about 100,000 lives each year?

When the Republicans captured Congress in 1994, all government regulations fell under unfriendly scrutiny. The GOP moved to roll back environmental, land use, logging, wetland, health, pharmaceutical, workplace safety, and other regulations. To expand the government's jurisdiction over tobacco was anathema to the agenda the nation had supposedly embraced in handing power to Gingrich and the Republicans.

But polls showed the tobacco industry had an Achilles heel—public opposition to teen smoking. About half of Americans didn't smoke and never had. A quarter once smoked and had quit. And one quarter continued to poison themselves with tobacco. Those who had quit smoking backed even the harshest of curbs on tobacco products. Those who never smoked didn't much care. But smokers wouldn't go along with any anti-smoking measures . . . except a ban on teen smoking.

When Clinton learned that the Food and Drug Administration (FDA), under its courageous leader David Kessler, was planning to issue a finding that nicotine was an addictive drug and that cigarettes were a drug delivery device, we began to work to steer the FDA toward a focus on teen smoking. Mississippi Attorney General Mike Moore and his lawyers Dick Scruggs and Steve Bozeman had already sued big tobacco, demanding that it reimburse states for the costs of treating the illnesses that smoking caused. In the Mississippi suit, paralleled by other states, Moore demanded that tobacco stop advertising to teenagers. No more Joe Camel.

Despite the worries of staff members like North Carolina's Erskine Bowles that tobacco companies would target Clinton if he let the FDA regulate tobacco and backed a ban on advertising, the president showed incredible courage in moving ahead on the issue. He backed Kessler, and held a press conference announcing the new regulations.

It was one of the most important moments of his presidency. With one stroke, Clinton had set in motion historic forces that would roll back smoking from 23 percent of the American public in 1995 to 18 percent today, and would cut teen smoking by about one quarter.

But how does Clinton describe this watershed? In a matter of two paragraphs, sandwiched between his battle with the Republicans on the budget and the defection of Saddam Hussein's two sons to the west. He notes that tobacco is addictive, speaks of the political power of the industry's lobby, worries about the impact of his position in Kentucky and North Carolina, and notes Gore's support for the new regulations. And then he moves on to the rest of the events of that day.

In July 1995, Clinton showed similar courage in his successful efforts to torpedo Republican pressure for the passage of a Constitutional amendment reversing the Supreme Court's ban on school prayer. I shuddered when Clinton told me he was determined to fight on the issue. "School prayer," I said, "is one of the only issues on which the Republican social agenda has a solid majority." We were already lagging in the polls; I didn't think this was an opportune moment for Clinton to take on this particular battle.

But the president had figured out a brilliant move around the Republican flanks. "Most of the stuff people want to have happen in schools is perfectly legal under the First Amendment," Clinton told me. "They don't need a new amendment to do most of the things they want schools to do." It was a brilliant idea. Rather than fight the prayer amendment on GOP terms—as a battle to bring God into schools—he was proposing to preempt them by explaining how much latitude the Constitution, as currently written, already provides.

He asked me to poll public opinion, to test what kind of leeway parents wanted their children to have to express their spiritual values in school. The poll showed strong support for measures that were entirely permissible under the First Amendment—morals and ethics classes in the curriculum, religious clubs after school, and a moment of silence at the start of each day. Voters may have been saying they wanted a prayer amendment, but it turned out that many of them didn't actually want their children to say a prayer. They wanted other forms of spiritual expression instead.

Armed with this insight, Clinton had Education Secretary Dick Reilly send every school board a list of what they could do to include spiritual values in their programs. It killed the school prayer controversy. The talk of an amendment died the day Clinton had Reilly send out the brochure. It was a masterstroke.

And yet again Clinton misses the importance of his own actions. In *My Life,* he simply notes that he sent out the booklet and lists what it said—without commenting on how the move brought the controversy to a close. He doesn't even mention the School Prayer Amendment he was trying to defuse.

In the aftermath of the Easter Accords that seemed to settle the troubles in Northern Ireland, I told Clinton that his major weakness—his desire to please everybody—had become his key strength in diplomacy. By appealing to each of the parties in the Ireland mess, and empathizing with their views, he gained their trust and brought them together—on the common ground he had granted them in his own mind.

Once again, Clinton just looked at me without seeming to understand what I was saying—and moved on to the next in his lifelong series of agenda items.

And thus we're left with this puzzling paradox: For all its faults (and we'll spend plenty of time on those), the Clinton administration made a number of significant contributions to American history. And yet—despite his fierce intelligence, his mastery of spin, even despite his legendary self-regard—*My Life* is marked by a strange unwillingness to trumpet them, to paint more than the most tepid and mundane portrait of his presidency. Was Clinton just mechanically shuffling through his appointment book as he generated chapter after chapter, rushing to finish the manuscript before his publisher's deadline? Or did he really fail to understand the significance of his presidency?

Don Baer, Clinton's brilliant director of communications, once told Clinton how he would describe his role in history. "Just as FDR made capitalism safe in a world that demanded social progress," Baer told Clinton, "you made liberalism safe and relevant to a world that prized free markets, low taxes, and limited government." Baer meant that Clinton had figured out ways (creating targeted tax credits, for example, instead of raising spending) to advance a social agenda within the constraints of the largely conservative backlash against big government that dominated American thinking in the wake of the Reagan presidency.

But Baer's efforts to lend a conceptual context to the Clinton presidency, like so many others, appear to have fallen on deaf ears. No such claim ever appeared in Clinton's speeches; nor does it appear in his memoirs. No surprise: Baer, after all, was offering an idea, not a story or a statistic. And Clinton's two-dimensional mindset never lent itself to such abstractions.

3

Timidity, Passivity, and Blame

The Negative Consequences of Clinton's Empathy

Bill Clinton's legendary capacity for empathy—his ability to internalize the feelings of others—has led him to spend much of his public life trying to alleviate the pain and hardship of almost everyone he encounters. Yet, in other situations, it has also discouraged him from taking action, leading him to overestimate difficulties, encouraging his passivity, and kindling his never-ending search for scapegoats when things went wrong.

Clinton's ability to see the world through different eyes often led him to exaggerate the seriousness of each new obstacle or adversary, to the point where his fantasy stopped him from taking decisive action.

Steeped in empathy, Clinton saw the views of his critics so clearly that he became like a figure in mythology: blind because he could see everything. In evaluating a proposed course of action, he would repeatedly play out the scenario in his own mind, vividly imagining the intensity of the negative reaction that a proposed action might trigger. He would visualize the condemnation and anticipate the firestorm, usually blowing it far out of proportion, until he awoke screaming from his own political nightmare and lost whatever courage he once had. Neither ignorant nor arrogant, he was not one to minimize obstacles; instead he magnified them until they robbed him of initiative.

The biggest surprise I had as I worked for President Clinton was the discovery of how profoundly he felt hemmed in by the challenges surrounding him, curbing his power, shrinking his mandate, foreclosing options, and dictating policies. The most powerful man in the world too often seemed a passive figure, buffeted by developments beyond his control. He would constantly complain to me of events, people, or circumstances that held him in check, forced his hand, or made action impossible.

At first, I had trouble understanding how he could view these barriers as insurmountable. It seemed incongruous that the president of the United States constantly came up against the word "can't" as he sought to lead the nation. My confusion grew as I came to test the permeability of these confines, and it became clear that many existed only in his mind, ready to fall in the face of a determined exercise of executive or political power.

I have three golden retrievers. I have often noticed that these hundred-pound dogs will never push aside a chair or ottoman that lies in their path. Instead they will go around or over it—and, if they can't, they'll whine until it is removed. Sometimes they remind me of Clinton.

In *My Life,* Bill Clinton recalls many, many times when he says he felt compelled to act against his better instincts by circumstances, adversaries, his own fears, and the White House staff—all seemingly beyond his capacity to face down. These obstacles seem to crop up every few pages in his memoir; while they are frequently real, just as often they appear imaginary. Occasionally the forces that seemed to dictate to him were truly omnipotent, but more often they could easily have been brushed aside.

Clinton's antenna, which picked up the slightest controversy on the horizon and magnified it into Armageddon, created an inertia in the White House that made decisive action difficult. The innate aversion to change that characterizes any bureaucracy, coupled with the president's excess of caution, dampened the bold action he needed to take to salvage his political career after the humiliating political defeat of 1994.

The examples abound:

- Clinton didn't mobilize the National Guard Military Police units to surround and protect black churches in the south from racist arsonists, because he was worried about criticism from the military that such action would undermine the Guard's readiness.
- He wouldn't ban administration officials from having contact with lobbyists representing foreign countries, because he was afraid too many of his top staff would protest.
- He did not do what President Bush and Senator John Kerry have both done—refused federal matching funds—for his 1996 campaign, and refused to abide by the expenditure limits that came with them because he was concerned about editorial criticism. Instead, he accepted the funds—and found a way to circumvent the limits.
- He rejected proposals to create a list of charitable organizations that were fronts for terrorism, because he was convinced he would be criticized by civil libertarians and that the list would be likened to the attorney general's list of communist fronts published in the McCarthy era.
- He did not submit legislation for uniform national testing in school to guarantee high academic standards—akin to the bill Bush got passed in 2001—because he was afraid it would be shot down by advocates of local control of schools.

One night, after a meeting in the residence with Clinton, Al Gore, and Chief of Staff Leon Panetta, I grew frustrated beyond endurance by Clinton's fear of doing anything, and confronted him directly. Once Al and Leon had departed, I went up to the president and grabbed him by the shoulders. "What the fuck has happened to you?" I screamed. "You used to take chances. You used to use issues to win elections. You used to have guts. What's happened to you in this building?" By now, I was punctuating my remarks by shaking his slack body.

"Be careful," he cautioned me. "The Secret Service will come in."

Steeling himself after this confrontation, Clinton slowly began to become more willing to act, more aggressive in seeking the kind of confrontations that would be crucial to his comeback. He bit the bullet and agreed to recommend a balanced federal budget in a nationally televised speech, despite Democratic concerns that this would undermine his criticism of the Republican budget cuts. He cast aside the warnings of some of his staff and took on the tobacco lobby, pushing tough federal regulations. He renegotiated the Bosnia agreements with the UN, which allowed NATO to launch air strikes without seeking approval from the world body. For the first time, Clinton was taking tough and vigorous action.

Once Clinton made up his mind and took action, however, he always had a person on hand to blame if things went wrong. This constantly updated catalogue of blame—perhaps Clinton's least attractive feature—was a constant during his presidency, and it is one of the few truly consistent themes in his memoirs.

Why did Clinton feel this compulsion to place blame? Was it that he was especially mindful of the risks behind certain actions, risks that could lead to real failure or dire consequences? Did he need others to take the fall if things went sour?

Certainly that was part of it. Every president must work within the realm of the possible, and it's often expedient to leave oneself an escape route, in order to protect the administration's power and profile. But with Bill Clinton there was something more at work. Responding most often to external stimuli, rarely to his internally generated priorities, Clinton saw each idea as having an author. When he embraced the concept, in his mind the person came with it. He acted partially out of respect for the merits of an argument, but also because he believed in the person advancing it.

This trait influenced Clinton's thinking in almost every aspect of his public life. When an old man would lament the high cost of medicine to candidate Clinton as he campaigned in some primary, the plaintive cry would still be resonating in Clinton's mind as he proposed legislation to address the problem. By the same token, when an adviser confidently proposed a certain line of action, Clinton would often be driven by his empathy with the proponent, his identification with the adviser's way of thinking, to adopt the advice. Few proposals ever became fully Clinton's own—at least until they proved successful. They were always borrowed from this or that adviser. And when things went wrong, he naturally primarily assigned blame to the advocate, and only secondarily to himself for adopting it.

As Clinton chalks up blame in *My Life,* for each of his mistakes, we realize that his decisions were really designations of one adviser's view as the right one. From then on, it was the staff member, not he, who was in charge. In her portrait of Mediator personalities, Helen Palmer notes how such people constantly sublimate their own views to those of others. But Palmer offers Mediators a crisp evaluation of their chosen coping strategy: "if you merge with another's agenda, you'll blame that person when things don't go well." As Palmer notes, a Mediator will say, in effect, "This was your idea, not mine. I just went along."

Bill Clinton treated his role in the White House more as magistrate than president, ruling on the opinions of others rather than hearing them out and then making his own decision. As a result, Clinton usually liked to act within the confines of the alternatives that were presented by his advisers.

There was a positive side to Clinton's relationships with his staff and friends: He would not tolerate yes-men, and sought constantly to surround himself with people who would criticize him, test him, and point out his failings. In *My Life,* he generously writes that one reason he enjoyed having me as an adviser is that I told him things that he didn't "want to hear." But this, too, had its disadvantages:

his universe was inevitably populated by people he could blame for any decision that went awry.

Clinton's best foreign policy adviser, Richard Holbrooke, failed to get the appointment as secretary of state during the second Clinton administration because he didn't realize how much the president preferred advisers who criticize him.

As the president shaped up his cabinet for the second term, he was forced to replace Warren Christopher, who held the position in the first term, as well as National Security Advisor Tony Lake. Lake and Christopher, I felt, had tended to treat Clinton as a novice in foreign affairs, which he truly was when he first took office. I used to chide him on the dominant role he let the duo play by saying that the president needed a "regent" to run foreign policy for him. "But when you turn twenty-one," I would assure Clinton, only half kidding, "Lake and Christopher will be glad to step aside and let you take over."

To take Christopher's place, I promoted the idea of choosing Holbrooke. He was an activist, and I knew he could bring Clinton aggressive ideas for a proactive foreign policy. On the day before Holbrooke's job interview with the president, he called me. "What do you think I should say?" Holbrooke asked.

"You have to criticize him," I answered.

"Won't he resent that?" Holbrooke replied. "Many presidents do."

"No," I told him. "He won't value you unless you criticize him. Walk right into the meeting and punch him in the nose. Otherwise he'll figure he won't need you. He'll glide right through the meeting with you. You need to be critical of him right away and bring him back down to earth. If you don't, he won't give you the job."

Holbrooke noted how unusual it was for a president to seek out criticism. "With Johnson," he recalled, "if you criticized him, it would be the last time you'd ever see him."

Holbrooke called me after the meeting.

"How did it go?" I asked.

"Wonderfully," Holbrooke beamed. "It was the best discussion of foreign policy I've ever had with him."

"Did you criticize him?" I probed.

"No, I didn't get to that," Holbrooke explained. "He had just come from a speech and he was in a relaxed, almost philosophical mood. We bonded on a level we never had before."

"You won't get the job," I predicted. "You didn't criticize him."

Later, before he made his formal announcement, Clinton told me that he thought Holbrooke, whom he knew I was supporting, was the "best qualified" to be secretary of state. That clinched it: I knew he was dead. It was Clinton-speak for "I'm going to appoint Madeleine Albright because I want a woman in the job."

Madeleine got the nod, and Holbrooke had to settle for an appointment as UN ambassador. To this day, I believe that had he been named either secretary of state or national security advisor, the Clinton administration would have been far, far more robust in dealing with Osama bin Laden in the years before 9/11.

Throughout 1995 and 1996, Clinton was discontented with his foreign policy team. "They give me no other options," he once howled to me, railing about their lack of creativity.

So why didn't *he* go out and invent new options? Why didn't Clinton just leave his advisers behind, evaluate the issues for himself, and carve his own way through the thicket, urging his counselors to catch up with his initiative? Isn't that what presidents are supposed to do?

Behind each new assignment of blame or fault lurks that essential Clinton flaw: his passivity. He *reacts*—to stimuli, in this case to crisis, and to advice about how to proceed.

And why did Clinton develop this lifelong habit of using others as proxies? Of relying on them to suggest ways and means to deal with his problems?

Because he could.

Because his charm, power, access to money, charisma, and electability all put him in a position where he could act through others, be guided by others, and could blame others when things went badly.

In Clinton's account of each of the first four major crises involving governmental force during his years in office, his passivity and need to affix blame are on consistent display.

Early in his first term, President Clinton was tested by four key decisions involving the use of government power. His performance was not encouraging.

His raid on the Branch Davidian Compound in Waco, Texas, led to a fiery inferno that killed eighty people. Abroad, a raid on the headquarters of Somali warlord Mohammed Aidid led to the death of nineteen American soldiers. His failure to use his power spawned catastrophe in Bosnia, as he allowed the genocide to escalate. And he set the pattern of token response to provocations from Saddam Hussein when he ordered a one-shot air raid, limited to one target, to punish the dictator for trying to assassinate former President Bush during a visit to Kuwait after he left office.

In his memoirs, Clinton condemns his failures with surprising frankness. But he blames his inability to do the right thing on circumstances purportedly beyond his control. Each time he swears that he knew all along what needed to be done, but could not do it because he was either blocked by outside forces or misled by his own advisers.

When I worked in the Clinton White House, I came to recognize that Bill Clinton's consistent complaint—that he was led astray by bad advice or forced into inaction by circumstances beyond his control—was too easy an excuse. I saw increasingly that his claim to be stymied over issues like Bosnia and Iraq was an attempt to justify his fear of action in these risky theaters. And when he did take action, as in Waco and Somalia, his arm's length approach simply allowed him to lay off the blame on somebody else after things went wrong.

To believe that Clinton was, indeed, paralyzed by bad advice or outside forces in these four crises, we would have to believe that he was more clerk than president—and wonder how a man so easily misled or daunted could have won the world's highest office.

I didn't buy Clinton's excuses then, and I don't buy them now.

In Waco, Mogadishu, Bosnia, and Iraq, Clinton had plenty of options. He had only to make up his mind to follow through on what he claims were his better instincts. These self-indulgent alibis, ventured as excuses to future historians for his past mistakes, should not be allowed to stand unchallenged. In these four early crises, he was cowed by fears of public backlash and partisan criticism. His empathy, the very quality that empowered him to act so effectively in many situations, here proved his own worst enemy.

Underlying all of this is the fact that Bill Clinton was congenitally uncomfortable with the use of force. Attacked for dodging the draft, and unaccustomed to the kind of force majeure with which the presidency is endowed, he instinctively shied away from confrontation and conflict. When he faced the necessity of using raw power, he saw potential disaster around every corner. In his mind, he could see the accusatory stares of widows or grieving parents, silently saying: *You sacrificed my husband or my son, when you yourself were too much of a coward to serve.* He could hear the partisan condemnations of his hypocrisy in asking others to risk what he wouldn't risk himself.

When David Koresh and his Branch Davidians killed four ATF agents and wounded sixteen others in Waco, Texas, on February 28, 1993, all eyes turned to Washington to see how Clinton would handle the first crisis of his presidency, just a month after he had taken office. Some felt he would order swift and sure retaliation; others wondered if he would try diplomacy. Instead, amazingly, he did nothing.

Day after day, week after week, month after month, the FBI surrounded Koresh and his followers, negotiating the release of some women and children, but leaving most within the compound. Koresh's offers to surrender proved disingenuous, and ultimatums and deadlines were allowed to pass. The political harm to Clinton seemed to mount with each day's front-page headlines, as Koresh flouted federal authority. Waco became a symbol of Clinton's weakness, as the FBI entrenched itself in stalemate and made no move to dislodge him or his followers.

Two months later, when the FBI finally did act, on April 19, the result was a total disaster. The entire compound was consumed in a mass of flames, killing eighty people, including twenty-five children. The government claimed that the Davidians had started the fire when the raid began, and that the flammable tear gas the FBI used to neutralize the armed men in the compound had spread the blaze. When Koresh's followers opened the windows of the building to vent the gas, the inrushing air merely fanned the inferno. Though the government denied it, some said that the FBI even fired upon people fleeing the compound.

That the Clinton administration could make so wrongheaded a decision as to storm the compound, when a siege would eventually have worked, was bad enough. But in *My Life*, Clinton lays the blame at the feet of his attorney general, Janet Reno, claiming that she talked him into the precipitate action. It was she, Clinton writes, who feared that Koresh might be sexually assaulting young children and plotting a mass suicide. Besides, Reno reported, the FBI was "tired of waiting" for Koresh to surrender, and the continued standoff was growing more expensive every day.

A careful review of his narrative reveals that Clinton did not pursue any serious alternatives with Reno—even though he'd had a successful experience with a similar situation in Arkansas. As governor, Bill Clinton had faced a serious decision about whether to storm a right-wing militia compound in northern Arkansas. In that case, too, the FBI had wanted to raid the compound to apprehend several murder suspects. As he describes it in his book, Clinton was actively involved in resolving the dispute and limiting the possibility of deaths of innocent people. He consulted with law enforcement authorities from neighboring states, met with the FBI, and critically considered the alternatives. Before he would permit any siege, he insisted that a pilot with experience in Vietnam fly over the mountainous compound and report back to him about the risks involved. Once he learned that it would be extremely dangerous and could lead to numerous deaths, he developed another plan and was able to blockade the compound and capture the suspects without any casualties. Clinton writes that he suggested that Reno adopt the same approach. Reno apparently dismissed Clinton's suggestion, citing the ability of the Branch Davidians to "hold out."

While governor, Clinton had immersed himself in the strategy for dealing with the Arkansas mountaintop cult and averted a tragic outcome. But now, as commander in chief, he acted helpless. Instead of calling in the FBI and local law enforcement for his own discussions and trying to broker another solution, Clinton caved in to Reno and gave her the go-ahead. When the raid backfired and turned into a fiery disaster, the president reports that he was "furious . . . for agreeing to the raid against my better judgment." Clinton later told the Danforth Committee, investigating the tragedy: "I gave in to the people in the Justice Department who were pleading to go in early, and I felt personally responsible for what had happened, and I still do."

Loyal to the last, Reno confirms Clinton's account. Telling her story in an Associated Press interview in 2000, the departing attorney general recounted a phone conversation with Clinton in which she briefed him on the plan for the raid and its dangers. The AP reported Reno's account: " 'I went through it with him, told him why I decided that we should go ahead,' Reno said of the Sunday phone call with Clinton on April 18, 1993. 'And he wanted, as I recall, to know what the questions were' that Reno had asked the FBI. Reno said Clinton asked her, 'Are you sure you've had all your questions answered' about the FBI's plan? Reno briefed Clinton on the 'conditions inside the complex, the status of negotiations and the reasoning behind the plan.' "

On April 20, 1993, the day after the raid, Clinton repeated that Reno had told him that "the plan included a decision to withhold the use of ammunition, even in the face of fire, and instead to use tear gas that would not cause permanent harm to health, but would, it was hoped, force the people in the compound to come outside and to surrender."

The president said Reno told him that "under no circumstances would our people fire any shots at them even if fired upon. They were going to shoot the tear gas from armored vehicles which would protect them and there would be no exchange of fire." Clinton asked "if the military had been consulted" And Reno assured him that they "had, and that they were in basic agreement."

But was Clinton really led astray by Reno's advice? Why did this president, who usually prided himself on a full mastery of all the details of his options before he acted, choose in this case to work only through his attorney general, respecting the chain of command in this area as he did in no other? Why didn't he convene a full Oval Office meeting, with the FBI, the ATF, the military, and his other advisers, to review the battle plan, subject it to scrutiny, and ask the probing questions himself? Why was he content just to ask Reno if she had asked the right questions, and if she was happy with the answers she got?

After all, Clinton had no extensive personal history with Janet Reno. He didn't really know her. She had been his third choice for attorney general, introduced to him by Hillary's brother Hugh Rodham and sponsored by Senator Bob Graham and Hillary's friends Vince Foster and Diane Blair. He knew that her background as a prosecutor didn't qualify her to supervise a paramilitary operation. I vividly remember how Bill Clinton once sat for days writing out an entire federal budget on a yellow pad in his lap, soliciting information from dozens of agencies in the process. Why the passivity in Waco?

And when the raid backfired, this president, who normally spoke to the nation every day, was strangely unwilling to step up to the microphone, waiting until the next day to speak to the public. Left out to dry by the administration, Janet Reno took full responsibility for the raid, appearing before the press and declaring bravely, "The buck stops with me"—a telling echo of the placard that more properly adorned Harry Truman's presidential desk: "The buck stops here."

The media was relentless in pounding at Clinton for failing to take responsibility after the attack. The *Wall Street Journal* accused Clinton of "dumping responsibility on to the barely-in-office Janet Reno," and said his "lack of grace in the face of the Waco tragedy raises anew issues about his instinct on matters of personal responsibility."

The *Washington Post,* noting any president's readiness to take credit for events they have scarcely influenced, said: "The flip side is that the president is also required, and rightly so, to accept responsibility when any agency of government is involved in something that turns out to be a catastrophe."

Clinton himself said after the attack that "It is not possible for a president to distance himself from things when the federal government is in control." But the fact is that he tried to do exactly that.

Clinton lashes back once again in *My Life,* claiming that George Stephanopoulos stopped him from immediately taking responsibility for the debacle in a public statement. George apparently feared that if any survivors were still alive, Koresh might be offended and murder them as well. "I didn't blame George," Clinton maintains. Yet, in effect, that's exactly what he did.

Clinton now claims that he was angry at himself for shirking responsibility. He complains that he relied on advisers even though his "gut" argued against allowing the raid in the first place, and against delaying the public statement taking responsibility afterward.

In *All Too Human,* Stephanopoulos confirms that he did indeed urge Clinton to hold back from speaking out in public. But his account skirts the central question: Why had Clinton listened to him, a barely thirty-year-old adviser with no experience in an executive capacity? Why did Clinton choose to be guided by a fledgling attorney general and a young, untested adviser?

Bill Clinton was no fool. He realized that the Waco standoff had become a political nightmare, as each day's coverage in the media seemed to cement Clinton's reputation for weakness. Waco had become a kind of domestic Iranian hostage crisis, draining Clinton's credibility as surely as the Iranian mobs had sapped Carter's.

And his political troubles weren't all in his mind. In their private newsletter of April 1993, Rowland Evans and Robert Novak reported that Clinton's "negatives are worse at this stage than any recorded since these measurements began to be kept. Democratic members of Congress from swing states and swing districts reported such negative feelings during their spring recess that the support level has continued to drop. Combinations of poor strategy, disorganization and just plain bad luck are conspiring to undermine the President's position."

So Clinton knew he had to act for political reasons. But he foresaw the potential for disaster when the FBI stormed the compound. So he waited until the bureaucratic forces proved irresistible to his attorney general, and bided his time until she called to ask his permission to authorize the raid. He didn't insist on an Oval Office meeting; that would have left his fingerprints too evident on the decision to attack the compound. He wanted to confirm the impression that anything that went wrong had occurred purely in Reno's sphere. And when the raid did blow up in her face, he hung back, grasping at the compliant Stephanopoulos's convenient hesitation as an excuse to do just what he wanted all along—to let Reno take the fall.

When Clinton did finally venture out to the microphones, it was to repeat what Reno had told him—and, essentially, to confirm that his attorney general, not he, was to blame. More than a decade later, in *My Life*, he repeats the story, asking history to look past his role as president and instead focus blame squarely on his attorney general.

So why did Clinton approve a plan that stopped his political hemorrhaging, but turned out to be deadly? And why did he let Reno take charge and blame her when the gamble failed, and then blame George Stephanopoulos for the fact that he had let Reno take the blame? All, once more, because he could.

Reno's loyalty in assuming the blame for Waco in 2000, years after the event, might have its origin in an interesting conversation she had with Clinton in the first few weeks of his second term. As I've noted elsewhere, Clinton told me that he despised Reno; he once told us that her appointment was the "worst mistake" he had ever made. As he shaped his second-term cabinet, he told me he was going to fire her. He sent her every signal of this intention, reappointing or replacing every one of his cabinet members but her. Clinton was obviously hoping that she would resign, to make it easier to get rid of her. But he couldn't get her to quit. So he scheduled a face-to-face meeting with her, at which, he told me, he planned to fire her.

Instead, he decided to let her stay.

Dumbfounded, I asked him why. "I told her," Clinton said, "that no attorney general had ever served for eight years, and that I thought it was not a good idea for anyone to do so. But she was desperate to keep the job. She says she'll quit [as attorney general] after a year—but she begged me to reappoint her first, so it won't look like I was firing her because of Waco."

I thought it odd that Reno and Clinton should still be talking about Waco, almost four years after the raid. But the very mention of the issue suggests that another dynamic might have been at play here: Reno may well have been demanding reappointment as her price for taking the fall for Waco—shouldering the responsibility that should have been his.

After the year ended, of course, Reno couldn't quit and Clinton couldn't replace her, because of Republican demands for a special prosecutor to investigate the campaign finance scandal. As long as Reno resisted these appeals, Clinton couldn't fire her. He knew that the Republican-dominated Senate would insist on a commitment to appoint a special prosecutor as its price for confirmation of any new attorney general candidate Clinton might designate. And Reno, for her part, resisted Republican calls for a special prosecutor because she knew that as long as she did so, she'd still have a job.

The results of the Waco raid were devastating. Beyond the scores of dead, who had expired in hideous pain, was the message the attack sent to cults and crazies throughout the nation: that the government was out to get them. So furious was the reaction to the fiasco that Timothy McVeigh cited Waco as the justification for his bombing of the Murrah Federal Building in Oklahoma City on the second anniversary of the raid. Would the Oklahoma City attack have happened had Clinton been wiser in his response to the Waco standoff?

And did Clinton's subsequent coarse explanation—that eighty people, including twenty-five children, had died "because some religious fanatics murdered themselves"—further fuel the disenchantment with Washington that led to Oklahoma City? This haunting question is not mentioned in his memoir.

"After Waco," he concludes, "I resolved to go with my gut."

But not really.

No sooner did he make the vow than he seems to have disregarded his "gut" once more, in his first real foreign military test. In June 1993, after Clinton was in office for barely five months, Somali warlord Mohammed Aidid murdered twenty-four Pakistani peacekeepers who were there as part of the UN mission to get food to the starving people of the region. Clinton ordered a retaliatory raid, but when U.S. troops closed in on Aidid in broad daylight, the Somali warlord's forces killed nineteen Americans and wounded eighty-four more. Then they dragged the body of a slain soldier through the streets of Mogadishu.

As with Waco, in *My Life*, Clinton elaborately lays the blame for the Somalia fiasco on others. Comparing it to JFK's Bay of Pigs disaster, he notes carefully that he had "approved" of the operation "in general but not in its particulars." That must be a new standard of presidential endorsement for a military operation. Clinton tries to cover himself by writing that he "did not envision . . . a daytime assault in a crowded, hostile neighborhood" when he okayed the raid. He assumed the rangers would try to catch Aidid away from civilians and his clan. The commander in chief appears to have had no idea exactly what kind of military operation he was authorizing.

Clinton even says that his chief of staff, General Colin Powell, said that he would not have approved of the raid either, had he known it was to be done during the day. But Clinton apparently never asked when the raid was to take place, and nobody imposed "any parameters" on General William Garrison in the conduct of the raid. As further proof that it wasn't his fault, in *My Life*, Clinton reports that the obliging Garrison took full responsibility for his decision to approve the raid.

Vowing to learn his lesson, Clinton writes that he was much more careful to learn the risks and the details of military operations before he approved them after the experience at Mogadishu.

This elaborate effort to deflect blame for the failure of the raid raises the basic question: Why didn't Clinton ask the right questions in the first place? The Waco raid had failed spectacularly only weeks before. He knew that the attack on Aidid was a dramatic departure from the humanitarian mission on which Bush had sent the American troops in the first place. Why did he assume that the raid would take place at night? Why didn't he ask? Why did he not inquire whether it would take place among the civilian population?

I refuse to believe that Clinton was that insensitive to the pitfalls of his first military action as president. He knew that Powell was only three days away from retirement. He must have realized that it was his own duty as president to ask the tough questions. And yet he did not—quite possibly because he suspected that the mission might blow up in his face, and he was anxious as ever to retain plausible, flexible deniability if things went south.

But the real disaster of Mogadishu was not the horrible casualties. It was Clinton's subsequent decision to cut and run.

Once the raid had failed, the world again waited to see what Clinton would do. Would he redouble the U.S. commitment and bring Aidid and his murderers to justice? The stakes were high; this was the first real test of Clinton's mettle as commander.

In the end, after a six-month period of "transition," he chose to pull out.

Always empathetic, Clinton claims in *My Life,* that he understood the feelings of the American troops who wanted to go back to "finish the job." He says he felt "sick" about the loss of American troops. So why did Clinton flinch? He claims that there was no support in Congress for a more extensive military commitment in Somalia. He writes that he wouldn't have minded battling in Congress about it, but that he was worried that such a fight might sap resources he needed for more important operations in Haiti and Bosnia.

Nonsense. Congress was in Democratic hands, and the leaders in the House and the Senate would never have embarrassed their president over his first foreign-policy crisis. Public opinion in the United States was outraged at the treatment of American soldiers, who were only in Somalia to feed the population; the public would have supported any military action under those circumstances. Finally, President Clinton had all the power he needed to order follow-on action. He didn't need even to ask Congress.

The real reason Clinton decided not to pursue Aidid was simple: He was afraid of getting stuck in a war in Somalia. He was determined not to be trapped into an escalating cycle of violence, where he believed no vital American interests were at stake.

"I keep telling him to get out of Somalia," Hillary told me in a phone call right after Mogadishu, "but nobody listens to me. It's Bush's final present to us. We should just get out."

Once again, Clinton's own aggressive draft dodging undermined his confidence and inclined him to avoid military retaliation. And his imagination at the peril of being dragged deeper and deeper into a dead-end war—the lingering prospect of a Vietnam-style "quagmire"—led him to abandon the battle where only minimal American interests appeared to be at stake.

But our interests in Mogadishu were much, much more vital than anybody realized at the time.

As the 9/11 Commission has recently reported, it turns out that Osama bin Laden was watching our reaction closely.

In an interview published in *Esquire* magazine in 1999, bin Laden commented on the Somalia withdrawal: "The youth were surprised at the low morale of the American soldiers and realized more than before that the American soldier was a paper tiger and after a few blows ran in defeat. . . . And America forgot all the hoopla and media propaganda about being the world leader of the New World Order, and after a few blows they forgot about this title and left, dragging their corpses and their shameful defeat."

Clinton was teaching the terrorists a tragic lesson about our government's resolve.

In Bosnia, too, Clinton sought to avoid military involvement, citing every excuse he could think of not to intervene to prevent the genocide of 250,000 Bosnian Muslims, who ultimately died at the hands of their Serbian tormentors.

The British and the French, who had primary responsibility for dealing with this European problem, had persuaded the United Nations to impose an arms embargo on both sides in the Bosnia civil war. As often happens, the embargo did little damage to Serbia's military capacities, since their army had inherited the extensive military hardware Yugoslavia had amassed under its former Communist regime. But the embargo did deny the means of self-defense to the poorly equipped majority Muslim population in Bosnia. Unarmed, they could do little to repel the invaders or to protect their villages.

Senator Bob Dole and the Republicans repeatedly urged lifting the embargo or, failing that, recommended a unilateral American decision not to respect it. Clinton agreed that the embargo was misguided, but notes in *My Life,* that he felt he had to respect it—once again against his better instincts—out of respect for the United Nations.

When Serb outrages continued unabated, he refused to bomb to protect the Muslims, because of opposition from the British and the French. Claiming that he did not want to split NATO, he determined not to send in American troops, because he felt the UN mandate "was bound to fail."

With European "peacekeepers" on the ground in Bosnia—each a potential hostage to the Bosnian Serbian Army—America's allies opposed air strikes and demanded a dual key approach, in which both the UN and NATO would have to agree before any air attacks. The result was a series of pinprick air strikes against highly restricted targets, which did nothing to deter the Serbs and only further enhanced their impression of the impotence of the West. In *My Life,* Clinton writes that he disapproved of the dual key approach because he realized we could never get UN approval for effective action, since Russia, a long-time Serbian ally, had a Security Council veto. History buffs will recall that World War I started when Russia went to the aid of her Serbian ally after Austria threatened invasion to retaliate for the assassination of the Austrian Archduke by a Serbian nationalist. The Russo-Serbian alliance ran deep.

So if Clinton realized the dual key policy was a prescription for inaction, why did he approve it? Again a fall guy emerges—this time Secretary of State Warren Christopher, who secured the agreement and negotiated the framework.

Hampered by the UN, President Clinton remained largely passive for two years as the Bosnian Serbs ruthlessly herded the Muslims into World War II-style concentration camps, murdering a quarter of a million people and systematically raping Muslim women in a sick effort at eugenic ethnic cleansing. It was not until the summer of 1995, after two and a half years of shocking inactivity, that Clinton finally stirred himself to take action.

Persuaded by the constant televised coverage of Serbian atrocities, Clinton began to realize, in the first half of 1995, how his inactivity was causing him political harm. I warned him frequently that his dithering was causing voters to see him as too weak for the job, and was driving up his negative ratings.

In the weeks after Oklahoma City, America had seen Bill Clinton at his best, consoling and healing the nation's wounds, and his approval ratings skyrocketed. But by May 1995, one month later, the televised images of Serbian rape, pillage, and slaughter were driving his numbers down again. America's seeming helplessness in the face of Serbian slaughter began to cost Clinton political capital. "The media are trying to force me into a war in Bosnia," he complained to me, moaning about the impact of each night's television news.

Finally, spurred into action by those declining numbers—which moved him far more than the Serbian atrocities themselves—Clinton at long last began trying to change the British and French position and end UN control over air strikes. In a long series of late-night telephone calls in the middle of 1995, which left him bleary the next day, he persuaded French president Jacques Chirac and British prime minister John Major to take away the power of the UN's secretary general, Boutros Boutros-Ghali, to veto NATO air action over Bosnia. Finally, the United States, Britain, and France drew a line in the sand, saying that if the Serbs attacked Gorazde, it would trigger a massive air retaliation. When they did, in the summer of 1995, Clinton finally acted—and within weeks the action broke the back of the Serbian military.

Those who condemn the Bush administration's exercise of military power to topple Saddam Hussein, and wish we had persuaded the United Nations to join us, should remember how waiting for UN approval hogtied the West over Bosnia. Boutros-Ghali's failure to approve air strikes cost one quarter of a million Bosnian Muslim men, women, and children their lives.

Why couldn't Clinton have moved sooner? Why hadn't he intervened as the body count multiplied? In *My Life,* he attributes his inactivity to the intransigence of our allies. But once his political fortune was on the line, he was quite up to the task of muscling allies into cooperation. Then, and only then, did the walls preventing action come tumbling down.

But Clinton knew he could persuade the British and the French to act whenever he wanted to. In *My Life,* he uses the UN, British, and French positions as excuses to evade responsibility for his inaction. The real reason he wouldn't act is that, once again, he was scared to death of getting mired in a war. Clinton's feigned helplessness in the face of the greatest European slaughter since World War II can be traced directly to his allergy to military action, born of his own lack of service and draft dodging. When political considerations finally impelled him to act, the ease with which he was able to persuade the Europeans to back massive air strikes—and the speed with which the bombings finally forced a Serbian surrender—belie Clinton's pretense of helplessness.

With Muslim lives on the line in Bosnia, America's failure to intervene once again convinced the fanatics who would launch the 9/11 attacks that the United States was a paper tiger that would never take action—certainly not to protect non-Christians.

Ultimately, Clinton acted in Bosnia. But he never did in Rwanda, where one million Tutsis were killed by the majority Hutus, many of whom were hacked to death. The United States did nothing, although Clinton frankly acknowledges in *My Life,* that a few thousand troops might have averted the horrific genocide.

The former president blames his failure to act on the distractions of Bosnia, Congressional opposition to military deployments, and the Mogadishu disaster six months before. But none of those was the real reason, as Clinton doubtless knows.

The real reason was that Rwanda was black. Bosnia was white. European atrocities *mattered* more than African atrocities—not to Clinton himself, but to the media, which covered the grisly deaths in Yugoslavia but devoted considerably less attention to the genocide in Africa. And without the media dogging him to take action, Bill Clinton—ever the reactor, rarely the initiator—wasn't about to pay attention.

Clinton's inaction on Rwanda wasn't racist. It was political. But it was an outrage just the same.

The imaginary obstacles between Clinton and action arose on one other telling occasion during the president's first year, when Saddam Hussein's plot to assassinate President Bush was discovered. In reaction, Clinton chose to deliver a largely symbolic air strike, targeting Iraqi intelligence headquarters. Why not a stronger response? Clinton writes in *My Life,* that he felt "we would have been justified in hitting Iraq harder," but Colin Powell persuaded him that wider attacks were likely to kill too many innocent people.

The first in a long series of ineffective bombardments of Iraq, Clinton's largely token retaliation convinced Saddam that he could push around the new administration without fear of any serious ground attacks in return. In the years that followed, Saddam loosened the belt that circumscribed him, knowing he had little to fear from Bill Clinton. Clinton's limited response made it very clear to Baghdad that Bill Clinton was no George Bush.

The 1993 attack on Iraqi intelligence headquarters was the first in a long series of ineffective air raids and other symbolic measures during the Clinton administration. With each new step Iraq took to defy the agreements it had made to end the Gulf War, the West responded in a limited, and ineffective, fashion. It was a series of unconvincing performances that proved that neither the United States nor the United Kingdom would show real toughness toward Saddam.

But never did Clinton do anything serious to stem the Iraqi move toward rearmament. Knowing that U.S. and U.K. ground troops would never intervene, and that whatever air attacks Clinton ordered would soon end, Saddam felt he could move with impunity. As these gentle attacks proceeded, Iraq moved further and further down the road to full oil production, the total expulsion of UN inspectors, and massive rearmament.

Each and every time Clinton faced the question of using force, he opted for the same formula: protect his political flank by proceeding only at the behest of his military, political, or law enforcement advisers, so that he would have a ready scapegoat should anything misfire. And in *My Life,* the fall guys are all on display. But behind them lingers the abiding image of a president uneasy with power, uncomfortable with military action, and unwilling to take personal political risks.

President Clinton failed to take responsibility after Waco, and he did not use his power responsibly in Bosnia, Somalia, and Iraq. In his handling of each of these fiascoes, Clinton offered an early warning of how he would fail in the later trials of his administration's battle against terror. Had Clinton acted with less sensitivity to the polls at the time of Waco, would the passions that ignited at Oklahoma City have been calmed? Would the bitter cycle of alienation that began to spiral with the raids on Ruby Ridge and other confrontations between the government and its citizens not have mushroomed into the bombing of the Murrah Federal Building?

And had the president showed more firmness in dealing with Somalia, would the nascent terrorist bin Laden have been more heedful of American power and less likely to gamble with his global terrorism?

Would hundreds of thousands of lives have been saved in Bosnia, and the tensions between the Christian and Islamic worlds have remained in check, had President Clinton overridden the dual-trigger approach earlier and demanded the effective use of air power in 1993, rather than wait until his hand was forced by public pressure in 1995?

And would Saddam have trimmed his sails if he had become convinced that Clinton would use the same firm hand toward him that the first President Bush had demonstrated in 1991? Would we have avoided sending the message that America was under new, weaker management, which kindled his determination to defy the global community?

These are some of the imponderables of the Clinton era. But one thing is clear. In *My Life,* the former president's squirming to avoid blame and to pin responsibility for these mistakes elsewhere reflects his own awareness that history will ask these same questions.

Clinton's need for scapegoats spilled over into all aspects of his presidency, and remains clear on each page of his book. Unsure of himself in foreign policy, he elevated blame to a fine art. But even on his home ground—domestic and economic policy—his world was populated by those he held responsible for his own mistakes . . . because he could.

Clinton needed people to blame, in the same way that a dolphin or a submarine needs to bounce sonar waves off the ocean's rocks and shoals in order to identify himself and determine his position. By blaming his advisers, adversaries, the media, and even his own party colleagues, he could locate himself and define who he was.

To grasp how Clinton used blame as an instrument of self-defense, one has to realize how essentially passive was his management style.

He would raise a topic by complaining loudly and furiously about it to all who were within earshot. Among his favorites: "I can't raise enough money." "Starr is after me." "We never get our message out." "My advisers never give me enough options." "The Republicans can articulate their message in thirty seconds. What's *my* message?"

After each long, voluble, and repetitive rant, he would retreat into silence as his advisers and colleagues proposed solutions. He met each idea with only with a blank stare. Clinton seemed, at times, almost to follow the psychiatrist's technique, keeping a blank face at all times so that the patient can read into his lack of expression exactly what he wants to see. Clinton would not betray his thinking by so much as a twitch, allowing his advisers and cabinet secretaries to project onto his screen their own views.

But there was another reason behind his passivity: It gave him full latitude to distance himself if a mistake was made. Understanding that he had to preserve his presidency at all costs, Clinton reached instinctively for subordinates to blame if things went awry. And his silence and passivity during the planning phases gave him a deniability he would use later if he had to.

Oddly, it always felt curiously good when you were being set up to take the blame should things go wrong. You felt the president was trusting you.

For example, when Clinton was pondering whether to sign the welfare reform bill in August 1996, he phoned me and complained about the legislation's anti-immigrant provisions. Shouting into the phone, he yelled: "If a guy comes here legally, complies with all our laws, gets a job, pays his taxes, does his work, and gets injured, under the [Republican] bill, he can't get disability benefits! His family won't be protected! Where is the justice in that?" As he pondered the fate of immigrants cut off from benefits under the GOP bill, he was at his empathetic best, cutting through a policy debate to feel the human pain underneath.

Of course he was right—but that was no reason to veto the bill, which required that beneficiaries work for their welfare checks and limit their stay on welfare to five years. "You can sign the bill and fix it next year," I counseled him. "You'll have a Democratic Congress back and they'll pass whatever fixes you need to get rid of those provisions."

"You mean I can say what I don't like about the bill even as I'm signing it?" he replied.

"Sure—lay it out there, and then campaign for the changes you're suggesting."

When he signed the welfare reform bill, he called me and said, "I'm signing this because I trust you." Who could avoid feeling a rush of intimacy with the president when he called with such a message? Only later did I realize that I was being set up for the blame should things go wrong. It was the same way Janet Reno must have felt during Waco.

As it happened, even though the Democrats lost Congress in the 1996 elections, Clinton was able to get rid of the anti-immigrant provisions in the bill during the next session anyway—thanks to pressure from Republican governors who didn't want a lot of impoverished legal immigrants on their hands.

My Life, like the Clinton presidency, is a catalogue of blame, in which he chalks up virtually every mistake of his eight years in office to other people. He blames himself only for listening to them.

For example:

- Why did he raise energy taxes in 1993, a move that did more to cost his party control of Congress than any other? He knew all along, he writes, that if he proposed such a levy the Republicans would beat him up with the tax issue. So why did he do it? To appease "the hunger of prosperous interest-rate setters," he says. Against his better judgment, he "gave in" to Treasury secretary Lloyd Bentsen and Vice President Al Gore and went along with the tax bowing to the power of "thirty-year-old bond traders."

  The reality is quite different. Clinton realized that he had to send a signal to the financial markets that he was willing to do the ultimate—raise middle-class taxes—in order to balance the budget. "I have to convince [Alan] Greenspan that I'm serious about deficit reduction, and the only way to do that is to show him that I'll take political risks to do it," he told me in a phone call as his 1993 economic package was taking shape.

But in *My Life,* he translates this need to reassure the Federal Reserve Board into a move to appease his Treasury secretary and vice president. In Bill Clinton's world, no move could be made without someone at the ready to jump in front of him and take the bullet—whether they liked it or not.

■ And why did he move so early in his administration to integrate gays into the military, a decision so controversial that it dominated the headlines for months at the start of his first term? According to Clinton, it was Republican Leader Bob Dole's fault. The senator forced his hand by proposing a Congressional resolution that would have removed his authority to lift the ban on homosexuals in the armed forces. With the Dole resolution coming before Congress, he felt he had to act quickly using his current authority.

"Dole made me do it," he screamed at me in 1993, when I told him what a public relations disaster it was to take the issue on so early in his presidency.

Of course, Dole had nothing to do with it. Even if he had actually introduced it, Dole's resolution would never have seen the light of day in a comfortably Democratic Congress, where Clinton's own party's leadership totally controlled the floor and committee agenda. So why did Clinton begin his administration with this proposal—which, he admits, led voters to think he cared more about the rights of gays than about the state of the economy?

The real reason wasn't Bob Dole at all. It was the enormous financial power of gay donors to the Democratic Party. As Al Gore once told me: "Gays and environmentalists are two of the leading sources of money for our party." And, in the opening days of the administration, Clinton had to try to appease them both.

By raising the issue early in his presidency, however, he made a massive mistake. As the *New York Times* reported two weeks after his inauguration, his opening days in office had been "dominated by the politically unwelcome fight over whether homosexuals should be allowed to serve in the armed forces."

- And why did Clinton break his campaign promise of a middle-class tax cut—the centerpiece of his battle for the Democratic nomination? This time, the bond market made him do it. He writes that he broke his commitment to cut middle-class taxes in a bid to influence the psychology of the market.

  Perhaps Clinton should look at why he made the rash proposal in the campaign. His chief opponent for the Democratic nomination, Senator Paul Tsongas of Massachusetts, warned that a middle class tax cut wasn't feasible with a huge deficit looming. He rightly accused Clinton of pandering and promising the moon. Rather than blame himself for making a campaign promise that he must have known was a fraud when he uttered it, Clinton blames the markets for his reversal.

- And who is to blame for his major defeat of 1993, the rejection by the Democratic Congress of his stimulus package just a few months into his presidency? This one was West Virginia senator Robert Byrd's fault. According to Clinton, the venerable senator insisted that no compromise was necessary, but that the administration could break the Republican filibuster. It turned out that he didn't have the votes; Byrd was wrong and the proposal went crashing to defeat.

  But it wasn't Byrd's fault, as Clinton doubtless realizes. It was Bill Clinton who doomed his own proposal, by so loading it with pork to buy Democratic votes that it became a laughingstock. Indeed, the very premise of the package—that we would spend public money not to any real purpose, but just to inject financial stimulus to hasten an economic recovery—was politically, and perhaps economically, flawed.

Americans don't approve of spending money just to see it spent, whatever the dictates of Keynesian economics. Without any real goal other than increasing spending, the package became a hodgepodge of swimming pools, basketball courts, and ice skating rinks in the districts of deserving Democrats. Republicans ridiculed the proposal, and the president who had made it.

The defeat of the stimulus package was devastating to the Clinton administration. In its first legislative test, and on its central issue—the economy—it lost even with Democrats in control of both houses of Congress. Clinton looked like a bumbler for losing, and a fool for making such a flawed proposal in the first place.

But Clinton blames it all on poor old Robert Byrd!

- And why did he and Hillary delay submitting their health care reform proposal to Congress for almost a year, while their staffs tinkered over every last comma in the 1,342-page bill they eventually sent to the Hill—a proposal so detailed that it became fodder for the late night comics? Even Clinton admits that his critics mocked the bill's length. So why did they write such a ludicrously detailed proposal, instead of sending rough outlines to Congress and letting the give and take of the legislative process shape something that could eventually pass? To hear Clinton tell it, it was House minority leader Dick Gephardt who was at fault. He was the one, Clinton writes, who said that the bill would have a better chance if it were specific and not just general.

- And, in a gesture that was to look more and more ridiculous as it became evident that Clinton couldn't get health care passed at all, why did the president go before a joint session of Congress and wave a pen in the air, saying he would veto any health care bill that did not provide for full coverage for all Americans? It wasn't his fault. He did it, he writes, because his advisers told him people wouldn't think he was strongly behind the bill unless he ruled out compromise.

But, as Clinton well understood, his obvious refusal to negotiate in good faith doomed the bill. When the sands were running out on his proposal, Clinton lamented that the GOP wouldn't come to the table to talk. But the bill's fate had been sealed by the president's line in the sand—a line that left him out in the cold!

■ And why did Clinton alienate the press by deciding to restrict their access to the White House? Oh, that wasn't his fault either. Someone high up in the Bush administration had suggested it, and Clinton doesn't recall participating in the decision to limit the media's ability to roam the corridors of the White House.

■ And why did he get such bad media coverage early in his Administration? Was it because of his refusal to release Whitewater documents, or his lying about ducking the draft, or failing to pass his economic stimulus package, or not taking responsibility for the Waco raid, or his do-nothing approach to Bosnia? No, according to Clinton the press was at fault, unfairly penalizing him for the restrictions he had placed on media access to the White House. It was their wrath that denied him the traditional honeymoon granted other presidents.

■ And why did the administration create a totally unnecessary scandal by firing the staff of the White House Travel Office, which made the arrangements for reporters to travel with the president? Whose fault was that? Not Clinton's. Hillary had gotten a complaint from a reporter about the Office's operations, and she and the president asked Chief of Staff Mack McLarty to look into it. After that, Clinton swears he forgot about the matter until his chief of administration in the White House, David Watkins, asked McLarty to fire them. The firings, Clinton says, were news to him.

■ And why did the media react so badly to the dismissals? Was it because Hillary denied, under oath, having anything to do with the firings, and was subsequently criticized by the Independent Prosecutor's Office for being "factually inaccurate"? Or did the media cover the scandal because it was increasingly evident that the Clintons were trying to steer the travel business to their close friend Harry Thomason? Or did the matter attract coverage because the Clintons charged that the head of the office had mishandled funds, an accusation of which he was acquitted after a trial? No, it was not due to any of these factors. In Clinton's account, the media was biased in favor of the Travel Office staff because they had been so well treated, particularly when the president went abroad. The reporters, he writes, felt that they should have had a voice in the decision on the firings.

- And why did Clinton order Air Force One to stay on the runway at Los Angeles airport while Hillary's hairdresser, Cristophe Schatteman, cut his hair? Who was responsible for the delays his decision may have caused (delays he denies occurred)? It was the Secret Service's fault. They told him twice, he writes angrily, that he would not cause any delays if he postponed his takeoff.

- And why was he attacked so aggressively during his administration? It was the fault of the Republicans, who never regarded his presidency as "legitimate," since he had been elected with only 43 percent of the vote after Perot siphoned off 19 percent to his third-party candidacy.

The Republican failure to acknowledge the legitimacy of his presidency touched a very raw nerve with Clinton. His heart sank on election night 1996, when he missed getting a majority of the popular vote by a few tenths of one percent. The legitimacy that would have come with such a majority affirmation proved elusive once more.

Why was he so spooked over the question of legitimacy? One wonders whether President George W. Bush—elected not only with a minority of the vote, but with one half million fewer votes than his opponent—ever felt illegitimate in office.

But Clinton felt the slight keenly, furious at the implication that his victory was some sort of accident owing to the division of the traditional Republican vote by Ross Perot's candidacy.

He often fumed at me that the reason he couldn't get a certain program through Congress, or that he could not get Republican support for his health care and economic programs, was that they thought he was an illegitimate president.

But it was up to Clinton, as president, to reach out to the other party to overcome the sense of illegitimacy that attached to his presidency at the outset. He should have governed in coalition with the GOP, going out of his way to meet with their leaders and negotiate legislative proposals. Instead, he was convinced that his majorities in Congress would insulate him from Republican opposition and guarantee him passage of his legislation.

In early December 1992, a month after the election, I met with the Clintons at the Arkansas Governors' Mansion, which was serving as the transition headquarters. In our meeting I warned them about the new reality in Washington: that a simple majority was no longer enough to pass legislation in the Senate because partisan filibusters, once reserved for civil rights bills, were now becoming almost routine. Without the sixty votes required to shut off debate and bring a bill to a vote in the Senate, legislation would not pass—and Clinton didn't have sixty votes.

But the president wouldn't reach out to the Republicans. He formulated his proposals only within his own caucus, consulted only with his party colleagues, and wouldn't bring any GOP leader into his councils or cabinet.

- And why did he appoint Louis Freeh to head the FBI, a choice he came to regret when his appointee gave ammunition to Republicans who were urging the appointment of a special prosecutor to probe campaign finance scandals? It was White House Counsel Bernie Nussbaum's fault. He had recommended Freeh. Clinton says that he heard from a friend that Freeh was too political and ambitious, but Clinton went ahead with the appointment anyway, saying he would have to trust Nussbaum's opinion.

■ And why did he not pardon former Arkansas governor Jim Guy Tucker and his close friend Webb Hubbell, who had been convicted by the hated Kenneth Starr, after he pardoned hundreds of others? This one is laid at the feet of his staff, who pressed him so hard that he gave up on the idea of pardoning his Whitewater cronies. He writes that the felt bad enough about his decision that he even apologized to Tucker, and vows, in *My Life*, to tender his regrets to Hubbell as soon as he can.

■ And why wasn't he more aggressive in answering Ross Perot's attacks on his record in Arkansas in the 1992 campaign, after the Independent ran ads showing how low the state ranked in most national measurements? Again, it was his staff's fault. He and Hillary wanted to reply, standing up for the honor of his home state, but he was "too tired and keyed up" to overrule his staff.

■ And why didn't he accept Boris Yeltsin's invitation to visit Russia right after the inauguration in 1993? Why did he turn Yeltsin down, even though the Russian leader was in political trouble at home and Clinton wanted to help him? Because National Security Advisor Tony Lake said he shouldn't go.

■ And why was Pennsylvania's popular but pro-life Democratic governor, Bob Casey, kept off the stage at the 1992 Democratic convention? Clinton was inclined to let him speak because he liked Casey. It was Democratic National Committee Chairman Ron Brown's fault that he was blackballed—as if Brown would not have obeyed Clinton's instructions.

■ And why did Clinton waffle when he was asked how he would have voted on the 1991 Resolution authorizing Bush to attack Iraq? Why did he offer such a gutless answer ("I guess I would have voted with the majority if it was a close vote. But I agree with the arguments the minority made.")? Why did he make what he said was one of his "worst" public statements? Indirectly, it was the fault of the two senators from Arkansas, David

Pryor and Dale Bumpers, who had voted against the resolution. Clinton felt he couldn't embarrass them by giving a straight answer—that he would have voted for the resolution.

- And why didn't he release the Whitewater documents the *Washington Post* was demanding—a step many felt would have nipped the scandal in the bud? His instincts were "to release the records," but White House counsel Bernie Nussbaum persuaded him not to.

- And why did he agree to let Janet Reno name a Whitewater special prosecutor when his inclination was to object to the appointment—a step he later rued? Turns out George Stephanopoulos and Deputy Chief of Staff Harold Ickes said it was inevitable, and urged Clinton to ask for a prosecutor.

- And when Clinton eventually agreed to let Reno appoint a prosecutor—Robert Fiske—why did he sign the newly adopted special prosecutor law, which allowed federal judges appointed by conservative Chief Justice Rehnquist to name a new person to the post? Clinton wanted Fiske to "be grandfathered" in, so why didn't he insist on that as a price for signing the bill? Whose fault was it that he signed the bill that made Ken Starr's appointment possible? White House Chief Lobbyist Pat Griffin and Counsel Lloyd Cutler get the blame; they assured him that the panel Rehnquist appointed would not move to replace Fiske.

- And who was to blame for the Oklahoma City bombing? This one is blamed on conservative radio talk show hosts. It was their "venomous" language that caused people like Timothy McVeigh to hate the government and act out against it.

- And why didn't he prop up Thailand when its currency started to fail, setting in motion the whole Asian financial crisis? It was Treasury Secretary Bob Rubin's fault: Clinton wanted to intervene, but Rubin talked him out of it.

- And whose fault was it that his 1996 reelection campaign took contributions that were funneled in by the Chinese intelligence operatives, triggering a huge scandal that dominated the media in 1997 and probably cost Clinton seven or eight points in the

1996 election? It was the fault of the Democratic National Committee, which failed in its duty to screen its contributions adequately. Clinton assures us of how angry he was to be victimized for something that was not his fault.

- And whose fault was it that he lied during the deposition by Paula Jones's lawyers about his affair with Monica Lewinsky? Jones's lawyers made him do it, because they failed to be specific in enumerating the sex acts they were asking about, so he ended up misleading them by denying "sexual relations" with Monica.

- And whose fault was it that he wagged his finger in the face of the nation on television and denied having sexual relations with "that woman," Monica Lewinsky? Why, it was at the "urging" of Harold Ickes and Harry Thomason. It was because of their bad advice that Clinton "reluctantly" went before the nation again with his emphatic denial.

- And, for that matter, why did he have the affair with Monica in the first place? The Republicans made him do it. He was so worn down by the "titanic" battle with Congress during the government shutdowns that he fell into the grip of his "old demons."

- And why was he so inept in his campaigning during the 1994 midterm elections? Basking in his higher poll ratings after he returned from negotiating the Middle East peace accord between Jordan and Israel a few weeks before the election, he called me to ask in which states I thought he should campaign as the race drew to a close. I told him to go back to the Middle East and do no campaigning at all. I warned that it would lower his poll numbers, making him look no longer presidential, but only political. A few days later he was zigzagging across the country, campaigning his heart out for the Democratic candidates for Congress. Why did he do it?

It wasn't his mistake. It was his staff's. In *My Life*, he says that he called his staff from the Middle East to tell them he wanted to stay in the White House and arrange for press events about his programs instead of campaigning. When he returned, he was "surprised" that he was scheduled to campaign for Democrats in ten states. Clinton never seems to have considered that he could have said no. (On election day 1994, when the Democrats lost control of both the House and Senate, Clinton was furious about the loss—and blamed his liberal staff, "the children who got me elected.")

■ And why did he make so many mistakes in the opening year of his presidency? It was the staff's fault again. They didn't have the right contacts among Washington's power elite, and their experience was too limited. True enough. But how about the president who appointed them? Why did he, a complete Washington outsider who had last worked in the city in his college years as a Senate intern, select a staff with such limited experience and contacts?

The answer is that Clinton nominated a staff that served primarily as ambassadors to factions within his own party. He realized that the Democratic Party leadership—and its rank and file too—had really wanted New York's governor, Mario Cuomo, as their candidate. But when he refused to run, Clinton stepped into the void. Knowing he was not their first choice, he fashioned a coalition government within one party, bringing in all of its factions to give them a stake in his presidency. He was haunted by the memory of President Jimmy Carter, who also controlled both the House and the Senate, but was undone by sniping from his own party (largely from then-House Speaker Tip O'Neill). With Democratic majorities in both Houses, Clinton felt he would need only to keep his party solidly in line to prevail.

So he named a staff that was primarily focused on appeasing the various factions in the party—without really examining their skill at finessing the Washington establishment as a whole. Budget Director and later Chief of Staff Leon Panetta was there to keep the House committee chairmen in line. Harold Ickes was his emissary to labor. Commerce Secretary Ron Brown handled the African American community. HUD Secretary Henry Cisneros dealt with Latinos. Stephanopoulos smoothed things over with his former boss, House Minority Leader Dick Gephardt.

But who among them knew anything about the Washington media, lobbyists, lawyers, and about that strangest of all creatures—Republicans?

None of them. And whose fault was that?

In *My Life,* as in Clinton's real life, nothing is ever his fault. He is victimized equally by his adversaries' maneuvers and his advisers' bad judgment. And yet, in the single most ludicrous statement in *My Life,* Clinton insists that he was brought up "not to blame others for my own problems or shortcomings."

The real problem with Clinton's refusal to take responsibility for any of the screw-ups in his administration, of course, is that if you don't take blame, you can never really change. If you never admit a mistake, you never learn from it.

But this one-man presidential chorus of blame highlights another sad fact: The truth is that Clinton was never the innovator, the driving force, or the creator of his own programs or initiatives. He was the jurist, the gatekeeper who allowed them to proceed or shot them down. The ideas came from others. He processed them. So when he blames others, it is not merely a device to deflect fault from himself. It is an accurate reflection of the fact that every idea came to him with a byline—usually not his own. If it proved to be successful, he would take the credit. If it proved to be a failure, he would apportion the blame to the author.

Clinton got his ideas from every possible source. He would scour op-eds, magazines, books, and periodicals looking for input. He would restlessly phone friends or advisers late into the night to get their thinking about important decisions he faced. His capacity to assimilate their advice was almost without limit. He could easily recall, verbatim, the text of his phone calls or ideas he had read. But the ideas would sit there in his short-term memory bank, undigested, unincorporated, while he pondered them. His mind was one giant in-box, with ideas piled high awaiting analysis.

I saw this phenomenon firsthand. Sometimes, during the years we worked together, I felt like a computer he would plug into five or six times each week, downloading the data he had accumulated and inviting me to assist him in sorting it out and analyzing it. But what was notable about these conversations was that each idea came from someone else. Each had an author. Clinton was just the editor, deciding which to include and what to drop.

For example, when Rev. Louis Farrakhan led African American fathers on a march on Washington, Clinton was in a stew about how to respond. Worried about embracing Farrakhan, whose extremist views were well-known—and who some charged with anti-Semitism—he was nevertheless attracted by the message of the march: that fathers should assume responsibility, and not rely on government or charity to bail them out.

Clinton had decided to go to Austin, Texas, on the day of the march to get out of town so he wouldn't have to have his picture taken shaking Farrakhan's hand. Once he was safely away, though, he also wanted to speak out about the message of the march, and identify with the many men who would visit Washington on that day.

He called me late at night and downloaded all the advice he had received, I suspect verbatim. *Jesse Jackson says that I should do this,* he told me. *E. J. Dionne wrote an op-ed where he said I should do that. And Ron Brown thinks I ought to do the other thing.* He faithfully rattled off this catalogue of third-party opinions, without comment or analysis. He had photographed their ideas in his mind but had not weighed them.

"You want to dis Farrakhan, but embrace his message," I answered, synthesizing the advice for him. "So speak out in support of the message, but condemn extremists and those who would divide us."

"Should I attack Farrakhan by name?" Clinton asked.

"No, it would overcome your embrace of his ideas, and drown out the positive story you want," I replied. "Just attack extremists without mentioning any names. The nation will know who you're talking about."

Clinton often saw our relationship as one of judge and advocate. I would make the argument, and then he would then issue his ruling. As he writes in *My Life:* "He [Morris] did me a lot of good . . . because I had good instincts about when he was right and when he wasn't." In the White House, Clinton would listen to my ideas without any reaction, verbal or otherwise. When I would spew out proposals to him, all I would get is a blank stare in return—not a nod of the head, not even a raised eyebrow. Nothing.

It hadn't been like that in Arkansas. Back then he was voluble, articulate, and would talk about ideas for hours. You couldn't shut him up, as strategy meetings degenerated into late-night bull sessions around the Governor's Mansion's copious refrigerator. But in the White House, he had turned laconic and taciturn. I didn't get it.

So one day I asked him about it directly—and his answer was revealing. "At the start of my term, we would have meetings all the time and I would participate like I did in Arkansas," he told me. "But then I began to read everything I had said—and a lot I hadn't—in the *Washington Post.* So I decided never to say anything with more than one other person present."

That made sense to me. This extroverted president had found it necessary to change his style of thinking and decision-making because of the ubiquity of leaks. But I still did not understand why he wouldn't engage me in conversation when I made policy or political suggestions to him—often when we were alone. Why the blank stare even then?

So I asked again. And I got only a stare in return. Then, as all his advisers did, I ventured my own opinions into the silence.

"I think your stare means 'You know that I basically agree with the thrust of what you are proposing, but we both understand the obstacles to moving in that direction.' Your stare means that it's up to me to deal with those concerns, so that you can do what I am suggesting. If I overcome them, you'll move ahead. If not, you'll wait until I do. Why don't you sit down and tell me what your concerns are? Because you have a pretty tough job, and don't have a lot of spare time to help me do my job for me. You figure we're the same age, and we've been to the same school of politics, and you're pretty certain I'll figure your concerns out on my own."

The president smiled, and said only this: "You're one bright son of a bitch."

There's an old saying that *Success has a thousand fathers, but failure is an orphan.* Bill Clinton stood that proverb on its head. His successes had only one father—himself. But his failures, to borrow a familiar Clinton phrase, were raised by a village.

4

Anger Without Management

Parallel lives are a major theme in *My Life*. But beyond the tension between Clinton's secret life as Saturday Night Bill and his public life as the Sunday Morning President, Clinton also leads another set of alternating lives: His usually sunny and optimistic demeanor is dogged at every turn by a dark and angry side. This side of Bill Clinton flares up often in private, but is rarely seen in public.

What frequently begins as mere frustration in Clinton's psyche slowly morphs into blame, and later metastasizes into anger. Once that happens, he unveils a raw and seething temper that explodes violently, uncontrollably, and unexpectedly. His is a primitive anger, manifested by red-faced screaming, a wildly pointing accusatory finger, and utterly self-righteous tirades. For those on the receiving end, it is a frightening and unforgettable encounter. For Bill Clinton himself, it is an exhausting and demeaning experience, usually followed by waves of guilt and, occasionally, a perfunctory apology.

On one level, Clinton recognizes his tendency to free-floating rage, and tries to keep it under control. On another level, however, he has proven unable or unwilling to keep that volatile and dangerous side of himself under permanent control—or to acknowledge the profound distress it leaves in its wake, as it slashes a path through its victims.

In a strange way, Clinton seems content to disassociate himself from this angry side. He behaves as though it is not connected to him, that it is not something he could change if he wanted to. He treats his temper like the weather: A storm comes and then it passes, and who could possibly be to blame? Certainly not Bill Clinton.

The weather in the Clinton Oval Office? As often as not, it was angry—very angry.

Throughout his presidency, Bill Clinton was almost completely successful in hiding this unattractive and chilling side. One reason he managed to keep this entire parallel life secret was that Clinton generally chose his victims cautiously. They had to be safe—usually people who were close to him, even symbiotic with him. People who wouldn't fight back, who wouldn't talk about it. People he had some control over. In short, people he didn't have to worry about.

Bill Clinton never showered open anger upon his enemies; that would have been too risky. He was never seen to attack his real adversaries—people like Newt Gingrich, Trent Lott, Ken Starr, or Bob Dole. He might have vented against them in private, but to their faces he was always controlled, civil, and courteous. He would never let his enemies witness one of his vicious tantrums. The possibility of jeopardizing his reputation—and his self-image—was likely too dangerous for him even to consider it.

Instead he has always selected his prey carefully, for the most part limiting his aggressions to his closest aides. Those were the people he could eviscerate without any concern for the repercussion.

Why would such a powerful man choose to abuse only those who were most devoted to him?

On one level, obviously, because he could—because he could use his position to demean those who got caught in his emotional crossfire, and those closest to him were easy and irresistible targets.

But on another, deeper level, Clinton vented his anger because he had to. There was so much of it to handle.

One doesn't have to be a Freudian psychiatrist to understand the likely genesis of his unresolved anger in the death of his father before he was born, and his abandonment by his mother until his fourth birthday. During those first few years he was virtually orphaned, a haunting trauma must have caused him certain, permanent pain. But in *My Life,* he never expresses a single word about his own feelings concerning his mother's disappearance during his childhood. In fact, the only thoughts he airs on the subject involve how difficult the period must have been on his mother. One prominent social worker and author we consulted, who prefers to remain anonymous, suggests that Clinton's failure to recognize his own loss—and the identification, instead, with the pain of the one who caused it—is a kind of "primitive, primordial [version of] Stockholm Syndrome."

Clinton writes only positively about his mother, insisting that she always "made me feel that I was the most important person in the world." This may well have been the beginning of Bill Clinton's amazing empathy for other people. Although he is frequently ridiculed for what became his signature expression, "I feel your pain," the fact is that Bill Clinton does have an uncanny ability to read the emotions of complete strangers merely by studying their faces—and to take on those emotions as his own. Feeling his mother's pain was the first lesson.

Both with and without his mother, Bill Clinton's childhood was a constant immersion in the potential for sudden adult rage, as he coped with his grandmother's and then his stepfather's volatile tempers. Confrontation, temper tantrums, domestic discord, and violence seem to have been the norms of Clinton's childhood. As a young child, he must have been terrified by the sound of adults yelling at one another. How ironic that this boy who clearly knew the pain that anger and violence could cause should become such an angry man himself.

From the anger in his grandparents' household, young Bill moved from the frying pan to the fire after his mother remarried and took the future president back to live with her and her new husband, an alcoholic car salesman named Roger Clinton.

Beyond the story of his stepfather's firing a gun over his mother's head, Clinton's memoir includes other awful stories of Roger Clinton's stepfather's rages. On another occasion, Bill opened the door to his parents' bedroom during a heated and loud argument to find Roger beating his mother. Bill says that he picked up a golf club and threatened Roger with it unless he stopped hitting Virginia.

Anger must have been a constant threat to the young Bill Clinton's stability. When would his stepfather next erupt? Would he batter his mother again? Was there a gun? Would his family fall apart? Was tonight the evening when everything would blow up?

Despite his own frightening experiences with the anger of others, as he grew up Clinton proved unable to control his own. Often his anger erupted when, in his view, others failed him. Rather than express his dissatisfaction in a civilized way, he would allow the slight to pass until his grievances accumulated and catalyzed into a rage. Decades later, I would watch the same thing happen time and again in the White House.

After one of these unpleasant tantrums, I met with Bill Curry, who worked with me there on domestic policy. Bill suggested that Clinton's patterns of fury were a residue of his childhood dealings with his alcoholic stepparent, who constantly disappointed him, but whom he could not challenge. Curry suggested a scene that was easy to imagine: Roger Clinton promising to take his stepson to the movies or some other event that weekend, but when Saturday rolled around showing up drunk and sullen, or not showing up at all. The young Bill Clinton doubtless would have known better than to remind his stepfather of his earlier promise, so he would let it slide. In Curry's opinion, this habit of not enforcing contracts stayed with him into his adulthood, and led to a pattern that culminated in searing hot rages.

In *My Life*, Clinton hints at such disappointment with his stepfather. He recounts numerous happy outings with Roger Clinton, including going by train to Missouri to see a baseball game, going fishing, taking a family vacation to another state, and taking him to cut down the family Christmas tree. But Clinton also recalls his sadness that all of these events only happened once: "There were so many things that meant a lot to me and were never to occur again." There is no indication that he ever shared that sadness with anyone at the time. It's far more likely that his fears kept him from mentioning it at all.

In *My Life,* Clinton absolves his childhood persecutors. His grandmother he recalls as a woman who loved him and meant well. His stepfather was not all bad, and was often quite lovely to be with. Despite her virtual absence for much of his first four years, Clinton consistently praises his mother.

He writes of his grandmother's confusion, his mother's ardent desire to make a better life for him, and his stepfather's fruitless battle with the bottle. In these early years, when most children see nothing more than their own needs, he seems to have had the genuine ability to look upon these towering figures of authority with empathy, not resentment.

But as he grew into adulthood, it became clear that forgiveness wasn't Clinton's only reaction to adversity. At any given moment, he was just as likely to meet challenges with rage. Yet he seems to have been aware of how ugly his tantrums could be. In the White House, Clinton hid his anger deeply, and his staff helped by covering for him. Anyone working there who leaked a story about the president's temper tantrums would only incur further wrath. Aides who leaked everything else would never dare speak out of school about his rages.

As I've recounted elsewhere, in 1990 I had my own haunting exposure to Bill's violent side, when he tackled me and knelt over my prone body, ready to punch me, before Hillary pulled him off, shrieking at him to control himself. The circumstances that led to the denouement were a typical source of anger: Clinton was infuriated that he was losing the Arkansas Democratic gubernatorial primary to an unknown challenger.

On the night Clinton attacked me, still shaken from the confrontation, I had called an acquaintance and confided to him what had happened. During the 1992 presidential campaign, while serving as consultant to a rival candidate, he leaked the story. Now I began to get calls from the press.

When I asked Clinton's Arkansas chief of staff and campaign aide, Betsey Wright, how I should handle the queries, the answer Hillary sent back was clear: "Just deny that it ever happened." As I would learn after the Clintons entered the White House, "say it never happened" became the standard way of hiding Clinton's parallel life of temper from the rest of the world.

For Bill and Hillary, protecting the family brand is paramount. The Bill Clinton brand is sunny and optimistic, not angry and snarling. So a story about Clinton tackling people and screaming at them must be squashed.

I will never forget Hillary's words to me as she tried to console me after her husband's attack: "He only does that to people he loves!" I didn't understand what she was getting at—it sounded flat-out crazy. In retrospect, I realize that she'd hit upon the truth: that Clinton only behaved violently and angrily around people he considered to be safe. I may have felt safe to him, but he no longer felt safe to me. I finished the campaign, but we were never on the same level again. Our friendship was shattered.

Years later, in the White House, Clinton began once again to show aggression toward me. As I gained power in the White House, he was becoming deeply frustrated. Sensing that he needed my advice, he grew increasingly concerned that my once secret role was becoming too obvious to the rest of the White House staff. So in front of the senior staff he screamed at me in a red-faced, finger-wagging, out-of-control rage. My crime? Getting too friendly with Al Gore. After a staff meeting in the White House Map Room (where cooler heads had planned World War II), he yelled as loudly as he could: "You have made the vice president your *employeeeee!*," dragging out the word like a man out of control. Shaking with rage, he harangued my back as I stalked out of the Map Room. Deeply upset, I left the

White House, packed my bags, and went home to Connecticut, planning and vowing not to return.

By the time I got home, Clinton had called several times. I didn't return his calls, but when he called again later that night I told him I could not work with someone who lost his temper like that, who felt free to assault me verbally. He was very apologetic and promised it would never happen again. But it did. After this second exposure to his wrath in the White House, I sent him a note explaining that my father had a horrible temper, and that I couldn't handle being around that kind of fierce anger. He apologized once again after reading the letter; only then did he stop inflicting his temper on me for good.

I was not the only one in the White House who was the object of the president's rage. George Stephanopoulos, apparently, was another safe receptacle for his fury. Clinton had an odd relationship with George. After 1994, he lost his trust in the younger man; he no longer valued his advice, and didn't even seem to like him very much. But he would never fire him, because he was afraid of what George might say or do once he was loosed from the bonds of loyalty. So, he boxed this brilliant adviser into a smaller and smaller role, and berated him mercilessly for the duration of George's time in the White House.

In his book, *All Too Human,* Stephanopoulos offers a detailed analysis of Clinton's temper, describing it as a "tornado" that was all too often directed at him. He recounts a prolonged and humiliating series of "tirades," "yelling," "screaming," and variations such as the "silent scream" (in which he coolly ignored the victim), the "morning roar" (in which he began the day with a complaint about something that annoyed him), the "slow boil" (a building undercurrent of deep, seething anger), the "nightcap" (a common reaction to late-night television or other late-breaking news), "the show" (in which he pretended to be angry for a particular audience), and the "last gasp" (a bout of self-criticism turned into anger at others). George recounts how the stress at the White House—including Clinton's anger—led to depression, insomnia, and a facial rash so severe that he grew a beard to cover it. Amazingly, Clinton tells us that he was surprised to read about this in George's book.

Clinton would rage about the media, his political adversaries, Newt Gingrich, Ken Starr, Colin Powell, Bob Dole, his own staff, the massive fund-raising burden he had to carry, the Congressional leadership and the Congressional Budget Office, Trent Lott, and a host of other icons of fury.

I easily recognized the various types of Clinton anger George described. Clinton was habitually in a foul mood.

Frequently, his anger was a cover for a mistake he had made himself. In 1995, he triggered a media outburst when he told a Houston audience that he agreed he had raised taxes too much in his first two years. When I questioned him about his gaffe, he exploded: "My fucking staff schedules me to give a speech at midnight. Midnight. After I've been up traveling and speaking all day. *Midnight!* Any time they do that, *any time,* I'll make a mistake. But will they stop? No, they won't. They cram my schedule with every request. Nobody ever says no. And the result: I make a mistake."

In 1996, on the train traveling to the Democratic National Convention in Chicago, he snapped at a reporter—which, predictably, made the headlines. This time, when I asked him about it, it was Mike McCurry who bore the brunt of the resulting temper tantrum. "Of course I snapped at the reporter. Fucking McCurry lets the press at me all the time. Twenty-four hours. Every time I turn around, there is a microphone in my face."

In Arkansas, his chief of staff, Betsey Wright, was the frequent object of his temper. But Betsey usually gave it right back to him, and he never seemed to mind. They were a strange pair. Sometimes they would scream across a table at each other, Bill yelling until he was red-faced and Betsey yelling right back. Then, after ranting at each other, they would go back to a serious discussion until the next explosion occurred.

In *My Life,* Clinton writes about his fear of anger, describing how he associated it with being "out of control" and was determined to rein in the "constant anger" he kept locked inside himself. As he recounts his own behavior during his presidency, Clinton mentions his fury only in passing, in much the same way he might describe a headache. Yet a close reading of his text shows that anger takes up a lot of space in Bill Clinton's life.

The instances of anger he does describe in his book are interesting in and of themselves. When he was criticized for holding up air traffic while he got a $200 haircut, he wrote that he "didn't handle it well, because I got angry, which is always a mistake."

He was "irritated," he writes, when Mack McLarty told him he had to end the interview with Larry King, until McLarty revealed the reason—that Vince Foster had killed himself. He was "angry" at Vince Foster for committing suicide, and he was "angry" at himself for not being able to help him.

When he delayed making any statement about Waco until after the FBI raid had turned bad, he was "furious" at himself for listening to George Stephanopoulos.

His "internal life," he says, was "full of . . . anger."

Overscheduling, he says, made him "irritable."

He was "angry" about Whitewater and had to struggle to control his feelings.

He "fumed" over policy criticisms from Mario Cuomo.

Jerry Brown "angered" him with charges of Hillary's conflict of interest.

He had to work hard to make sure that his "anger" over the Starr investigation did not hamper his ability to get his work done. Clinton writes that Whitewater challenged his "normally sunny disposition."

He was "burned up" at having to pay Paula Jones.

He "griped too much in the morning."

Sometimes his anger is trotted out as a justification for his own conduct. When he criticized the Starr investigation in his speech to the nation after his grand jury testimony, he was still too "angry" to be as sorry as he should have.

Now that he has left the White House, Bill Clinton apparently feels a little more able to lash out at someone in public, someone who is not safe. This happened most recently during a BBC interview about his book on June 22, 2004. When the BBC's David Dimbleby asked him why he would have an affair with Monica Lewinsky at a time when he knew that Starr's office was investigating him, he lashed out, giving the public a rare glimpse of vintage Clinton in his anger mode. "Wagging his finger and getting visibly agitated," the BBC reported, "Mr. Clinton expressed anger at the media's behavior."

It was a surprising loss of control. Clinton could have simply stuck with the humble demeanor he had shown in other earlier interviews about the book. He could have admitted he was wrong to have gotten involved with Lewinsky, that it was an arrogant act he wasn't proud of. He'd said that before.

But this time the interviewer set him off. He turned on Dimbleby, confronting him with one of his favorite defenses: It was the media's fault, not his. "Let me just say this," he said. "One of the reasons he [Kenneth Starr] got away with this is that people like you only ask me questions." He grew angrier as he continued: "You gave him a completely free ride. Any abuse they wanted to do. . . . They indicted all of those little people from Arkansas, what did you care about them? They're not famous. Who cares if their life was trampled, if their children [were] humiliated?"

Warming to his theme, feeling the anger coursing through him, Clinton carried on: "Nobody in your line of work cared a rip about their story. Why? Because he [Starr] was helping their stories. And that's why people like you always help the far right, because you like to hurt people, and you like to talk about how bad people are and talk about their personal failings." Clinton's fury at Ken Starr had defeated the filter that he normally relies on to curb his wrath. For a brief moment, the world saw the dark side of Bill Clinton.

It's no surprise to realize that Clinton is still enraged at Kenneth Starr. What's surprising is that he showed it.

Still, as he always does after any public display of rage, Clinton quickly found his footing. After his outburst on the BBC, he went on to complete the interview in a civil and friendly way, even suggesting that he would come back for more. He charmed the interviewer, and the outburst was forgotten.

Once again, the weather had cleared; it was no longer angry out.

5

AWOL on Terror

Clinton's Disastrous Passive Mode

September 11, 2001, was the worst day of the Clinton presidency, even though it was 233 days after the former president left office. For on that day, when our country suffered cataclysmic terrorist attacks in New York and Washington, Americans immediately began to ask the vital question: How could this have happened? As investigators probed the reasons we were unprepared to stop the terrorists' infiltration, it became clear that the failure to capture or kill bin Laden ranked among the most egregious, and deadly, lapses of Bill Clinton's tenure.

Clinton once told me that he would have to have a war to be regarded as a great president. After 9/11, I realized, he'd had a war on his hands all along. He just didn't fight it. He didn't really even know it was there.

The report of the bipartisan 9/11 Commission, released in the summer of 2004, highlighted the weak, incompetent, hesitant, and inconsistent attempts of the Clinton administration to kill or capture Osama bin Laden. The report's account shows the president and his advisers at their worst.

The report's publication, which came right in the middle of a presidential election campaign, led to a partisan wrangle over who was more at fault for the lack of preparedness before 9/11: Clinton or Bush? The question of their relative negligence, of course, is immaterial; there is enough blame to go around. But while Bush can be held accountable for his failures during the eight months preceding the terrorist attacks, Clinton must answer for his negligence during a period of eight years.

To read the accounts of when, how, and why Clinton failed to kill or capture bin Laden is to invite a migraine at best, a heartache at worst.

The Clinton administration had been aware of Osama bin Laden since 1993, when the State Department added him to their TIPOFF list that identifies potential terrorists. There appear to have been at least four serious opportunities to get bin Laden, each lost by the Clinton administration:

- By 1997, the CIA Counterterrorism Center had been working on a plan to capture bin Laden for some time. Working with contacts from local tribes, they had identified bin Laden's fortress-like compound and developed a plan to grab him, take him to the desert and hold him there for some time, then transport him to the United States or possibly another Arab country. On February 13, 1998, just three weeks after the Lewinsky scandal broke, CIA director George Tenet reviewed the plan with Clinton's national security advisor, Sandy Berger. During the next few months, the CIA operatives rehearsed the operation, concluding the last dry run on May 28.

  A day later, however, Berger and Tenet decided to scuttle it. According to the 9/11 Commission, the key reason for the no-go decision was a fear that bin Laden might be killed, rather than just captured and returned to the United States.

  Advised of the cancellation, the operation's planner was told that "cabinet-level officials thought the risk of civilian casualties—'collateral damage'—was too high" and had worried that "the purpose and nature of the operation would be subject to unavoidable misinterpretation and misrepresentation—and probably recriminations—in the event that Bin Laden, despite our best intentions and efforts, did not survive." Most pointedly, the Commission noted, Tenet and Berger were worried that if bin Laden did not survive, the operation could be construed as an assassination."

In addition, Berger was apparently worried that if bin Laden were actually captured, there was insufficient evidence to hold him—and that there was a "danger of snatching him and bringing him back to the United States only to see him acquitted."

Their worries were rooted in the fact that President Clinton had not approved the use of lethal force against bin Laden. It was only later, on August 20, 1998, after the attacks on U.S. embassies in Africa, that Clinton signed a Memorandum of Notification authorizing the CIA to "use force" to capture bin Laden.

The cancellation of the raid to grab bin Laden was a huge blow to antiterrorism activities. In the words of the 9/11 Commission Report, "no capture plan before 9/11 ever again attained the same level of detail and preparation. The tribals' reported readiness to act diminished. And bin Laden's security precautions and defenses became more elaborate and formidable."

In *My Life,* Clinton disingenuously omits the concern for bin Laden's safety in the proposed commando operations. He simply says that he signed several Memoranda of Notification authorizing them to kill bin Laden, but never mentions that he did so only after our best chance to kill or catch the al Qaeda leader had already passed—because of worries that it might look like an assassination.

■ Having rejected the notion of snatching bin Laden, the government's attention turned to trying to kill him in an air strike. While American operatives could not shoot bin Laden on the ground without express presidential approval, an air strike aimed at one of his bases would not be considered an assassination, even if he were killed in the incident.

Responding to the African embassy bombings, the United States fired salvos of cruise missiles at targets in Afghanistan and the Sudan on August 20, 1998, two days after Clinton's Grand Jury testimony. According to the 9/11 Commission, "the strike [on Afghanistan]'s purpose . . . was to kill Bin Laden and his chief lieutenants." And it might have succeeded. Tenet felt that it had only missed bin Laden by a few hours. How had he known to escape? He was likely tipped off. The Commission reported that "Since the missiles headed for Afghanistan had had to cross Pakistan, the Vice Chairman of the Joint Chiefs was sent to meet with Pakistan's army chief of staff to assure him the missiles were not coming from India. Officials in Washington speculated that one or another Pakistani official might have sent a warning to the Taliban or Bin Ladin."

In *My Life,* Clinton confirms the 9/11 Commission Report's account of the August 20 missile strike, but says that the U.S. military official was only supposed to have told his Pakistani counterpart about the American strike "a few minutes" before our missiles were over Pakistan, so as not to give him time to alert the Taliban or bin Laden. Apparently, a few minutes were all that was needed.

The failure of the August 1998 air strikes to kill bin Laden chilled Clinton's willingness to order more attacks, especially after many GOP leaders accused the president of staging the attacks to distract attention from his grand jury testimony on his relationship with Monica Lewinsky. The movie *Wag the Dog,* released just months before, depicted just such a scenario—a president using a foreign crisis to distract attention from a sex scandal—and many Americans saw the attack in these terms. The Commission noted that these factors "had a cumulative effect on future decisions about the use of force against Bin Ladin." The report also noted that "President Clinton and Berger also worried . . . that attacks that missed Bin Ladin could enhance his stature and win him new recruits."

■ Having considered and rejected a ground operation and been unsuccessful in an air strike, the Clinton administration considered bribery. The 9/11 Commission reports that "two senior State Department officials suggested asking the Saudis to offer the Taliban $250 million for Bin Ladin. [National Security Council staff expert Richard] Clarke opposed . . . a 'huge grant to a regime as heinous as the Taliban' and suggested that the idea might not seem attractive to either Secretary [of State] Albright or First Lady Hillary Rodham Clinton—both critics of the Taliban's record on women's rights. That proposal seems to have quietly died." Clarke is the author of the book *Against All Enemies,* a critique of the Bush administration's antiterrorism policies.

■ The next chance to kill bin Laden with an air strike—and the best one—came in May 1999, when, according to the 9/11 Commission, "CIA assets in Afghanistan reported on Bin Ladin's location in and around Kandahar over the course of five days and nights. . . . If this intelligence was not 'actionable,' working-level officials said at the time and today, it was hard for them to imagine how any intelligence on Bin Ladin in Afghanistan could meet the standard." One senior military officer told the Commission "this was in our strike zone. It was a fat pitch, a home run."

But, incredibly, Berger and Tenet decided not to strike. The officer planning the mission said that "when the decision came back that they should stand down, not shoot . . . 'we all just slumped.' "

Why was the strike called off? The 9/11 Commission conceded that the decision "may now seem hard to understand," but cites two factors:

Six months before, on December 18, 1998, there had been another chance to kill bin Laden, after intelligence reports said that he would be spending the night at a home that was part of the governor's residence in Kandahar, Afghanistan. The 9/11 Report indicates that back then some thought had been given to the idea of launching a cruise missile strike against Bin Ladin, but that no strike was ordered because of concern over how many innocent bystanders might have been killed or wounded. Subsequently, the

United States found out that the strike would not have killed bin Laden because he had left the room unexpectedly. The episode cast a cloud over efforts to kill bin Laden by bombing, and cooled enthusiasm for the May, 1999 strike.

The second reason the 9/11 Commission gives for the cancellation of the strike was that the United States was embarrassed by the air attack in Belgrade, Yugoslavia, which had mistakenly hit the Chinese Embassy, causing an international furor and street demonstrations in Beijing. Apparently, the incident had left American officials gun-shy about bombing, so they cancelled the plans to kill America's most wanted enemy.

Clinton blames the cancellation of the air strikes on unreliable intelligence. But the 9/11 Commission obviously did not agree with Clinton's negative assessment of the available information. The former president, doubtless knowing that his failure to eliminate bin Laden will haunt his legacy, does not mention the real reasons the strikes were cancelled—timidity, hypersensitivity to public reaction, and fear of failure.

Was the cancellation Tenet's fault, Berger's fault, or Clinton's fault? The 9/11 Commission places most of the blame with Tenet, but notes that when he told Berger that the attack was off, the national security advisor did not urge that the attack proceed.

But the ultimate blame must be placed at Clinton's doorstep, for the atmosphere of caution that surrounded such decisions. Anxiety over potential civilian deaths—and over potential public criticism if the raid should fail to kill bin Laden—should not have scuttled this opportunity to kill the man who was already planning 9/11.

What is the common denominator behind all of these missed opportunities? Political caution. The first attempt to snatch bin Laden was cancelled out of concern for global public opinion if he should be killed in the process. The second attempt—the air strike that was actually launched—may have failed because we felt we had to brief Pakistani military authorities to forestall a hair-trigger decision to retaliate against India. The effort to bribe the Taliban was called off because it might have been regarded as bad public relations to be dealing with the regime, especially by the feminist first lady and secretary of state. And the May 1999 attack never happened, because of concern that global public opinion would consider the U.S. bomb-happy.

The common element in all of these bungled plans was an oversensitivity to public opinion and political circumstances, and inadequate attention to the importance of killing bin Laden.

A big part of the problem was the role Sandy Berger played in making these decisions about bin Laden. In all my many dealings with Berger, I found him to be cautious, political, and hesitant to incur public ire. I was constantly challenging his warnings that some aggressive foreign policy move might hurt our political standing. Berger reflected the political caution of many amateurs, who concentrate on avoiding potential mistakes rather than taking overt action.

Berger thought he knew a lot about both politics and foreign policy. But he was really out of his league in the former, and temperamentally unsuited to the latter. Paralyzed by political risk, he was always hesitant to take direct action. It was in the hands of such a man that Bill Clinton delegated the decision to strike or not to strike at Osama bin Laden.

In early 1997, as Clinton assembled his second-term cabinet, he had a choice among Holbrooke, Albright, and Berger for his top two foreign policy positions. He chose Albright as secretary of state partly because he wanted to name a woman, and also because he liked her affinity for action, particularly in the Balkans. But to offset Albright he put the cautious Berger into the national security advisor slot, and shuffled the more action-oriented Holbrooke off to the United Nations. And this was no accident: Clinton knew exactly what he was doing when he appointed Berger. He wanted Sandy's caution.

In an odd footnote to the failure to catch bin Laden, in 2003 Sandy Berger was accused of smuggling classified documents out of the National Archives. Berger was designated as the Clinton administration's representative to review documents at the Archives prior to testifying before the 9/11 Commission. According to published reports, the Archives staff became suspicious of Berger when he asked them to leave while he made phone calls (wonder whom he called?) and made repeated trips to the bathroom. The staff claimed that they saw him stuffing documents in his socks and pants. On his next visit, they marked documents so that they could tell if any were missing. They claim the marked papers were missing when they checked the files afterward. When Berger was called about the documents, he claimed to have taken them in error, and returned some of them. Others, he said, had been thrown away and could not be retrieved.

Is it plausible that the former national security advisor to the president did not understand that classified documents could not simply be lifted out of the National Archives and taken home? Of course not. Some reports suggest that the documents that were taken had handwritten comments by various principals in the Clinton administration. Could that have been what Berger was interested in? It will be some time before we know the answers. Berger apparently hired a lawyer in October 2003 to represent him on the matter. (He has denied any improper motive.)

Today, as creatures of 9/11, it's easy for us to grasp the danger of inaction. But in the 1990s, before bin Laden knocked down the World Trade Center, smashed the Pentagon, and hijacked a plane that crashed in Pennsylvania—in a series of coordinated attacks that killed 2,973 people—there were other lessons of history that loomed larger in Clinton's mind.

Indeed, the era during which Clinton came into political consciousness was marked by a string of military failures and missions that backfired, each carving on his psyche the need for caution. The Vietnam War, of course, looms as the chief example of the risks of military action, but others repeatedly drove home to Clinton the need for caution—among them Kennedy's failure at the Bay of Pigs, Carter's failed hostage rescue mission, and the Lebanon barracks bombing in the Reagan years.

Lacking in military experience himself, Clinton was frightened by the risks of armed action, worried that his draft dodging would be dredged up again if he sustained casualties, and fearful that a military failure would make him look weak. In writing about his decision to approve the raid in Somalia, which resulted in the deaths of nineteen American servicemen, he cites the Bay of Pigs; comparing his flawed trust in his generals with that of JFK in the 1961 Cuban fiasco, he says he knew how Kennedy felt.

Even when he approved military action, as in the Balkans and Kosovo, Clinton opted for high-altitude bombing to avoid casualties; likewise, he confined his military actions against bin Laden to missile strikes from afar.

In our weekly sessions on foreign policy, Clinton would always express his concern about becoming embroiled in a foreign military operation that could sap his popularity and destroy his presidency. With impeachment nipping at his heels in his second term, he felt he had no margin for error.

But, in a larger sense, the failure to kill bin Laden was a direct result of the presidential impeachment process, which paralyzed the nation's political structure during Clinton's second term. Mindful of the widespread condemnation for wagging the dog in his first strike at Bin Laden, Bill Clinton would never have taken the political risk of a commando raid or repeated bombing with civilian casualties in the midst of impeachment.

When it came to fighting terrorism, in a very real sense, for most of Clinton's second term America was without a president—as surely as it was after Woodrow Wilson suffered a debilitating stroke in the closing year of his second term.

Can we assign real blame for 9/11 back to Clinton's behavior in conducting an affair while he was president, with all of its dangers? For that matter, should any of it fall to the Republicans, for insisting on their pound of flesh through the mechanism of impeachment? Does it rest on Clinton for not stepping aside, perhaps invoking the Constitutional amendment that permits a president to temporarily hand over power to his vice president if he is disabled and prevented from doing the job?

Or does it rest on us all, for taking one side or the other in this no-win battle over Lewinsky and perjury, while Osama was preparing to strike?

During his second term as president, Bill Clinton began to see more and more vividly the dangers that the gathering storm of terrorism posed for the United States. With the bombing of American barracks in Saudi Arabia, the attack on the U.S.S. *Cole* in Yemen, and the bombing of our embassies in Africa, the threat became sadly apparent.

But during Clinton's first term, when prompt action might have nipped the al Qaeda threat, the president was curiously disengaged on the subject of terrorism. Indeed, the word "terror" or "terrorism" occurs only rarely in *My Life*'s account of his first term. Apart from references to terrorism in Israel or Ireland, the Tokyo subway attack, or the domestic terror attacks in Oklahoma City and at the Atlanta Olympics, the former president only mentions the topic six times in the three hundred pages he devotes to his first administration. He notes it twice as an issue at a G-7 meeting of world leaders; he alludes to his September 1996 UN speech, which addressed the threat of global terrorism; he mentions his air safety initiative after the crash of TWA 800; and he laments Congress's delay in passing his anti-terror package, which was proposed in the wake of Oklahoma City.

As the 9/11 Commission noted, though, "Terrorism was not the overriding national security concern for the U.S. government under either the Clinton or the pre-9/11 Bush administration."

Clinton believed that his unique contribution to foreign policy was to re-orient it away from its traditional focus on military/diplomatic/intelligence issues to what he saw as a more fitting post–Cold War focus on jobs and trade. Viewing global affairs as a subset of economic policy, he was determined not to be distracted by what he often dismissed as paranoia left over from the era of confrontation with the Soviets.

In a previous book, *Off with Their Heads,* I recounted Clinton's doleful first-term history in failing to wage the war on terror. But it is important to revisit here the historical record of Clinton's failures on terrorism during his first term, in light of two new developments: the new evidence unearthed by the 9/11 Commission, which casts new light on the president's inadequate response to the threats we faced, and Clinton's own words in *My Life,* which underscore his own lack of comprehension (even after 9/11) of the challenges he should have met.

I came to see just how limited Clinton's focus on terrorism was when the time came to prepare for his October 22, 1995, speech to the United Nations General Assembly. In my draft of the speech, I labeled Iran, Iraq, Libya, and North Korea "rogue nations," saying that the threat they posed was the successor to the dangers we had faced from fascism and communism. The National Security Council raised hell at the inclusion of this language, so similar to that later used by President Bush in his "axis of evil" reference. Meekly complying with their advice, Clinton made only a general allusion to terror in his remarks.

Why did Clinton show such hesitation over the phrase during his UN appearance? Because his empathetic antennae were warning him of the danger of appearing to "politicize" his foreign policy. He was probably deathly afraid that the National Security Council staff—Tony Lake and Sandy Berger and their minions—would leak that Clinton was getting advice from his political consultant on what to say to the United Nations. So, rather than risk having to run that gauntlet, he held his silence.

(A little while later, when nobody was looking over his shoulder, Clinton was preparing to address a San Francisco audience gathered to commemorate the UN's fiftieth anniversary. Phoning me from the West Coast, he asked: "Do you still have that language about rogue nations from the UN speech?" I told him I did. "Fax it to me here at the hotel," he said, "but don't tell anyone you are doing it." This time, he included it in his speech.)

One reflection of his inability to focus on terror early in his term is that Clinton devotes only one paragraph to al Qaeda's first attack on American soil, the bombing of the World Trade Center thirty days after he took office. By contrast, he devotes ten pages to the issue of gays in the military. As these two issues vied for his attention in the opening weeks of his presidency, his memoirs indicate which gained the upper hand.

In his curt description of the 1993 bombing—launched by the same group against the same target with the same goal as the 9/11 attacks—he notes how pleased he was with the prompt arrests, and that he and his national security team decided thereafter to devote more time to the terror issue.

The fact that Clinton never visited the site of the bombing (pleading that there was "no opening" in his schedule)—even though he toured nearby New Jersey four days after the blast—and that he warned New Yorkers not to "overreact" to the bombing, all confirms how low a priority he accorded it.

Indeed, after 9/11 George Stephanopoulos noted that, the day after the 1993 bombing, "It wasn't the kind of thing where you walked into a staff meeting and people asked, 'What are we doing today in the war against terrorism?'"

Clinton's approach to terrorism during his first term in office, formulated in those early days of 1993, was to stress the law enforcement aspects of the problem. He saw terrorism as a crime, not as a war. His focus was on those who actually blew up buildings and the criminals who sent them, rather than on the nations that harbored, funded, nurtured, and encouraged them.

He failed to understand that terrorism is like an HIV virus that courses through the bloodstream, posing a threat but doing no damage. The virus itself does not create symptomatic AIDS. It is only when it latches onto a cell that it is able to use the DNA of the cell to propagate and spread disease through the body.

By themselves, terrorist gangs can pull off suicide bombings in restaurants and other such low-level attacks. But they cannot knock down buildings. It is only through drawing on the support of a nation-state that they can spread death and destruction more widely. A nation offers them secure borders within which to train terrorists, a budget financed by taxation and confiscation, a ready-made military including aerial and naval hardware, a population to conscript into service, diplomatic missions around the globe through which to infiltrate other nations, an intelligence service to give them a head start on their plots, foreign currency reserves, and worldwide export-import trade channels whose shipping can provide a cover for smuggling terror material to other countries.

Just as the most recent successful treatments delay the onset and severity of symptomatic AIDS by stopping the virus from permeating the cellular boundaries, so Bush, unlike Clinton, moved the focus of his anti-terrorism efforts to stopping nations from harboring or supporting terrorism.

But Clinton chased the terrorist criminals and disregarded the nation-states, a path as ultimately fruitless as swimming after HIV viruses in the bloodstream.

The administration's limited response to the 1993 WTC bombing made a big difference in the war on terror. Because Clinton never elevated the investigation to the level of a true national priority, it was conducted by the U.S. Attorney's Office in New York City. With only a local staff to handle the investigation, it plodded along, and only very gradually did the full dimensions of the terrorist organization emerge.

According to the 9/11 Commission Report, it wasn't until 1997 that American intelligence agencies realized that bin Laden was, in fact, the mastermind of the anti-American terrorist jihad rather than just its "financier." That alone explains why Clinton didn't approve the use of force to capture bin Laden until 1998.

The low priority assigned to the investigation of the 1993 bombing also led to another missed opportunity to deal an early blow to terrorism. In late 1995, as the 9/11 Commission explains, "when bin Laden was still in Sudan, the State Department and the CIA learned that Sudanese officials were discussing with the Saudi government the possibility of expelling Bin Ladin. U.S. Ambassador Timothy Carney encouraged the Sudanese to pursue this course." Unfortunately, though, the Saudis didn't want him. Under pressure from Sudan, bin Laden left for Afghanistan.

Why didn't the United States jump at the opportunity to get our hands on this terrorist? Because, according to the 9/11 Commission report, the U.S. ambassador to the Sudan "had no legal basis" to ask Sudan to hand him over.

And why not? Because the 1993 World Trade Center bombing investigation had not proceeded to the point where we could have indicted bin Laden—a sorry result of Clinton's failure to focus full federal resources on penetrating the conspiracy. Clinton left the cops to chase the robbers, never integrating the U.S. Attorney's efforts to investigate the 1993 bombing with the anti-terror initiatives of his Washington agencies.

It was not until June 1998 that a grand jury, convened by the U.S. Attorney for the Southern District of New York, finally indicted bin Laden. And when they did so, the 9/11 Commission Report notes, their efforts were "on their own separate track, getting information but not direction from the CIA." Content to have found the bumbling Laurel and Hardy operatives who actually planted the bomb, Clinton was in no rush to probe more deeply. He had his suspects and the pressure was off.

The 9/11 Commission reports that Sudan's minister of defense, Fatih Erwa, "has claimed that Sudan offered to hand Bin Ladin over to the United States." The Commission reported that it "has found no credible evidence that this was so." Despite this finding, in a February 2002 speech Clinton indicated otherwise. Speaking to a business group, Clinton clearly stated: "The Sudanese wanted America to start dealing with them again.

"They released him. At the time, 1996, he had committed no crime against America so I did not bring him here because we had no basis on which to hold him, though we knew he wanted to commit crimes against America."

Whether Sudan offered up bin Laden or not, it is clear that the United States could just as easily have asked for bin Laden to be sent to the United States rather than Saudi Arabia. But we didn't, because we did not yet realize how dangerous he was. Even worse, due to the snail's pace of the 1993 WTC bombing investigation, bin Laden was yet not officially wanted for anything in the United States.

Another indication of Clinton's lackadaisical approach to terrorism was his failure to meet with CIA director R. James Woolsey. Incredibly, Woolsey said that he did not have a single private meeting with the president during all of 1993 or 1994. In *My Life*, the CIA director is mentioned only once, at the time of his appointment.

As we've noted, the president's decision to abandon the mission in Somalia in 1993 after nineteen Americans were killed at Mogadishu sent a signal of weakness that led bin Laden to call the U.S. military a "paper tiger" in a 1999 interview. American appeasement at that crucial juncture encouraged bin Laden to move ahead with his terror plans.

If the bombing of the World Trade Center did not alert Clinton to the massive danger that terrorism posed, the bombing of the Murrah Federal Building in Oklahoma City two years later should have served as a wake-up call. In *My Life*, Clinton discusses his anti-terrorism initiatives in the aftermath of the attack, but he fails to concede that his decisions after Oklahoma City failed to create measures that might have averted 9/11.

As soon as the smoke cleared in Oklahoma, the FBI began pressing Clinton to expand their ability to wiretap and search terrorists to unearth their plots before they could strike—seeking, according to the *New York Times*, the ability to "infiltrate such [terrorist] organizations or use informers to keep track of their activities."

Under pressure from civil liberties groups, though, Clinton backed off the proposal and refused the FBI request. Clinton refused to abandon the requirement of probable cause before a warrant could be issued for surveillance against terror suspects. He refused to allow search warrants based on a suspect's membership and activity in a terrorist group. Even when the FBI offered to ban the resulting evidence from use in criminal prosecutions, limiting its use to intelligence purposes, he would not loosen the rules.

And that is why, when the FBI's Minneapolis office was alerted to the flight lessons being taken by Zacarias Moussaoui, alleged to be al Qaeda's twentieth hijacker, Federal agents were denied access to his laptop computer—because Clinton had not changed the rules in the aftermath of the Oklahoma City bombing.

And, astonishingly, on Moussaoui's computer were the names of the other nineteen hijackers, and the locations where they were taking flying lessons! That alone would have been all that was needed to break the plot wide open.

Clinton missed another key opportunity to take action that could have stopped some of the 9/11 terrorists when he refused to use the motor vehicle licensing system to track illegal immigrants and terrorists. On March 16, 1995, I urged the president to "make states issue driver's licenses [to immigrants] that expire when [their] visas do." Noting that half of the nation's illegal aliens had evaded the system by overstaying their visas, I suggested that the computers at the various state motor vehicle departments be interfaced with the INS and FBI computers, in order to identify illegal immigrants and wanted terrorists. I proposed a system providing for "automatic referral from motor-vehicle agencies to the INS" for deportation when routine traffic stops revealed drivers without licenses who were here illegally.

Clinton was initially interested in my proposal, but was warned off it by George Stephanopoulos, who counseled the president that it would alienate his Hispanic base. Unwilling to upset a core group within the Democratic Party—a group whose votes were necessary to winning key states like Florida, California, Texas, New York, and Illinois—Clinton chose instead to do nothing.

And that is why, when 9/11 hijacking leader Mohammed Atta was stopped by police near Miami for driving without a license five months before the fatal day, he slipped through our hands. Without a computer interface, the traffic cop had no idea that Atta was here illegally, his visa having expired earlier in the year. Under the proposal Clinton rejected, Atta would have been bound over to the INS for deportation and might not have been in the United States to lead the 9/11 hijackers on their grisly mission. Instead, the matter was treated as a routine traffic offense. He was summoned to appear in court, but never did; a bench warrant was issued against him, but never enforced.

Two other 9/11 hijackers, Nawaf Alhazmi and Ziad Samir Jarrah were also pulled over for speeding, but no one knew to take any further action against them.

In *My Life,* Clinton never even mentions the issue of a national database of aliens who had overstayed their visas. Of course, we should keep in mind that before 9/11 most Americans gave no more thought to terrorism than Clinton did. But it's no mystery that the average citizen never dwelled on the threat. The astonishing thing is that our president appears to have been no more worried about it than the rest of us.

But Clinton's biggest failure in fighting terror during his first term was how far he fell short of making our air traffic system safe.

National sensitivities to aircraft terrorism had been sharpened by the TWA crash on July 18, 1996, which many attributed—prematurely, as it turned out—to terrorism. (The true cause of the crash has never been established.)

Responding quickly to public concerns, with the election only four months away, Clinton named Vice President Al Gore to head a commission to explore ways to make air travel safer. In *My Life,* Clinton notes that he responded to the crash by requiring hand searches of more luggage, more screening of bags, and the inspection of every plane cabin and cargo hold prior to flight. After Gore's commission reported its recommendations, Clinton issued an immediate order that all bags be matched to passengers on an airplane as a precondition of takeoff—a measure based on the happy assumption that no terrorist would blow up a plane on which he was flying.

Indeed, in the wake of the Gore Commission, a new technology called the Computer Assisted Passenger Prescreening System (CAPPS) was developed to identify possible terrorists for special scrutiny, based on such facts as how the ticket was paid for and whether or not the trip was one-way. As the *New York Times* indicated, though, "at the time, CAPPS was intended only to foil suitcase bombers, and was used to assure that no baggage was loaded onto a plane unless its owner was on board."

The 9/11 Commission confirms that only passengers checking bags were eligible to be selected by CAPPS for additional scrutiny. And, the Commission notes, this extra screening involved only "hav[ing] one's checked baggage screened for explosives or held off the airplane until one had boarded." But, as the Commission notes, the algorithm CAPPS used to identify suspicious passengers "included hijacker profile data." So why was only checked baggage screened under the new rules set up by the Gore Commission? Why was carry-on luggage—which a hijacker might certainly use—ignored?

The Commission also noted that "primarily because of concern regarding potential discrimination and the impact on passenger throughout, 'selectees' were no longer required to undergo extraordinary screening of their carry-on baggage as had been the case before the system was computerized in 1997." The Commission noted that "this policy change also reflected the perception that nonsuicide sabotage was the primary threat to civil aviation." Indeed, the final report of the Gore Commission, issued in 1997, did not address the possibility of terrorist airplane hijackings—an omission so grave that it should subject both Clinton and Gore to a harsh judgment in history.

CAPPS actually worked on 9/11.

It did identify eight of the nineteen hijackers as "suspicious." But because the entire system was designed only to ensure that passengers flew with their own baggage on board, it did not flag these men for the more intrusive security check that might have stopped them from boarding the flights.

The consequences of these limitations on CAPPS are sickening.

9/11 ringleader Mohammed Atta "was selected by . . . CAPPS," but, according to the 9/11 Commission, "under security rules in place at the time, the only consequence of Atta's selection by CAPPS was that his checked bags were held off the plane until it was confirmed that he had boarded the aircraft. This did not, by any means, hinder Atta's plans."

And, while three other members of the hijacking team that would take over the flights that crashed into the World Trade Center were "selected by CAPPS" when they boarded the planes in Portland, Maine, their "selection affected only the handling of their checked bags, not their screening at the checkpoint."

Meanwhile, according to the 9/11 Commission Report, three more hijackers were flagged by CAPPS in Washington as they attempted to board American Flight 77, which would crash into the Pentagon. Two were also "selected for extra scrutiny by the airline's customer service representative at the check-in counter. He did so because one of [them] did not have photo identification nor could he understand English, and because the agent found both of the passengers to be suspicious." Because of the lax air safety rules put in effect during the Clinton years, however, "the only consequence of their selection was that their checked bags were held off the plane until it was confirmed that they had boarded the aircraft."

Beyond the CAPPS system, the Gore Commission left other gaping loopholes in our air safety system. The hijackers' weapons on 9/11 were short knives, mace or pepper spray, and box cutters. Why were they allowed to take such weapons aboard? According to the 9/11 Commission Report, "While FAA rules did not expressly prohibit knives with blades under four inches long, the airlines' checkpoint operations guide (which was developed in cooperation with the FAA) explicitly *permitted* them" (emphasis added). Why? Because the agency did not consider them "menacing," most local laws permitted people to carry such knives, and they would have been hard to detect "unless the sensitivity of metal detectors had been greatly increased."

Indeed, the Commission reported that "a proposal to ban knives altogether in 1993 had been rejected because small cutting implements were difficult to detect and the number of innocent 'alarms' would have increased significantly, exacerbating congestion problems at checkpoints."

When Gore was pondering his recommendations, many on the White House staff were pressing for a far more extensive overhaul of the air safety system. In fact, on July 24, 1996, I conducted a survey for President Clinton in which we tested the three main air safety initiatives that were subsequently adopted by the Bush administration in the shadow of 9/11. Even in 1996, voters heartily approved of X-raying all checked baggage, federalizing the air security workers, and requiring photo identification to fly. Clinton and Gore were seriously considering these additional safety steps, but were deterred by opposition from the airline industry, sensitive to spooking would-be travelers.

Even when the Gore Commission hit on a good idea that might have hindered the 9/11 hijackers, it was not implemented. The Commission called "on the FBI and CIA . . . to provide terrorist watchlists [to the FAA] to improve prescreening." But the FAA "no-fly" list contained only twelve names of terrorist suspects, even though the watch lists of the other agencies had the identities of "many thousands of known and suspected terrorists." The 9/11 Commission found, incredibly, that "the longtime chief of the FAA's civil aviation security division testified that he was not even aware of the State Department's . . . list of known or suspected terrorists (some 60,000 before 9/11) until he heard it mentioned during the Commission's January 26, 2004 public hearing."

Bill Clinton's and Al Gore's pathetic efforts to foil air hijacking make a mockery of the president's proud proclamation to the Democratic National Convention in 1996 that "We will improve airport and air travel safety. . . . We will install the most sophisticated bomb-detection equipment in all our major airports. We will search every airplane flying to or from America from another nation—every flight, every cargo hold, every cabin, every time."

But if Clinton did not take strong measures to counter air-hijacking terrorism in 1996, why did he not do so later in his term, as the evidence mounted that al Qaeda might be contemplating a terrorist action involving passenger planes? As the 9/11 Commission reported, a Presidential Daily Brief that Clinton received on December 4, 1998, was headed "Bin Ladin Preparing to Hijack U.S. Aircraft and Other Attacks," and "cited information indicating that Bin Laden and his allies were preparing an aircraft hijacking and other attacks in the United States to free three jailed Arabs, including the mastermind of the 1993 World Trade Center bombing, Ramzi Yousef and 'Blind Sheik' Omar Abdel-Rahman."

Knowing that he had rejected the more comprehensive air safety measures discussed two years before, why didn't Clinton pick up those initiatives and act on them?

Bill Clinton wrote his memoirs three years after 9/11, the greatest aviation disaster in history. He knew that the system he had bequeathed to Bush was riddled with holes. Yet, he spends only a single paragraph on the topic in his 1,000-page memoir. Nothing could more eloquently attest to the fact that he just didn't get how important it was—even, apparently, in retrospect.

As a result of his failure to reform aviation security, even if President Bush had full knowledge of the dates, times, and places of the terror attack, he may not have been able to prevent them. Without competent air traffic safety measures in place—and skilled federal employees to administer them—it's unlikely that we would ever have caught the hijackers in time.

Clinton also missed a key opportunity to learn more about bin Laden and al Qaeda after the group showed its face with an attack, during the summer of 1996, on American troops living in Khobar Towers in Saudi Arabia. The bombing killed nineteen and left an eighty-foot crater in its wake.

A full investigation of the attack might have revealed much about al Qaeda's operations and the threat that it posed. As soon as the bomb exploded at the U.S. base, American law enforcement officials were worried that the Saudis would cover up the affair and that they would never learn who was really responsible. Their concerns were well founded. Eight months before, terrorists had killed five Americans in an attack on another building in Saudi Arabia that had been used by the U.S. military to train troops from the kingdom. The Saudi government quickly arrested four men it blamed for the attack and executed them—never permitting American officials to interrogate the suspects.

The dead men told no tales.

Suspecting a link between the two attacks, and desperate to avoid premature executions, FBI Director Louis Freeh hurried to Saudi Arabia—and returned twice more—to make sure we would be able to question any suspects. But the Saudis stonewalled anyway, probably anxious to prevent us from discovering evidence that one of their nationals, Osama bin Laden, had been behind the attack.

Unbelievably, in *My Life* Clinton cites the eventual Saudi execution of those responsible for the Khobar bombing as an achievement, making no mention of their repeated refusals to permit American interrogation. Why didn't Clinton demand an aggressive interrogation of the Saudis, allegedly our allies?

Again, it was likely due to his aversion to conflict and his desire to please everybody. Bill Clinton just wasn't the man to lean on the Saudis. Even if he'd tried to do so, he would doubtless have heard the warnings ringing through his own mind: that with one signature the kingdom could strangle global oil stocks, sending the already-rising price of gasoline through the roof (and Clinton's popularity to new lows). Having raised gasoline taxes in 1995, he was already vulnerable on gas prices; Republicans were compounding his problems through showy efforts intended to repeal the Clinton gas tax and bring down prices at the pump.

Even during the Clinton years the search for Osama bin Laden wasn't the only front on the war on terror. On Clinton's watch, Iran, Iraq, and North Korea were the most serious rogue nations we faced. And Clinton's record was no better on any of these three fronts than it was in tracking al Qaeda.

Throughout 1996, a fierce debate raged in the Clinton administration over a bill, sponsored by New York Senator Alfonse D'Amato, that authorized the United States to invoke tough sanctions against any foreign company that invested in helping to develop Iran's petroleum industry (it was already illegal for American companies to do so).

The D'Amato bill was a revolutionary concept. It permitted the United States to extend its reach to foreign companies, penalizing them by denying access to various American programs and benefits if they helped Iran. It raised a firestorm of criticism in Europe, where ongoing trade with Iran was a highly profitable part of their economy.

Clinton got a provision included in the bill that allowed him to waive the sanctions in specific situations where it served the national interest. With this proviso, he signed the legislation with great fanfare right before the Democratic National Convention. Framing it as the centerpiece of his anti-terror policy, he told the wildly applauding convention: "We are working to rally a world coalition with zero tolerance for terrorism. Just this month I signed a law imposing harsh sanctions on foreign companies that invest in key sectors of the Iranian and Libyan economies. As long as Iran trains, supports, and protects terrorists, as long as Libya refuses to give up the people who blew up Pan Am 103, they will pay a price from the United States."

Some price! Every time an opportunity arose to impose the sanctions, Clinton caved in to pressure and waived them. As a result, not a single company was penalized. When Total S.A. of France, the giant Russian natural gas company Gazprom, and the state-owned Petronas of Malaysia signed a contract with Iran to invest in a $2 billion gas field, Clinton waived the sanctions!

In *My Life*, Clinton omits mention of the bill, his signing ceremony, his reference to the sanctions in his speech, the debate over imposing sanctions, and his later waivers. Undoubtedly conscious of how his record would look today—and may look in the future if Iran succeeds in developing a bomb—he felt silence was his best option.

On Iraq, Clinton constantly backpedaled, allowing Saddam Hussein to pump his petroleum under the so-called Oil for Food program. When Clinton took office, Iraq was blocked from selling oil on the world market and was swarming with UN inspectors; Saddam and his shattered military posed little international threat. By the time he left office, however, Saddam had kicked out all inspectors, and was happily pumping more than two million barrels a day, generating daily revenues of $40 to $60 million to fund his military rebuilding.

How did Clinton let Saddam off the mat?

Each year brought a new demand from the Iraqi dictator to loosen sanctions, increase oil production, or to limit inspections. Saddam would announce that he was planning to refuse to honor some aspect of the UN requirements unless his demands were met, and the world would convulse in crisis. The United Nations Security Council would huddle in executive session. France, China, and Russia—Saddam's allies, bought and paid for by bribes from the Oil for Food program—would press for concessions. But Clinton would stand tall against Saddam before the world audience, and Saddam would seem to give in.

Then, when nobody was looking, Saddam would get much of what he asked for.

First, Saddam persuaded America and the United Nations to let him sell half a million barrels of oil daily, allegedly to pay for food for Iraqi children. Then he got the ceiling raised to one million barrels, then to two million; finally, he got it eliminated entirely.

Having secured the money, Saddam then proceeded to wriggle out of restrictions on how to spend it. He began by demanding that American officials be barred from the UN inspection team, claiming that they were spies. Then he restricted where the inspectors could go. Ultimately, he kicked them out altogether. Clinton and Tony Blair responded furiously. In *My Life,* Clinton catalogues the four-day bombing that ensued, noting that the coalition flew 650 air sorties and fired 400 cruise missiles. Of course, what did Saddam care? He'd gotten rid of the inspectors, and all without having to suffer a Gulf War–style American-led invasion. After four days of bombing, he was free to pump all the oil he wanted and use the money to arm to the teeth.

Game, set, match to Saddam.

But the story that goes unmentioned in Clinton's memoirs concerns the corruption that underscored the whole Oil for Food program to begin with. Why did the world tremble when Saddam announced that he would refuse to extend the program? Was it because of global concern for the Iraqi children who would starve? Not likely. Subsequent documents, released in the aftermath of the U.S. invasion, show massive fraud in the program, including payoffs to highly placed officials in the governments of Chirac of France and Putin of Russia and direct payments to each leader's political party. In fact, even the director of the Oil for Food program has been accused of receiving payoffs from Iraq. Current estimates place the total oil revenues diverted into bribes to French, Russian, and UN officials at $10 billion of the $62 billion the Oil for Food program generated. Ten billion dollars can buy a lot of complicity!

Though he knew all this at the time he wrote *My Life,* Clinton makes no reference to the shenanigans that went on under his nose.

Clinton's irresponsibility in dealing with North Korea is perhaps the worst such story. When Clinton took office in 1993, he was confronted with massive evidence that North Korea was seeking to develop nuclear weapons, diverting nuclear fuel from its Yongbyon reactor and planning future diversions to build up enough material to produce up to five atomic bombs.

Clinton's foreign policy people frantically worked to build global support for tough economic sanctions against the vulnerable regime in North Korea. Impressively, they got Japan to agree to sanctions that would bar Koreans living there from sending money home to their relatives—a key source of foreign exchange for the isolated North Korean government. With Japan and South Korea on board, the United States seemed poised to bring maximum economic pressure on Pyongyang.

Then former President Jimmy Carter pulled the rug out from under Clinton by traveling to North Korea in search of a peaceful alternative. Clinton did not ask Carter to go, but could not very well request that he stay home after the former president had arranged the trip and presented Clinton with a fait accompli. Carter went right from his meeting with the North Koreans to CNN's studio to announce that he had secured Pyongyang's approval for a "very positive step," and urged the administration to withdraw its proposal for sanctions.

Carter, it turned out, had been flim-flammed. And in the process he robbed the Clinton administration of whatever momentum it had built up for effective measures against North Korea.

In *My Life*, Clinton celebrates the framework agreement with North Korea, signed on October 21, 1994, in which Pyongyang agreed to freeze all activity at its nuclear reactors and to open them to monitoring, to ship nuclear fuel rods out of the country, and to dismantle its nuclear facilities. In return, the United States, Japan, and South Korea agreed to ship North Korea 500,000 tons of heavy oil per year.

After Carter had tied his hands, though, Clinton proved far too eager to go along with the phony "Framework" Agreement his negotiators reached with North Korea. Anxious to have a foreign policy achievement to take to the voters, Clinton announced the agreement just before the 1994 elections—and then proceeded to let the North Koreans off without adequate inspections. The North Korean promise to discontinue its nuclear program wasn't worth the paper it was written on.

After he left office, the former president then notes, he learned that North Korea had begun to violate the agreement in 1998. But Clinton must have known of the violations while he was still in office. After all, the readers of the *New York Times* did.

On August 17, 1998, the *Times* broke a story on its front page that North Korea was cheating, and that American intelligence knew about it. The next day the *Washington Post* reported further information about the violations.

So Clinton surely knew all about them. But he did nothing.

Is Clinton lying in his memoirs when he says he didn't know? Well, read what he says carefully. He doesn't say he didn't know. He just says that he "learned" about the North Korean operations after he left office. As usual with him, it depends on what the definition of *is* is.

Another reason Clinton didn't act aggressively when he learned about North Korea's betrayal was his own vulnerability to the pending impeachment. If he admitted that one of his top foreign policy accomplishments had been found to be a sham, it would have immeasurably weakened his case for remaining in office. And had he tried to rally America to any real action against North Korea, of course, he would just have been accused of wagging the dog.

As with Iraq and bin Laden, the fact that America didn't have a true president during much of Clinton's second term—but rather an incumbent hanging on by his fingernails—doomed us to passivity in Korea, while our problems there and elsewhere grew larger and less tractable.

On these four main terror threats that faced the United States during the 1990s—al Qaeda, Iran, Iraq, and North Korea—Clinton ignored the problems for too long, or fell victim to elaborate ploys that fooled him into believing he had solved, or at least alleviated, the problem.

Why was he so gullible? Why so inactive?

The real reason is rooted deep in Bill Clinton's past. The president's own record of draft dodging, to which we'll turn in a moment, made him deathly afraid of putting American troops in harm's way. He was haunted by the prospect of facing mothers and fathers whose sons and daughters had perished on his watch.

As a result, Clinton did everything he could to avoid direct risk of American combat deaths. And, as laudable as his desire to save lives may be, it often led him into wishful thinking and credulousness. He was willing to believe North Korea, because he hated to think of what he would have to do if he didn't. He pounded Saddam Hussein with aerial attacks, because it allowed him to look tough without having to send in ground troops. And, in the ultimate test, he decided not to send U.S. soldiers on a mission to kill or capture Osama bin Laden, or even to approve further air strikes that might have killed him.

In light of Clinton's aversion to military action, we must ask again the question that was raised throughout the 1992 campaign: Should Clinton's lack of service in the military have disqualified him from the presidency?

Clearly not. Neither George W. Bush nor Ronald Reagan were hampered in their conduct of the military by their own lack of service in combat units. Presidents can run the Pentagon without having been there.

But it is also clear that Clinton's political weakness—stemming from public awareness that he had taken deliberate action to avoid military service—made him cautious to a fault in approving armed operations that entailed any potential danger to U.S. casualties or, even in some cases, of any foreign civilian deaths.

It was this political sensitivity, this heightened vulnerability to criticism, that disabled Clinton throughout his presidency.

6

Ducking the Draft

If missing the opportunity to prevent 9/11 was the greatest failure of Clinton's presidency, his sensitivity to the charges of draft-dodging was the biggest cause of the hesitancy, irresolution, and weakness that characterized his ineffective response to terror.

Why revisit the draft issue now? Because in order to grasp why the question so paralyzed his hand, one must understand what it was that he was covering up—what it was that so haunted his mind.

The draft issue was more than a simple campaign scandal. In fact, it was at the root of Clinton's problems as president. His deliberate deception in releasing the details of his draft status during the 1992 campaign sowed a legacy of distrust with the national media that would set the tone for his daily pounding in the press for the next eight years.

The draft was the Original Scandal—the one that first introduced Bill Clinton to America's media. It was there, in his mishandling of the issue, that the press took his measure and decided it could not trust him to tell the truth.

If he lied about Gennifer Flowers, the media was inclined to forgive him. They had heard his voice on the tapes, but they also wondered about the credibility of a woman who had been paid to tell her story. Moreover, many reporters believed that the personal lives of the candidates were not fair game. The draft, on the other hand, could

hardly be considered a purely personal matter. It was a totally legitimate issue for a presidential candidate; the responses a candidate
would offer the media on the subject were a good indication of character and trustworthiness. It was in these responses that the legacy of
media distrust, of which Clinton complains loudly in *My Life,* was
first developed.

But neither the Clintons nor their aides ever fully understood the
permanent damage that they inflicted on themselves during this
scandal, and how it would come back to haunt him in the future.
Journalists who had been blatantly deceived by Clinton and his
campaign staff would never trust them again, and would not easily
discount stories of further scandals as they unfolded. Clinton may
have won the short-term battle over the draft, but in the long term
he lost. Never again would he be given the benefit of the doubt.
Never again would his word mean much to the media.

And, now, when we are asked to take Clinton's word—one thousand pages of it—we should note that nowhere is the disjuncture between *My Life* and real life more pronounced than in his account of
the draft story. In both his version of what went on when he was
ducking service, and his rendition of how the scandal played out in
the media, we see Bill Clinton at his untruthful worst.

The way Clinton deals with this scandal is a textbook illustration
of his ability—witnessed over and over again—to weave prejudicial
facts and questionable conduct into a politically acceptable and appealing story. He's very good at it, which is no surprise considering
that he's been doing it all his life—in his campaigns, his presidency,
and now in his memoirs. In *My Life,* he has idealized his role, he has
minimized his negatives, and, it is clear, he has learned no lessons.

Indeed, without the extensive contemporaneous record in the
press, one would barely recognize the situations he describes. For it is
his own reality, a curious and truncated one, that he shares with the
reader. His version of history provides a fascinating view of how Clinton thinks, learns, and operates. And, most important, in this version
he unconsciously reveals his previous lies, omissions, and spins.

Clinton's misleading statements, contradictions, and distortions created chaos during every one of his personal crises; only his amazing communication skills, and ability to persuade the public, ultimately saved him—until the next crisis came along. He emerged battered, not beaten, but with an ever-growing reputation for untrustworthiness.

To understand the divergence between Clinton's latest account of the draft and the facts, one must begin by going back to his college days and unravel what really happened. Like most of Clinton's important life experiences, his actual draft history was complicated, convoluted, calculated, and covert. Only in his retelling has it come to seem incredibly simple—simple and incomplete; simple and inaccurate.

The reality is that, because of political and family influence, Clinton was able to avoid the draft; he was given special treatment that was not available to his peers. By misleading ROTC officials, he was able to win himself a deferment. By living at Oxford, but apparently doing little or no work as a graduate student at Oxford (for his second year), he managed to preserve his student deferment. Then, when the draft rules changed in his favor, he resigned from ROTC—but not before he was reasonably sure he wouldn't be called.

But there is more. Clinton's draft woes took place only five years before he ran for Congress from Arkansas. Already actively contemplating a political career, he took care to make it appear that he was, indeed, rejecting deferment from the draft—at the very moment when he was pulling every string he could to stay out of the military.

Did Bill Clinton do anything illegal in dodging the draft? No. But he certainly violated the essential principles of ethical conduct. He wove a complex quilt of misstatements designed to get him into ROTC, with the sole purpose of ducking service. And when the scandal broke as a key issue in the 1992 campaign, his lies and obfuscations almost cost him the election.

One way of debunking the story of Bill Clinton's avoidance of the draft as he tells it in *My Life,* is to trace the conflicting details that he reluctantly, slowly, and misleadingly provided during his 1992 presidential campaign. A simple review of the record reveals that, in his recent attempt to retell his story for the permanent record, he has revised not only the "facts" of the case, but even the spin. In 1992, his message in a nutshell was: "I didn't dodge the draft, and I never sought or received special treatment." After more and more conflicting details emerged, he later admitted that there was much more to the story. But that's as far as it went.

Now, in *My Life,* his revisionist view of the events casts him as a principled—although selective—latter-day self-styled conscientious objector, who was not against all wars, just fervently opposed to the Vietnam War. He depicts himself as an intelligent and sensitive young man struggling with a complicated moral issue, giving no thought to its ultimate implications for his political career.

In Clinton's memoir, his work as a clerk on the Senate Foreign Relations Committee becomes a daily statement of his opposition to the war. Like Walter Mitty, he now paints a grandiose self-portrait of his job at the Committee, noting that he was one of the few people in the country who had access to the true information about Vietnam. If he hadn't had that exceptional access while working on the Committee, Clinton now claims, he "might have made different decisions about military service."

Are we to believe him? Was his determination to avoid service so principled, so informed by his work at the Committee? How does his exalted account of his job jibe with another revelation he offers in *My Life*—that he used to take naps at work downstairs in the document room? Or that his chores included delivering papers to the Committee members, adding names to the mailing list, clipping newspapers, and occasionally driving Senator Fulbright?

Bill Clinton, like many of his peers, didn't want to go to Vietnam. But the situation was more complicated for him, for even then, at the age of twenty-two, he was carefully planning and preparing for a career in public life. Clinton recognized that he could not openly resist the draft. That wouldn't fly in Arkansas. So he had to find a way to stay out of the draft, without jeopardizing his future ability to become a public official. (Remember, Clinton became attorney general of Arkansas only seven years after his draft eligibility ended.)

The fact that Clinton had not served in the military during the Vietnam War would not have proscribed his candidacy. He was not alone. Thousands of young men were either granted deferments or were saved from induction into the armed forces by receiving a high lottery number. Many of them went on to become elected officials, with little or no stigma attached to their lack of military service.

But what clearly rankled voters was the idea of a politician who had either taken extraordinary and deliberate steps to stay out of the military, or received special treatment to avoid the draft—this *was* deadly to a presidential candidate. As George Stephanopoulos put it: "Failing to serve in the military was not disqualifying as long as you didn't 'pull strings.' You didn't have to be a war hero, but you couldn't be seen as a draft dodger."

This was something the political side of Bill Clinton understood instinctively—understood it, in fact, even as he was pulling those strings.

THE FACTS: 1964–1970

On his eighteenth birthday, August 19, 1964, Bill Clinton registered for the draft in Hot Springs, Arkansas, as he was required to do under the Selective Service Act. Like all other college students, he was automatically eligible for a student deferment, and in November 1964 he was classified as 2S—a status he maintained until late in his senior year at Georgetown University.

During his work as a part-time clerk at the U.S. Senate Foreign Relations Committee, he became friendly with the other staff members. In *My Life,* Clinton describes his growing sympathy with the anti-war movement, fueled by a combination of what he learned while reading and writing papers at school, information he had access to at the

Foreign Relations Committee, and his personal sorrow in seeing high school classmates on the casualty list. According to Clinton's memoirs, he was by no means a radical; his opposition to the war did not manifest itself in passionate political, cultural, and moral objections. While others were involved in student protests, joined the Students for a Democratic Society (SDS), and worked for Eugene McCarthy, Clinton says, he acted otherwise. In discussing the counterculture of the late 1960s, Clinton writes that although he was "sympathetic to the zeitgeist," he did not agree with the "radical rhetoric." He writes of his short hair and distaste for loud music. He disavows hatred for President Johnson, and says he was afraid "culture clashes" would not hasten the end of the conflict. "I just wanted to end the war."

In his senior year, Clinton was chosen as a Rhodes Scholar, and planned to go to Oxford University in England in the fall of 1968. But in February of that year, President Johnson suddenly abolished all student deferrals for graduate students, except those in medical school. So on March 20, 1968, Clinton's draft status became 1A, making him eligible for induction after his graduation from Georgetown at the end of the semester.

What did he do? As the record shows, he marshaled all of the influence he could to delay his induction. Robert Corrado, one of the members of the Hot Springs three-man draft board at that time, recalled that the board received calls from an aide to Senator Fulbright, urging them to keep Clinton out of the draft. Documents in Fulbright's official papers, identified by the *Los Angeles Times*, verified the staff contacts on Clinton's behalf. As Corrado remembers, at one point the chairman of the draft board, William Armstrong, held back Clinton's file, stating: "We've got to give him time to go to Oxford." Clinton's influential uncle, Raymond Clinton, lobbied Armstrong, as well as Fulbright, and later Lieutenant Colonel Trice Ellis, commanding officer of the local naval reserves, on Clinton's behalf.

In the summer of 1968, Uncle Raymond arranged to create a special reserve commission for Clinton as an enlisted man in the naval reserves, even though no such slots were available for anyone else.

(With his poor hearing, he had failed a physical for the Naval Officer Program.) This solution was not ideal—it meant he would eventually have to serve two years of active duty—but it would have bought him a year-long delay. But Clinton never had to accept that opportunity, for Uncle Raymond also succeeded in convincing the Hot Springs draft board to ignore Clinton's file for a while, giving him time to go to Oxford.

As a result of the efforts to keep Clinton out of the draft, the Hot Springs draft board allowed Clinton to wait eight months—until January 31, 1969—to complete the preinduction draft physical. This delay allowed him to go to Oxford instead of going into the army. According to the *Los Angeles Times,* Clinton was the only person in his draft board who was ever allowed to defer his physical for such a long period of time.

After he eventually passed the physical, Clinton was available for immediate induction, and on April 30, 1969, while still at Oxford, Clinton received a draft notice that ordered him to report nine days earlier, on April 21, 1969. He immediately called the draft board and was informed that he was entitled to complete the semester, but was ordered to report for induction on his return. The board then sent him a second induction notice, for July 28, 1969.

Back in Hot Springs on June 26, Clinton cast about desperately for any and all alternatives to the draft. He tried the National Guard, but there were no openings. He "looked into the air force, but learned [he] couldn't become a jet pilot because [he] didn't have fusion vision."

Then, on July 17, 1969, just eleven days before he would have to report for induction, Clinton went to Fayetteville to meet the director of the ROTC, Colonel Eugene Holmes, who immediately accepted him into the program. Since he had also been accepted to attend the University of Arkansas Law School, he would not have to report for active duty until after graduation from law school. When Clinton signed his letter of intent to join ROTC, it waived his induction notice and led to his reclassification as 1D, a reservist, on August 7, 1969. His induction was apparently cancelled after a personal meeting with Colonel Willard Hawkins, who "had the authority to rescind a draft notice."

The ROTC deferment got Clinton out of the October 1969 draft, which took two younger men from Hot Springs instead. (The policy at the time was to draft the oldest first.)

Meanwhile, Clinton decided not to go to law school but to return to Oxford for a second year, starting in the fall semester of 1969.

But by now rumors were swirling that President Nixon, who had succeeded Johnson, was planning a major change in the draft. On September 14, 1969, the *Arkansas Gazette* ran a story indicating that the president was planning to suspend the draft or limit it to nineteen-year-olds. And, on September 19, Nixon did actually suspend the draft calls for November and December, and spread out the October quotas over three months. Nixon also noted that he had asked Congress to establish a draft lottery, and said that if it failed to do so, he would sign an executive order eliminating the draft for all men between twenty and twenty-six. And on October 1, 1969, the Nixon administration announced that graduate students would be allowed finish the academic year before they could be inducted.

In fact, Clinton was hardly a serious graduate student. He received no degree, attended few classes in his second year, and traveled for several months during the school year. While his classmates—like Strobe Talbott—wrote serious works, he hiked around England and read novels and poetry with no particular concentration on any subject.

But the graduate deferment was a gift: Clinton no longer needed his ROTC deferment to stay out of the military. It had served its purpose in keeping him out of the October draft, and henceforth he would be protected by the graduate deferment he got for attending a second year at Oxford.

But Clinton still had two problems:

1. He didn't want to have to go into the military, as he was required under the rules of the ROTC program.

2. He needed to minimize the future political damage that might arise if he appeared to have ducked the draft.

He wanted, in other words, to have his cake and eat it too. But how to do it?

Nixon's decision to extend the graduate deferments opened the door to a solution. Now Clinton could ostentatiously resign from the ROTC and seem to put himself back into the draft—while knowing all along that his graduate deferment would protect him. After the end of his second year at Oxford, the draft would be winding down anyway. Nixon, anxious to defuse the antiwar sentiment on campus, was clearly ending the draft system.

So now Clinton moved to implement his grand design. He called his stepfather and asked him to tell Bill Armstrong, the draft board chairman, to reclassify him as 1A, knowing full well that his graduate deferment would kick in and save him from induction.

Later, when he was running for president, Clinton eagerly used the political cover he had arranged for himself, telling the *New York Times* that he had had an attack of conscience and "put himself back in the draft because he felt a moral obligation after learning that some high school classmates were killed." In *My Life,* he characterizes himself as thinking: "I don't believe in deferments. I cannot do this ROTC thing."

Clinton's new, politically clever strategy allowed him to quit the inconvenient ROTC program, thus ducking the eventual military service it would have required—while minimizing what might later prove politically embarrassing evidence that he had ducked the draft.

But this solution still left Clinton with one problem: Anyone who looked carefully into his record would know that he hadn't really subjected himself to draft vulnerability, since he had only gotten reclassified 1A *after* Nixon had reinstated the graduate school deferment. But count on Bill to have a story to cover himself: He claimed he had written a letter to Bill Armstrong, the chairman of his draft board, asking him to be reclassified 1A—but forgot to mail it. He claims he wrote the letter in late September 1969, weeks *before* Nixon extended graduate school deferments. Had he actually mailed the letter when he said he wrote it, he would have subjected himself to draft eligibility before he knew that graduate school would keep him deferred.

And yet this man—whose memoirs reflect that he saved every scrap of paper and object he ever owned—does not produce a copy of this letter he claims to have written to Armstrong and admits he never mailed.

On December 1, 1969, even Clinton's theoretical vulnerability to the draft ended. Nixon had gotten his lottery passed, and by dint of his date of birth Clinton was fortunate to receive number 311 out of 365.

As soon as the draft was no longer a threat, on the very next day, December 2, 1969, Clinton applied to Yale Law School. On the following day, he sent what later became an infamous letter to Colonel Holmes, thanking him for "saving" him from the draft, stating his opposition to the war, and notifying him of his decision to resign from the ROTC program. In his letter to Holmes, Clinton mentions another letter that likely never existed, claiming that he had asked the draft board to reclassify him 1A on September 12. If this were the case, it would have constituted another action taken before he knew Nixon was extending graduate deferments. Like the Armstrong note, however, no such letter has ever surfaced.

Clinton's letter to Holmes is surprisingly honest about his political motivation in seeming to subject himself to draft vulnerability. Clinton begins the letter by noting that he "came to believe the draft system itself is illegitimate," and that "no government should have the power to make its citizens fight and die in a war they oppose." But then he writes that he "decided to accept the draft in spite of my beliefs for one reason only, to maintain my political viability within the system," adding that "for years, I have prepared myself for a political life characterized by both practical political ability and concern for rapid social progress."

Embarrassingly, Clinton told Holmes that he "loathed the military"—a statement in sharp contrast to his later accolades for the institution. It was another statement he would later have reason to regret.

THE SPIN: 1992 EDITION

How in the world did Clinton get elected president after the facts surfaced about his draft-dodging behavior during Vietnam? Developing a damage control strategy that students of politics will study for decades, he evolved tactics that would serve him time after time as he faced accusations and scandal.

It was a four-pronged strategy: First, deny as long as you can, hiding behind a smokescreen of legalistic, specific, and pedantic language. Then attack the press for raising the issue, and throw dirt at your opponent. At the same time, take care to depersonalize the issue: Tell the people this isn't about your misconduct, it's about the evil entrenched interests, who are trying to destroy you because of your innovative policies. Finally, to ensure your lasting recovery, create a myth about the attacks, investing them with a deeper meaning.

Before he ran for president, Clinton had always handled the draft issue easily. Running for governor in 1978, he claimed that he had never received a deferment—that he had decided to "subject himself to the draft."

While the explanation had the virtue of simplicity, it was also untrue. He had, in fact, received two induction notices, and he had avoided the draft by enrolling in ROTC under the hapless Colonel Holmes after the draft board was lobbied by his uncle and by Fulbright's office.

But no one had ever seriously challenged Clinton's version of the events of 1968 and 1969, and he had no reason to expect anything different as he ran for president in 1992. While he consulted anxiously with me many times about how he would handle charges of drug use and womanizing, he never even mentioned the draft as a problem. When any questions came up, he referred reporters to Colonel Holmes, who did not disclose any of the details of his draft history.

But in December 1991—two months before the New Hampshire primary—Dan Balz of the *Washington Post* interviewed Clinton for an article contrasting him with his opponent, war hero Bob Kerrey, who had lost his leg in Vietnam.

Stephanopoulos describes his vague sense of impending doom about the draft issue when he overheard Clinton tell Balz that it was a "fluke" that he hadn't been drafted in August 1969. "*Fluke* was too provocative a word, almost a taunt. I don't know all of the details, but I doubted it fit the word *fluke*." Several weeks later, George suggested that they needed more answers from Clinton about the draft, because it was an issue that wasn't likely to go away. He hit a very raw nerve. "You would have thought that I called Bill a draft dodger. Hillary spoke first and she was incensed. 'Bill's not going to apologize for being against the Vietnam War.' Ignited by her intensity, Clinton launched into a red-faced tirade against the war and said he'd rather lose the race than say it was right."

Of course, this nondenial avoided the key issue of whether he had ducked the draft—and in the process answered a question George hadn't asked: How had he really felt about the war?

Rather than simply asking Clinton what he did to avoid the draft, the campaign made a big show of hiring an outside research firm to review the candidate's draft history. In essence, Clinton was investigating himself. But it made sense: Instead of telling the truth—even to close aides and associates—the Clintons needed first to see what information was out there. Of course, the Clintons themselves weren't interviewed; first they had to find out what could be gleaned from the public record, or through interviews with people familiar with the details, probably so they could mold their story to fit. And of course, though he obviously relied on a wealth of diaries, papers, and tapes as he recited the dates and details of every incident about the draft in his book, in 1992 Clinton simply claimed he couldn't recall what had happened and was searching for documents—the same documents he relies on in *My Life* twelve years later.

Then the Clinton version of the draft story began to come apart. Colonel Eugene Holmes, the bedrock of Clinton's alibi, turned on him, saying "There is the imminent danger to our country of a draft dodger becoming commander-in-chief of the armed forces." Holmes was not someone Clinton could easily dismiss. A thirty-two-year army veteran, he had survived the Bataan Death March, been a Japanese POW for three and a half years, and won the Silver Star and two Bronze Stars.

On February 6, 1992, the *Wall Street Journal* ignited a national uproar by quoting Holmes, reporting that candidate Clinton had joined ROTC only to avoid the draft, and had never really intended to serve. "I believe that he [Clinton] purposely deceived me," Holmes said, "using the possibility of joining ROTC as a ploy to work with the draft board to delay his induction and get a new draft classification."

Holmes disclosed the political pressure to which he had been subjected in the late 1960s to persuade him to avoid drafting Clinton. He said he got "daily calls" about the young man's draft status, and had been told by the draft board that Senator Fulbright's office was pushing for Clinton's admission to the ROTC program. In response to the pressure, Holmes said, he "then made the necessary arrangements to enroll Mr. Clinton in the ROTC program."

Now Clinton was in the dangerous territory that George Stephanopoulos had warned about: That he had sought and received special treatment.

Clinton's strategy? Deny, deny, deny.

But he was careful to avoid an outright lie, and left himself an escape. The day after the *Journal* story broke, he told the *Washington Post* that he "never *knowingly* received favorable treatment" [emphasis added]. As always, Clinton's wording was deliberate. By hanging his denial on the word "knowingly," he could wriggle out without calling Holmes a liar. As the *New York Times* summarized his position: "if he ever received special treatment from his draft board, he never asked for it or knew about it."

Then the other shoe dropped. Three days later, on February 10, 1992, ABC News—showing a pro-Clinton bias—slipped the campaign a copy of Clinton's 1969 letter to Colonel Holmes, telling him he had quit ROTC and had used the program to duck the draft. ABC's ethical lapse gave Clinton several days to prepare a response, and then permitted him to release the letter himself on February 12.

(Some published reports suggest that Clinton friend Rick Kaplan, who was then the executive producer of *Prime Time Live* at ABC, gave Clinton the heads-up on the letter, making it possible for Clinton to get control of the story. Kaplan went on to become the head of CNN, where he led its decline from the most popular cable news station, losing half of its audience to Fox News Network. Kaplan was listed as a Lincoln Bedroom guest at the Clinton White House.)

How did Clinton explain away his own words, admitting that he had misled Colonel Holmes and thanking him for "saving" him from the draft? Stephanopoulos remembered that when he read the letter he felt it suggested that Clinton had maintained his ROTC position only until he received his high lottery number, and knew he would not be drafted. To George, it looked like the campaign was over: "That's it. We're done."

The questions about his draft history—and his disingenuous responses to the press—almost derailed Bill Clinton's nascent presidential campaign. Even more than the Gennifer Flowers story, the draft issue resonated with the voters, and turned them against him. Just a week before the New Hampshire primary, Clinton's support plummeted in that state after the press began to cover the many discrepancies in his story. "I was dropping in the polls like a rock in a well," he writes in *My Life*. "I was already in third place, and it looked as if I might fall into single digits."

"The Flowers thing isn't hurting me," Clinton told me at the time. "But the draft is killing me."

Desperate to stanch the bleeding, Clinton made an appearance on *Nightline,* where Ted Koppel pressed him on the "coincidence" that he had learned of his high lottery number on December 1, applied to Yale Law School on December 2, and wrote to Colonel Holmes on December 3. Koppel suggested that these were the actions of a person who was "fairly confident" that he would not be drafted.

As he was preparing for *Nightline,* Clinton had called me at the Madison Hotel in Paris, where we were spending a week on vacation. It was the hotel's custom to hold all calls before 7:00 A.M., allowing callers only to leave a message. Apparently, Clinton had called several times in the very early morning, and had been insistent about speaking to me. Finally, the desk clerk, Alain Ginger, came and knocked at our door at about 6:30 A.M., saying that a *Monsieur Cleen-tun* was on the phone and that it was urgent. The candidate apologized for waking me up, saying, charmingly, that he had stayed up late just so he could call. I listened to his tale of woe, and suggested he use the line that saved him on Koppel's show. At the peak of the *Nightline* inquisition, Clinton delivered it perfectly, saying that he was being asked only two questions: "about an affair I never had and a draft I never dodged."

After the election, when we visited the hotel again, I told Alain that *Monsieur Cleen-tun* was now President Clinton. He asked me to get the president's autograph for him, and Clinton was gracious enough to provide one for me to bring to Alain the next time I visited Paris. For many years it hung in the hotel's office, and Alain still regales guests at the Madison with the story of his phone call with President Clinton.

Clinton survived the draft stories; his second-place finish in New Hampshire was strong enough that he dubbed himself the Comeback Kid. But the reprieve would be only temporary, for Clinton hadn't told the full story, and the press kept digging.

In April, the *Los Angeles Times* reported that Clinton had actually received an induction notice before he joined ROTC. Stephanopoulos noted he had been kept in the dark along with everybody else: "What I didn't know was what had not been reported; that Clinton's version picks up *after* he had received an induction notice from his local draft board."

Clinton had actually denied this twice before, claiming that he had never been called up. Now, caught in a lie, Clinton backtracked: "I gladly would have told you this if I thought it was relevant," he said. And he got away with it!

In May, the Clinton campaign reported that they were "still searching for records that would document how he received a draft notice before he enrolled in ROTC." All the campaign had to do was to ask Clinton himself: He knew the answers and he had the documents to explain the whole story. In early September, another draft story surfaced. This time there was evidence that Uncle Raymond had intervened on his behalf with the draft board and the navy reserve. According to the *Los Angeles Times,* his uncle had lobbied Senator Fulbright, the draft board, and Lieutenant Commander Trice Ellis of the local navy reserve unit. As a result, Clinton got a "standard enlisted man's billet, not an officer's slot."

This time, Clinton dodged the bullet by claiming he knew nothing about his uncle's efforts. "It's all news to me," he said. "This is the first I've heard of any of this." Campaign flack Paul Begala told the *New York Times:* "This thing about the navy, he has never heard of."

But Clinton kept stumbling over the facts. Three days later, he had to admit that he knew all about Raymond's intervention after retired Navy Lieutenant Trice Ellis told the *Arkansas Gazette* that he had personally told Clinton about it. Then the Clinton campaign went into full-scale doublespeak. Dee Dee Meyers, the Clinton campaign spokesperson, denied denying the story. The *New York Times* reported: "Meyers said that Clinton's earlier responses had been meant to be taken as answers to the larger accusations by the *Los Angeles Times* concerning a broad lobbying effort on Clinton's behalf, not a response to a specific matter [i.e., the naval reserve issue]."

Clinton kept his own campaign as much in the dark as possible. Meyers told the *Times* that the campaign launched an investigation into what Ellis had told Bill Clinton and could not confirm the facts at that time. Given what we now know, it appears their investigation did not include asking Clinton if it were true.

Several weeks later, on September 19, 1992, another admission leaked out: Clinton conceded that he had asked Fulbright's office for help in getting into the ROTC program in 1969. Lee Williamson, a top aide to Fulbright, claimed that any help was "limited to advice." But the statements of Colonel Holmes and his assistant, Lieutenant Colonel Clint Jones, contradicted Williamson's statements. Subsequent documents in Fulbright's archives showed that Williams had made notes indicating a phone call about the terms that Clinton had wanted with ROTC, including permitting him to go to Oxford in the fall of 1969.

Finally, reduced to an incoherence reminiscent of Yogi Berra, Clinton said, "Even if all this stuff is true, it doesn't change anything about what I knew or did at the time." Huh?

So, to summarize:

- At first Clinton said he got out of the draft because he was lucky.
- Then he said it was a "fluke," and that he did nothing to evade the draft.
- Then he said he might have gotten special treatment, and others may have intervened on his behalf, but he didn't know about it.
- Then he had to admit that he had joined ROTC to duck the draft, but that he had never gotten an induction notice.
- Then he admitted he *had* gotten an induction notice, but didn't tell the press because he didn't think it was relevant.
- Then he said his uncle may have made calls for him, but that this was the first he had heard about them.
- Then he admitted that he knew about the calls, and denied ever denying that he knew.
- Finally, he had to admit that Fulbright's office had interceded on his behalf.

After the stories about his special treatment and his uncle's intervention appeared, Clinton decided on a tactic he would return to throughout his presidency: *Blame the press and attack your enemy.*

On September 8, 1992, the *New York Times* reported that Clinton had "lashed out at the press" for its coverage of the draft issue, blaming them for emphasizing irrelevant issues about him while ignoring potential scandals about George Bush. On Don Imus's radio show, Clinton had blamed Republicans and "assorted enemies" for spreading stories about him.

It might have served him to remember that the same press corps he was lambasting would be the same crew that would cover him for the next eight years.

THE SPIN: 2004 EDITION

The controversy about the draft issue resurfaced constantly throughout the 1992 presidential campaign. Clinton's less than truthful reaction to questions about his conduct came close to destroying his presidential aspirations.

Yet, in a familiar Clintonian disconnect, he devotes less than two pages to the draft issue in *My Life,* most of it devoted to a warm and fuzzy description of the many Friends of Bill who swarmed into New Hampshire to tell the voters what a great person he was. Amazingly, he also writes that he was "unprepared" for the issue, and that he "mistakenly" claimed he'd never had a draft deferment.

"Unprepared"? Really? This is typical Clinton, taking an issue as intimate to his public life as the draft, and re-framing it into something detached completely from him. It's as though he views his personal conduct regarding the draft in the same category as a public policy position he hadn't been properly briefed on or studied carefully enough. And "mistaken"? After obsessing on avoiding the draft throughout his two years at Oxford, could he truly have forgotten he'd had a deferment, and mistakenly deny that he had one? Of course not. What he actually meant was that he hadn't sufficiently developed and memorized the spin he would use to defuse the draft issue.

During the 1992 campaign, Clinton claimed that he was searching—unsuccessfully—for records that would either confirm or deny the stories that were surfacing about the draft. He gave the impression that if only he could find the documents—particularly those pesky induction notices—he would be able to set the record straight. And yet his memoirs make it clear that Clinton possessed critically relevant records all along; he just didn't want to go public with them, for they actually *would* set the record straight . . . and not in Bill Clinton's favor.

As Clinton reveals in *My Life,* he kept a detailed diary during his time at Oxford. He quotes the diary frequently throughout his Oxford period, and specifically refers to diary entries to discuss his Army physical on January 13, 1969. Even when he doesn't actually quote from the diary, it is clearly the source of many of his recollections. And in that diary Clinton describes, in clear detail, how he got an induction notice—the very one he couldn't recall in 1992, and which he hired a research firm to track down.

He writes that the war "came directly home" to him when he received his induction notice on April 30, 1969—the one that ordered him to report on April 21, nine days earlier. He reports that he called home so the draft board would know "that I had not been a draft resister." The board let him finish his academic semester and told him to return and report after it was over.

And, lo and behold, Clinton also reveals that he knows all about his second induction notice, too—the one issued for July 28, 1969. The research firm apparently could not find a trace of that one, either, but he seems to have known about it all the time. He almost dares us to catch him.

The naval officer reserve program that he seemingly knew nothing about in 1992 surfaces, too, in his memoirs. Here he reveals how he failed his navy officer physical because of a previously undetected hearing problem. This would likely explain why his uncle was frantically lobbying for an enlisted naval reserve slot for him: Failing the officer's physical would prevent him from becoming an officer, but perhaps he could get in as an enlisted man—lining him up for delayed naval military service, which would be better than the impending draft.

Here we have the essence of Bill Clinton, the lifelong spinmeister: a man who jealously hoarded the records of his life, suppressing them when his political career was at stake, then reaching back into his personal archives when he needed them to paint his verbal portrait for history. If those archives inadvertently revealed his deceptions along the way—illuminating how he deliberately duped us in 1992, for example—what did it matter? By then he was just where he wanted to be: beyond accountability.

Clinton's early chicanery in seeking to duck the draft, even as he was laying the basis for claiming he'd voluntarily subjected himself to it, underscores the duality that runs through his life: the split between his life of public service, which he trumpets for all to hear—and his political side, which he'd rather we not see.

The Politician and the Boy Scout

Bill Clinton's Parallel Lives

One of the elements of *My Life* that garnered the most press upon publication was Clinton's portrait of the dichotomy between his "parallel lives"—the one on public display, the other shrouded in secrecy. What Clinton fails to convey is that this habit of living not only characterized his personal life, but extended through the entire range of his political career as well. Just as he hid his private misconduct from others, he was always anxious to hide the means by which he sought and kept public office.

Clinton led yet another set of parallel lives—those of a public official and would-be statesman on the one hand, and a politician on the other. He lived his political career with the conviction that if anyone saw how he sought to get and keep power, it would look dirty and inappropriate—and he would somehow seem less brilliant. Politics was better left out of the official version of his life, and indeed it is almost absent from his memoirs. Every politician makes hidden moves he would rather not read about on the front page of the newspaper, but in *My Life*, Clinton cordons off virtually his entire political life from public view.

In the pages of his autobiography, decisions seem to spring from Clinton's brain without any political consideration. Politics, if we believe this account, stopped at the door to the governor's office—and then at the front steps of the West Wing.

For a man whose entire political career was defined and enabled by polling and television advertising, he makes scant mention of either. In contrast, he often makes a deliberate effort to conceal that there was any political calculation behind his public moves. The life traced in *My Life,* could have been lived by a civil servant; there is no real clue that its author is a politician.

Bill Clinton was, and is, very much a politician—a reluctant but very talented politician who understood the importance of the game but never wanted to be seen playing it. Proud of his public service and—in his own mind—sincere about wanting to do the right thing, he saw politics as a sullied necessity, forced on him by an unjust world that did not immediately recognize his obvious merit. In a perfect world, he would have no need of politics. But as his political career began, he saw early that he would have to stoop to conquer.

Clinton's discomfort with politics is suggested by the fact that early in each of his major tenures in public life—first as governor and later as president—he made the same mistake: forgetting that political calculation was as important in governing as it is to getting elected in the first place. As soon as he took each office, he dropped politics the way a pole-vaulter drops the pole that bore him aloft—disavowing it as an inconvenient reminder that he needed help to jump that high.

Clinton walked away from politics, trying to govern as a Boy Scout. But each time he did, he ran into catastrophe; soon he was calling back his political handlers to help him meet the challenges of governing. Their presence was an embarrassment—a reflection of the dirty business he had hoped to leave behind in the campaign, and an assault on his vanity, as he once described it to me.

But Bill Clinton had to work hard at politics. It didn't come easily. Relating to people was second nature; he oozed an effortless charm.

But the maneuvers, confrontations, feints, and strategies of politics were hard for him to learn.

Despite his reputation as a master politician, the fact is that Bill Clinton had almost no common sense when it came to politics. Whenever he confronted a new political situation, he always screwed it up—without exception. He lost his first campaign for Congress. He was defeated after only two years as governor. Clinton acquired the nickname the "Comeback Kid" after almost blowing his presidential candidacy in the snows of New Hampshire, the nation's first primary. He lost Congress after his first two years as president. And even as a fledgling ex-president, he found himself in hot water over his last-minute pardons as he was leaving office. In each case, of course, he went on to ultimate success, absorbing the lessons of his errors, righting himself, and doing a politically competent job. But he always seemed to have to make a mistake—a big one, a public one—before he got anything right.

Bill Clinton's lack of personal experience, and his dependence on empathy and data to learn about reality, made him politically obtuse. His extraordinary intellect and memory bailed him out, as he learned from his mistakes and remembered the lessons. In this respect Clinton is like a blind man who walks briskly into a room, confident that he can see any obstacles in his path, though he is actually unable to see a thing. He trips over every chair, table, and couch in his path, and emerges battered, bleeding, and limping. But as he falls and gets up, he memorizes the location of every piece of furniture, so that the next time he enters the room he is able to stride surely through. The third time he enters, he's able to run through the room unscathed. Though you'd swear he can see, in fact it's just that his memory and intellect are guiding him through.

Clinton's memoirs are replete with stories that illustrate this early naïveté when up against a new challenge. And they also show his growth and increasing wisdom as he recovered from his own mistakes. It was only when the early screw-ups would not go away—as with his scandals—that they continued to trip him up.

John Kennedy reportedly said that his good judgment came from experience—and that his experience came from previous bad judgment. Like Kennedy, Like Clinton.

A relatively flawless performer like Reagan has little to teach us about politics. He always got it right the first time. Clinton's political career, on the other hand, offers dozens of political lessons—about what to do wrong, and how to correct it.

Clinton's failures of political judgment in his opening years as governor and as president can be traced back to those twin sources he drew upon for help in understanding the outside world: empathy and data.

His empathy gave rise to his inability to prioritize. To him, all the pleading voices sounded the same; the pain he heard in all their stories felt alike. Being a creature of external stimuli, Clinton had no internal method of assigning priorities, ranking the importance of the various problems or proposals that competed for his attention and investment. He never ranked problems in order of importance, working on the most pressing problems first and then moving down the list. Rather he pivoted, swinging this way and that to placate and appease each crying demand or heart-rending plea.

For any politician, setting priorities involves a kind of ruthless triage. But Clinton was never comfortable choosing between clashing demands. He was fine when it came to setting his *top* priorities; that came easily. The problem lay in defining what would rank lower down—what problems would have to wait while he ministered to those atop his list. That he could never bring himself to do. It was easy to say yes to an important program. The problem came in rejecting its competitors for public funds.

And Clinton's dependence on data gave rise to his inability to see through the superficial statistical arguments and understand the political realities that lay beneath. Statistics, after all, do not always govern human behavior. People behave irrationally. Taxes that collect equal revenue can have very different political impacts. Bill Clinton had to learn this lesson the hard way—twice.

His failure to prioritize got Clinton in trouble, during his first term as governor and his first two years as president. Each time, he tried to do much too much.

In his account of his first term as governor, Clinton says that he was constantly "in a hurry" to address each of the state's problems, but that "my reach often exceeded my grasp." And in recounting his failures in the opening year of his presidency, he cites much the same problem: He was attempting to "do too many things at once," as he recalls, "creating an impression of disarray."

I told Clinton that his first budget as governor looked like a political platform, with a paragraph for each cause and a program to placate each constituency. A hodge-podge of ideas and programs, it had no message or theme. And the same could be said of his first years as president. He had a bill for every problem, a response to every demand.

And each time, as governor and as president, he damaged his credibility by doing the same thing—raising taxes. He heard every plea for help, and his empathy made him respond with a new government program for each. But when he added up the numbers, they exceeded his revenues. Unable to rebuff the crying demands he witnessed as governor, or the importuning of the bond market he heard as president, he settled on the most expedient course: a tax increase.

But each time he failed to understand the political impact of the taxes he was raising. The politically harmless ones—like tobacco— were the same to him as the deadly increases, like the gas tax or the car license fees he raised in Arkansas. His dependence on data made all tax increases alike in political impact, differentiated only by their varied revenue yields. But a tax that yielded half as much money often cost twice as much political capital, and that distinction was lost on him.

As Clinton took office as governor of Arkansas, he faced the same choice that often faces incoming state chief executives: Should he give priority to schools or to roads? These two traditional areas of state focus compete for attention in virtually every southern statehouse, pitting the teachers' union against the highway contractors in the ultimate food fight. Clinton decided to help education, raising school funding by 40 percent over two years. And he was able to do it without raising taxes. Had he left it at that, he would have been reelected easily.

But then the highway contractors came calling with their stories of bad roads, broken-down cars, and farmers who lost money because of the difficulty in getting their goods to market. So Clinton tried to please the highway lobby, too. He feared antagonizing them, because he knew their campaign contributions bought lots of support in Arkansas' legislature, and he realized that their appeals to rural Arkansas might undermine him if he neglected their needs. He had no trouble saying yes to schools, but he couldn't bring himself to take the next step and say no to highways.

Then Clinton made a fatal mistake: He financed his road construction program with a virtual doubling of the fees motorists paid when they renewed their driver's licenses ("car tags" in Arkansas parlance).

As he often did, Clinton thought up a complex way of raising car tag fees to minimize the political damage. He proposed predicating the fees on the value of the car. This progressive indexing allowed him to come down hard on yuppies who owned BMWs, who could care less about the pocket change the fees represented, without touching the fees farmers paid on their old, beat-up clunkers. Predictably, though, the legislature failed to see the virtue in more heavily taxing the BMW owners, who financed their campaigns, and rejected Clinton's complicated formula. Instead, they just raised everybody's renewal fee.

Clinton caved in and signed the increase in car tag fees, because the highway lobby's pressure was irresistible—and because he heard the howls of the disgruntled farmers who had bad roads, but was curiously deaf to the more anguished yelps they could be counted on to make when they saw their fees double.

Clinton overlooked another important fact: Highway projects take years and years to complete, but car tags have to be paid every

THE POLITICIAN AND THE BOY SCOUT   149

twelve months. Long after he was dead and buried by voters out-raged about the fee increases, voters would enjoy driving over the new roads they paid for—even if Clinton was interred underneath the macadam.

Besides, Clinton reasoned, the license fee increase was really very small. For the average heavy, old, used car, Clinton pushed it up from $19 to $36 per year. Even in a poor state, how fatal could a tax hike of $17 per year possibly be? Clinton did the math and figured out that it cost people only thirty-three cents per week. For better roads, he wondered, who wouldn't mind paying that?

But the data didn't tell him that this fee was always paid at one shot, and it hadn't been raised in decades. So each farmer would pull up to the motor vehicle bureau, get out of his pickup truck, and walk in to pay for his new car tags. There, he would learn that the fee was twice what he expected to have to pay, courtesy of the new governor. Some of these farmers, as Clinton recalls in *My Life,* only brought enough cash with them to pay the old fee, and had to go back home to get more from the cookie jar—a trip that gave them plenty of time to learn to hate Bill Clinton.

Car fees, more than any other issue, cost Clinton the governorship in 1980, when he became the youngest ex-governor in the nation. In *My Life,* the former president frankly admits his political blindness during his first term as governor. His first two years in office, he notes, were "a policy success and a political disaster."

Later, of course, he recovered, regaining the Governor's Mansion and becoming a successful leader for the state. But then he won the presidency in 1992—and made the exact same mistake on becoming president that had sunk him when he first became governor: He raised taxes on cars.

As Clinton took office, he correctly assessed that high interest rates on long-term debt such as home mortgages posed an overriding barrier to prosperity. No matter how much the Federal Reserve Board cut short-term rates to stimulate the economy, bonds with longer maturities continued to sell only at high interest. Investors were worried that the large budget deficit would cause inflation. So if the government wanted to borrow their money for a long period of time, it would have to pay high interest rates in order to hedge against inflation. Also, with the budget deficit as large as it was, the competition for capital was itself driving up rates. Both to reassure investors that inflation was tame, and to free up money for private sector borrowing, the deficit had to come down.

Clinton personalized the challenge in *My Life,* grousing that he had to bring down interest rates in order to please "thirty-year-old bond traders." But the problem wasn't the young men and women on Wall Street so much as it was the old man at the Federal Reserve Board: Alan Greenspan. As a one-man judge and jury, it was Greenspan, more than anyone else, who would signal to the markets when he felt inflation was truly under control and the boys in Washington were actually going to cut the deficit.

Greenspan wanted the deficit reduced, but he wasn't satisfied with just any deficit reduction. He wanted it reduced by a tax increase. And not just any old tax increase: It had to be a tax that caused real political pain.

The old fox at the Fed knew that if the deficit came down just because spending was cut—well, hey, what comes down this year can go up again next year. It had to be the product of a tax hike. After all, taxes, once levied, usually stick around on the statute books for a long time. And he wasn't going to be appeased by just raising taxes on upper-income Republicans. That kind of politically inexpensive tax increase wouldn't convince him that the new Clinton administration had the political will to really bring down the deficit. No, Clinton would have to walk the plank to satisfy Greenspan; he would have to raise a tax that would raise hell. He wanted the administration to show it had the courage to impose a broad-based tax that hit the average person in the checkbook.

Clinton was willing enough to raise taxes—on rich people who would never vote for him anyway. He was happy to raise the top tax bracket, the so-called millionaire surcharge, up to 39.6 percent (actually on all incomes over $250,000). But Greenspan had something more drastic in mind.

"He wants me to raise taxes that really hurt," Clinton told me as I returned a page from him in a Manhattan pay phone in the early part of 1993. "He won't be satisfied until I raise taxes that hurt me politically."

"But you get most of your revenue from the tax bracket increases. Why do you need to raise taxes that cost you politically?" I asked.

"Because Greenspan is making me do it," he replied hotly.

(At this point, a man began to rap on the phone-booth glass, signaling that I should get off the phone; I'd been in there talking with Clinton for fifteen minutes. Eileen, who was standing outside, told him, "He can't get off. It's an important call." The stranger replied, "Who's he talking to? The president of the United States?" "Yes he is," she answered.)

In truth, Clinton understood Greenspan's viewpoint. He even grasped the points the bond traders were making: With his indefatigable empathy, he even felt the market's pain. He understood too well why income taxes wouldn't appease it. He realized that he was going to have to bite the bullet.

Another president might have pushed back, demanding a more politically acceptable tax. But Clinton so internalized the concerns of the economists he spoke with that he realized he would have to feel some pain himself for the deficit reduction to be real. As so often with Clinton, his empathy with the other side made confrontational negotiation impossible.

So Clinton tried the same dodge he had tried in Arkansas, when he had to raise taxes for highway construction. There he had proposed a complex formula to raise fees based on the cost of the car; now, he wanted to tax all energy sources based on their BTU output. It was a tax that nobody but Al Gore could understand. It was supposed to save the climate while cutting the budget deficit. He could have raised tobacco taxes or liquor taxes or beer taxes and survived politically, but Gore talked him into raising energy taxes instead.

And then the same thing happened in Washington that had unfolded in Little Rock fourteen years before: Congress wasn't going to buy into the complicated Al Gore BTU tax. They couldn't understand it, and they didn't like it. So they simplified things, just as the Arkansas legislature had once done, and told Clinton they would let him raise gas taxes by a nickel. No BTU tax—just a simple old gas tax increase.

Now Clinton's lack of common sense came into play. He no more realized how much people would gripe about the gas tax than he had understood in Arkansas how they would resent the car tag increase.

"Haven't you learned not to mess with people's cars?" I asked Clinton in our chat over the pay phone in 1993.

He hadn't. Clinton had talked himself into believing that his increase in the Earned Income Tax Credit (EITC) would offset the impact of the gas tax increase. He even reports, in *My Life,* how he had his economists run a computer model for each Congressman's district, showing how much more his constituents would get from the higher EITC than they would have to pay in gas taxes.

It was a ludicrous calculation that only a policy wonk could love. It ignored a few facts:

- The Earned Income Tax Credit conferred big checks on a few people, while the gas tax hit everybody who drove a car; the number of voters harmed grossly outnumbered those who would be consoled by the EITC.
- Almost all the voters who got the EITC were Democrats anyway; the gas-tax payers were a broad cross-section of the country.
- Voter turnout among EITC recipients was probably miniscule anyway.
- No one had ever heard of the EITC—but the Republicans made sure *everyone* knew about the gas taxes.

With his unique combination of misplaced empathy for those pressuring him, and misguided reliance on data that defied common sense, Clinton stumbled into the fatal error: He raised gas taxes. And, to make matters worse, no Republican supported his plan—he had to jam it through on a party-line vote, making totally clear that it was a Democratic tax.

The result is history: He drove the Democratic Party over a cliff in the 1994 elections, costing them control of Congress. And not just for two years: The Democrats have yet to regain both houses, and probably won't until at least the reapportionment of 2010.

Clinton learned his lesson too late. In *My Life*, he points to the tax increases of 1993 as the key factor in the defeat of his Congressional candidates the following year. Interestingly, Hillary Clinton seems not to have gotten the message. In her memoir, *Living History*, she gives lots of reasons for the 1994 defeat, but forgets the major one: tax increases. Bill learns from his mistakes. Hillary doesn't make any.

The other big debacle of Clinton's first two years, of course, was the failure of Hillary's health-care reform initiative.

The problem started when Bill Clinton had to decide which of his two basic campaign promises to keep in his first two years: his pledge to "end welfare as we know it," or his promise to extend health insurance to all Americans. As a practical matter, he couldn't tackle these two great tasks at the same time. One had to come first; the other would have to wait. Had he opted for welfare reform, he might have projected an image as a centrist from the beginning of his administration. But with Democrats running both houses of Congress, he decided that health care reform would be the easier sell—a decision for which both Clintons would be labeled permanently as liberals.

I actually doubt that Clinton himself, with his reluctance to prioritize, really made the decision to stress health care over welfare reform. I suspect that Hillary made it for him. After all, she was looking for something to do. Her first choice—to be appointed attorney general or secretary of education—was scotched when the staff found an old anti-nepotism law on the books that was passed to embarrass JFK after he appointed his brother Bobby as attorney general. Hillary spoke to me about serving as her husband's chief of staff, but then abandoned that notion. Eventually, she settled on heading a task force. And her liberal friends probably talked her into making it about health care.

So health care it was.

From the start, the health care program was crafted with an intense focus on what Hillary and her utopian guru, Ira Magaziner, thought would be the ideal system. Very little consideration went into how to pass it. With a Democratic majority in both houses of Congress, they assumed that passing health care reform would be possible.

Asked whether Senator Daniel Patrick Moynihan (D-NY), chairman of the Senate Finance Committee, might not object to the administration's program, one staff member (who wisely remained off the record) was quoted as saying "He's cantankerous, but he couldn't obstruct us even if he wanted to. We'll roll right over him if we have to."

Indeed. Apparently the Clinton White House wasn't familiar with the savvy senator from New York, who knew how to get even with his critics. Moynihan was livid that Clinton had ignored his pet issue—welfare reform—to give priority to health care. Saying that the president had campaigned on welfare reform, he now dismissed Clinton's promise as "boob bait for the Bubbas," and threatened to hold health care reform "hostage" unless the administration proved it was serious about fixing the welfare system. And, for good measure, he answered "Yup" when asked if a special prosecutor should be appointed to pursue Whitewater.

Far from being rolled over, Moynihan was the one who bottled health care reform up in his committee, never letting it die a decent death on the Senate floor.

I tried to point out to the Clintons the problems they would face in Congress, despite the Democratic majorities in both houses, during a meeting on December 2, 1992, at the Governor's Mansion in Little Rock, Clinton's transition team headquarters. With filibusters becoming routine in the Senate, and their majority still short of the sixty votes needed to shut off debate, the Clintons had a tougher road ahead of them than they expected.

"With the Democrats now controlling the presidency and both houses, the Republicans will start to use the filibuster on every important bill," I told the Clintons. "You'll need sixty votes and you don't have them."

Clinton spoke vaguely of rallying public opinion to force the Republicans into line, or of peeling off liberal Republicans to join a solid Democratic majority and shut off a filibuster. But it was clear he had no idea what he was up against.

Liberal Republicans were a slender reed on which to rely. Generally weak, and used to caving in to the GOP majority, they weren't about to help Clinton pass health care. In fact, the only Republican vote Clinton got was Jim Jeffords of Vermont, who later broke with his party to become an Independent. The Clintons kept Hillary's task force deliberations top secret—even litigating to protect them from scrutiny—and refused to listen to Republican views or to incorporate their ideas into the utopian construct. And yet they were shocked when Jeffords was the only Republican who backed them.

In *My Life*, Clinton—naively or disingenuously—contrasts the kid-gloves treatment of his anti-crime bill with the sharp partisanship that greeted his health care proposals. But the crime bill, which featured an expanded list of death penalty offenses, extra funds for prison construction, limitations on parole, and gun control provisions, was formulated in good-faith negotiations with the Republicans. Health care, on the other hand, emerged from Hillary's think tank fully formed and impervious to amendment.

So without any thought to how to pass health care, Hillary and Bill proceeded to alienate every constituency in their path as they formulated their utopian scheme. Insurance agents? Hillary dismissed them to me as "middlemen who drive up the costs of the system." Doctors? They were making too much money anyway. Small businesses? They were the culprits who weren't giving their employees health insurance.

President Clinton took a curiously passive role in the health care reform fight, letting Hillary shape the strategy and tactics on her own. When the initiative failed, he blamed the Republicans, a charge he repeats in *My Life*. But the fact is that the Clintons lost the battle not only in Congress but in the court of public opinion as well. When the bill died, it lost not because of a Senate filibuster, but stuck in committee, when the administration couldn't even get the votes of the Democratic majority to report the bill out to the floor. It never made it as far as a GOP filibuster.

Why was Clinton so inept in his first two battles—over the economy and health care? In each case, he listened to advisers with limited political ability: his naïve economic gurus and his still-unseasoned wife.

In the first two years of Clinton's presidency—as during the opening of his first term as governor—he failed to appreciate the importance of politics in getting things done. His approach in both instances was to plunge ahead with what he felt was right, and let the politics take care of itself. With Democratic majorities in both houses in Little Rock and in Washington, he felt he could push through what he wanted. As it happened, he was wrong.

To correct this naïveté, Clinton formulated what has been called the "permanent campaign"—using techniques like polling and advertising to continue the campaign long after the election is over and before the next one has begun. He eventually came to realize that the ways and means of winning elections were also crucial to successful governance.

After the health care reform was beaten, I suggested to Hillary that she settle for what was then called the Dole Bill and was eventually passed as the Kennedy-Kassebaum bill, guaranteeing coverage to people who changed jobs. But she wouldn't hear of it. Clinton, for his part, admits that if he had simply postponed action on health care after defeat became inevitable, he might have averted the debacle of the 1994 elections.

The 1993 tax increases fueled the Republicans' ardor, and the failure of Hillary's health care proposals in 1994 made Clinton look weak, liberal, and incompetent. But the issue that really drew out the activists on the right was gun control.

Clinton pioneered landmark federal gun control legislation. He pushed through a ban on assault rifles, and forced passage of the Brady Bill, which required a waiting period and a background check before a dealer could sell a handgun. As a result, felons, fugitives, and mental patients were screened out and prevented from buying deadly firearms. The legislation is one reason that violent crime rates have dropped in half since the early 1990s.

But Clinton's lack of political instincts made him misunderstand the snake pit he was stirring up with the passage of new gun control laws. The right is animated by gun owners, who passionately believe that the Second Amendment gives them the right to arm themselves as they please. While the Supreme Court does not share their reading of the Constitution, they are determined to defeat gun control advocates, and they often succeed.

Clinton writes that he was persuaded that a vote for gun control wouldn't harm Democratic congressmen from rural districts. As an Arkansas boy, he should have known better. Though he was warned by the House Democratic leadership—Speaker Tom Foley, Majority Leader Dick Gephardt, and Judiciary Committee Chairman Jack Brooks—that gun control legislation would cause a disaster for rural Democrats, Clinton disregarded the warnings.

Once again, he was persuaded by a story. Senator Howell Heflin, an Alabama Democrat, had been fooling his state for years, running as a conservative and voting as a liberal. Heflin told Clinton that he would defend his vote for a ban on nineteen types of assault weapons by citing a provision in the law that prohibited limits on other types of weapons. It was a foolish argument that nobody but Clinton thought would stand up against an attack by the National Rifle Association (NRA).

In an epitaph for the Democrats who lost their seats in the 1994 debacle, Clinton admits his error—scant comfort for a party that lost control of the House and is not likely to regain it for decades. (The last time a new party took over the House—the Democrats in 1954— they held it for forty years.)

~~~~

In explaining the 1994 defeat, Clinton correctly writes that he failed to force the Democrats to develop an "effective national counter message" to Gingrich's calls for less government. Admitting that the future speaker was the better politician, Clinton accepts that he blew it in his first round with Newt.

. . . And then there were a host of more minor catastrophes that can be attributed to Clinton's political naïveté as he entered the White House:

- Clinton got into trouble right off the bat with his expensive in-auguration as president. Eight hundred thousand people attended the celebrity-studded festivities, which featured eleven inaugural balls and cost between $25 and $30 million. Never one to miss a bet, Clinton raised $33 million at the receptions.

  As he and Hillary danced at each ball, he gave Americans the impression—later confirmed by his Martha's Vineyard vacations—that he was into hobnobbing and hanging out with celebrities from Hollywood's establishment, a far different milieu from the traditional Democratic base that had elected him.

  Americans may go to the movies in droves, but they hate Hollywood values—or the lack of them. By spending lavishly on his inauguration, and being photographed with every possible movie star, Clinton gave off an image that first befuddled and then enraged social populists, who thought they'd elected a guy who stopped at McDonald's while jogging in baggy shorts.

- Clinton couldn't pick an attorney general. His first candidate, Zoe Baird, was shot down when it turned out she had employed two illegal immigrants in her home and didn't pay her part of their Social Security taxes until just before her appointment. Failing to realize that the Senate would find hiring illegal immigrants—not to mention failing to pay taxes on them—offensive, Clinton submitted the nomination anyway.

  Clinton looked incompetent when he had to withdraw her name, but then he compounded the error by nominating and then also withdrawing a second candidate: Kimba Wood, a renowned and respected U.S. District Court judge. When it turned out that the judge had a Trinidadian babysitter who was here illegally, Clinton panicked and killed the nomination (before it was actually officially announced and sent to the Senate). In this case, though, it turned out that Judge Wood—who had made a name for herself by her toughness in dealing with financier Michael Milken—had done nothing illegal. She had paid all the taxes, as required.

  So Clinton got it from both sides. Failing a second time made him seem like a bumbling fool, and dropping Wood, who had broken no law, made him look vicious. (Clinton does not mention Kimba Wood in *My Life*. She's one of the ghosts who have disappeared from his official story.)

- Then Clinton screwed up another appointment at Justice by nominating his old law school classmate, the African American radical Lani Guinier, to head the Civil Rights Division. All hell broke loose when the Republicans discovered that Guinier had written articles advocating what she called cumulative voting. Her idea was that if voters had to fill three seats on a city or town council, they could vote for three candidates—as they can now—or cast three votes for one candidate. Guinier's thought was that this abandonment of "one man, one vote" would allow minorities to bloc-vote for their candidates and propel them into office.

In *My Life,* incredibly, Clinton admits that he never read Guinier's articles when he sent her nomination to Congress for confirmation! After a firestorm erupted, he sheepishly writes, he decided to read them after all. Once he saw what his old friend was proposing, he, like the rest of America, began to realize how pernicious her ideas really were, and withdrew the nomination. But not before Clinton had been slowly roasted alive for making the crazy nomination in the first place. Their friendship did not survive the incident.

Then, after two years of unremitting error, it came as a shock to the Clintons when the Democrats lost control of Congress in 1994. In that moment, though, Bill Clinton learned the same lesson he had learned before, in Arkansas on election night 1980, as he watched his governorship slip away: that politics is as essential to governing as it is to campaigning.

But he still didn't want anyone to see him doing it.

And yet, while at the time Clinton seemed to have learned this lesson, his memoirs suggest that he remains uncomfortable with it. In *My Life,* curiously, nearly all of his political consultants and advisers seem to disappear after his inauguration in January 1993. In the early months of his presidency, Clinton caught severe criticism for giving his political consultants passes to enter the White House at whim, even though they were not government employees. James Carville, Mandy Grunwald, Stanley Greenberg, and Harry Thomason were singled out by critics as having inappropriate unfettered access to the administration. There was no allegation of wrongdoing, other than Thomason's alleged involvement in the Travelgate scandal, but questions were raised. After that, the consultants were required to file financial disclosure forms with the White House Counsel. But consider how Clinton recalls these advisers in *My Life.* In most cases, he has little or nothing to say about any contribution they may have made in the eight years of his administration.

James Carville: After the election of 1992, Clinton makes only the following mention of his well-known former adviser:

- He was not interested in serving in the government.
- He was present in the solarium with other friends immediately after Clinton's Grand Jury testimony.
- He urged Democratic congressional candidates to run anti-impeachment ads after a survey showed that voters were 20 percent more likely to vote for a Democratic candidate who favored censure of the president than a Republican who favored impeachment. (The Democrats did not take back the House.)

Mandy Grunwald:

- She attended a retreat for staff and consultants at Camp David in January 1993.

Harry Thomason, the president's good friend:

- He and his wife stayed with Hillary when her father was dying.
- It was at his urging that Clinton made the infamous "I did not have sexual relations with that woman" statement about Monica Lewinsky.
- He was present in the solarium after Clinton's Grand Jury testimony.
- He and his wife produced three biographical films about Clinton for the Democratic conventions.
- He was on Air Force One for the last flight home with the Clintons.

Paul Begala, the campaign consultant who joined the administration:

- He came to the administration to work on the message about economic programs.

- He agreed with Laura Tyson about the level of the deficit.
- He was present in the solarium after the Grand Jury testimony.
- He announced that he was leaving; Clinton had relished having him there.

Stan Greenberg, his pollster, whose firm was paid millions by the Democratic National Committee:

- He attended a staff retreat in January 1993.
- He, like Carville, conducted a 1998 survey that confirmed that voters were more comfortable with censure than impeachment.

As for his pollsters, Mark Penn and Doug Schoen, Clinton recalls that I brought them in, that they stayed for the rest of his presidency, and that Penn counseled him to campaign in large cities at the end of the 1996 election.

All of these consultants served him ably, but none gets the attention he or she deserves. Once again, Clinton seems jealous of his advisers, anxious to take credit for their ideas and suggestions, He wants them to be invisible to everyone else, for the same reason that the magician conceals how the rabbit got in the hat: to preserve his air of mystery and power.

8

Politics Is Not Spoken Here

After 1994, Clinton got the message and integrated politics more fully into his governing style. Like a kid who had flunked math, he knew he needed a tutor—and, if all else failed, the answers to the next test. But he wasn't proud of his needs. So he preferred to take his political advice in private, behind closed doors. As part of his other, parallel life.

And he went to great lengths to keep it secret: Even now, he still leaves most of it out of his memoirs. For Clinton, a career politician, to exclude politics from his life story is a bit like watching a self-made millionaire tell his story without mentioning money.

Why the omission? Obviously part of the reason is a desire to make all his actions and proposals appear to be above politics, motivated by no selfish calculation of interest or ambition. All politicians would rather that their personal motives not show through the speeches they are making.

But in Clinton's case the reason for concealment ran deeper—it involved issues of self-esteem. He needed to feel good about his own political skills, and was embarrassed that he had put together such a poor record in his first two years on the job as president. So he was always very, very anxious to make sure that he personally got full credit for what he did and said. In *My Life,* he may be happy to blame his bad decisions on his advisers, but at the time—especially when it came to *good* decisions—Clinton reacted with fury whenever staff members or advisers leaked to the media that the president had made a decision based on their advice.

One reason Clinton felt comfortable working with me was that I didn't talk to the media while I worked for him. Bob Woodward, journalist par excellence, chased me around Washington trying to interview me for his books about the Clinton administration, but I turned him down, despite my huge respect for what he accomplished for democracy in saving us from Nixon. While he kept promising I could talk off the record, I knew that the moment I opened my mouth I would regret it. "You're better at interviewing than I am at being interviewed," I explained to him.

But Clinton's jealousy about letting his internal operations show in public got me in trouble anyway. One Sunday morning, Clinton woke me up with an early phone call. Screaming into the telephone, he demanded to know if I had read the front-page article in that day's *Washington Post.* "No sir," I replied, "I'm in Connecticut at my home."

The offending article reported the questions and results of a focus group we had conducted about Clinton's image. The paper reported that we had asked if people felt the president was weak, or prone to flip-flop on issues, or personally immoral. I had not spoken to any reporter, but that wasn't good enough. I had spoken to two senior staff members. Clinton screeched at me for talking with his staff, telling me I might as well have sent out a press release.

"Are you saying I can't trust your own staff?" I asked, throwing the blame back at him.

"You can't. You *can't.* Don't you realize you can't?" he yelled as he slammed down the phone.

Clinton's vitriol ran deeper than just that one leak. He was feeling emasculated by his staff, and this was just another insult.

Clinton's insistence on maintaining separate lives as statesman and politician sometimes led to ridiculous extremes. In January 1995, he called and asked me to come to the White House residence at night to help him write his State of the Union address. When I arrived, he handed me a pen and a yellow legal pad of paper. I was astonished. When I worked for him in Arkansas, in the precomputer days, I usually had at least a typewriter at my disposal when I needed to draft a speech or an ad for him. "My handwriting is terrible," I pleaded, "and I don't know if I can write that much by hand."

"But I don't want you to use the White House computer system," Clinton answered. *Aha.* Everyone in the White House knew the president couldn't type. So if an address appeared miraculously on the computer system, his staff would know another hand had been involved.

"Do you have a IBM Selectric typewriter around here anywhere?" I asked.

Clinton sent for an usher, and a few minutes later the man returned, blowing the dust off a Cro-Magnon relic. As I typed each page, I had to take the paper down the hall of the residence and deposit it on Clinton's desk, where he sat meticulously recopying the speech in his own left-handed scrawl so that he could present it to his staff the next morning as his own effort. In my previous account of this episode—in *Behind the Oval Office,* written while he was still in office—I took pains not to embarrass the president by camouflaging the operation, saying that he was editing the manuscript as he copied it. As my original draft (which I still have) and the final address prove, though, Clinton made almost no changes to what I had written.

At one point, as Clinton was walking back to my typewriter with me to discuss an upcoming passage, he confided: "I like you because you are secret."

The key was that he wanted the staff—and by extension all of Washington—to believe that the words I had written were *his* words, *his* ideas, *his* thinking. No president likes people to think of him as a parrot, reading a speech prepared by some faceless drone in the back office. But Clinton's possessiveness went beyond that. He wanted even his top staff, his intimate associates, all to believe that his work was one man's creation—his own. When I heard that Clinton had shown reporters stacks of handwritten notebooks as proof that he had written *My Life* himself, I remembered our collaboration—and imagined him copying 957 pages from someone else's typed manuscript!

Clinton's penchant for hiding his political life from public view extended to our entire relationship. In all the years we worked together in Arkansas, my name never once appeared in the press. I recently looked back at copies of old polls and memos about our jointly developed concept of "The New Covenant" in the 1980s. I had to smile when I read Clinton's analysis that my theory of "triangulation" was really just a different way of expressing the policies he had been advocating as governor and as a candidate. True, but the reason for the similarity was that I had developed many of those ideas for him during our work together. (In general, though, I have no complaints about how Clinton treats me in his memoirs.) In any event, while I worked for him, I stayed in the background, and understood that was what Clinton wanted. (When one fellow consultant who worked for Clinton talked with the media about his work for the president, he was fired.)

So hidden was my involvement in his political life in Arkansas that no book mentioned it until I agreed to be interviewed by David Maraniss, the Pulitzer Prize–winning reporter for the *Washington Post*. When his account of Clinton's prepresidential years, *First in His Class,* was published in 1995, the role I had played in Arkansas was prominently featured. Maraniss told me that his editor, on reading his manuscript, told David that I must have conned him, since he had checked me out and found that nobody had any record of my working with Clinton for all those years, despite the dozens of biographies that had already appeared.

When I went back to work for Clinton in late 1994, he wanted to continue the secrecy. Since my political consulting practice was by that time exclusively Republican, and I would lose every client I had if it came out that I was working for Clinton, I was just as happy with the arrangement. (Moreover, I didn't know if I would last with Clinton as a presidential adviser, and wanted to be sure it would work out before I burned my GOP bridges.)

I assumed the code name "Charlie," a moniker I chose in honor of my closest friend in the Republican Party, political consultant and lobbyist Charlie Black. When I called the White House and got one of Clinton's assistants, Nancy Hernreich or Betty Currie, I would tell them Charlie was on the phone. One of them would tell the president; as often as not, he would leave the meeting he was in to take the call in his study adjacent to the Oval Office. I have always wondered whether the FBI spent any time trying to determine just who Charlie was.

Clinton ultimately decided to reveal my role to his staff because he felt I couldn't operate effectively in secrecy. But after my work became known in April 1995, after five months of secret collaboration, my impact was impaired by staff rivalries and jealousies. At one point, Chief of Staff Leon Panetta threatened to quit unless Clinton reined me in. I stayed, and so did Leon.

For my part, I couldn't understand why Clinton kept appointing staff members who didn't agree with the centrist approach he and I were pushing. "You keep appointing Stalinists," I complained. The final blow was when my only ally on the staff, Erskine Bowles, left and was replaced by Hillary's confidante, the certified liberal Evelyn Lieberman.

"Why are you systematically appointing people I can't work with?" I asked Clinton in one late-night phone call in December 1995 as I threatened to leave. "We've done some good work," I said, "and now maybe it's time to let Harold [Ickes] bring you the rest of the way in." Clinton knew that Harold was my worst nightmare, the furthest left-leaning of the liberals on his staff.

Eileen reminded me that Clinton couldn't appoint staffers who would work with me, because it would make all too evident the closeness of our relationship. So during a January 1996 visit to the Oval Office, I suggested that I could work like a "little bird on your left shoulder, whispering in your ear," while avoiding contact with the White House staff. "Now you've got it," he beamed. We were back to the working protocol from the Arkansas days.

Once we'd restored our old back-channel arrangement and I started staying in the background again, Clinton opened up my access to him to unprecedented levels. He was all too happy to get the answers to the math test in private, with nobody watching. To Clinton, getting advice and conducting polls were a form of cheating, one he wanted concealed. And he was particularly anxious to hide the fact that so many of his political moves came from someone else's advice.

And he was very, very good at concealment. The practice Clinton had gained in the art of hiding his affairs carried over easily into cloaking his political strategies, tactics, motives, and moves from the rest of the world.

If Clinton was anxious to obscure how much he relied on polling to shape his domestic policies, he was absolutely paranoid about anyone thinking he was using surveys to shape foreign policy.

In a curious reference in *My Life,* Clinton writes that I "wanted to politicize foreign policy too much." The real story is rather different: I worked at his direction to politicize it as much as possible—but in secret.

As a condition of agreeing to come back to work for him after the debacle of the 1994 elections, I asked that the president meet with me, face to face, once each week. He agreed, and thus began our now-famous weekly strategy meetings at the White House residence, usually held on Tuesday or Wednesday nights.

At first the meetings were held in the president's East Wing office, otherwise known as the Treaty Room, since it was there that President William McKinley had signed the agreement ending the Spanish-American War. Loaded with his library books—many of which we had recommended to each other—the room was decorated with dark red walls and the president's heavy mahogany desk. The president and I would sit facing one another—he in his favorite wing chair and me in the matching one opposite, across a glass coffee table.

When the meetings expanded to include others, they would take seats on the coach to his left and on chairs brought in to his right.

After a while, as the word of their importance got out, the meetings became larger and the venue was moved to the yellow oval room next door, decorated in a light Louis XIV style that belied the pragmatic content of the issues under discussion. But Clinton cautioned me never to speak about foreign policy issues in the presence of the other attendees. "Give me advice on them, poll them, but don't ever speak about them with anyone else present but you and me," he directed.

And so, after every strategy meeting, I would stay for at least another hour to discuss foreign policy issues alone with the president. Sometimes I would have to deceive others in the meeting into thinking I was leaving, only to sneak back in through another doorway once we had parted on the street outside.

For every White House strategy meeting, I prepared a detailed memo to the president, which we called, euphemistically, the "agenda." Far from a list of topics to be discussed, it was the text of the advice I planned to give at the meeting, annotated with polling data to sustain and support it. The agenda, which routinely ran to more than twenty pages, was distributed in numbered copies to each of the participants at the meeting, and collected again at the end of the session. Only the president, the vice-president, Chief of Staff Leon Panetta, Deputy Chiefs of Staff Harold Ickes and Erskine Bowles, and I kept copies.

(These agendas comprise the fullest accounting of the actual political strategy behind the moves the president made during the 1995–1996 period. At this writing, I have received no request to donate them, or copies of them, to the Clinton Library, an omission that mirrors the president's desire to screen his political activities from public view. Excerpts from them are available in the paperback version of *Behind the Oval Office*.)

At the back of each week's agenda, however, I included a private agenda dealing with foreign policy issues. At Clinton's direction, this private agenda was included in only the copies I gave to him and to Gore; I never discussed their content with anyone else.

I did not have, and never sought, security clearance, so the discussions of foreign policy were usually rather one-sided. I would talk and Clinton would listen. I assumed that his conversation was limited by his inability to share classified material with me. To my knowledge, he never shared any with me.

But the private agendas covered the entire gamut of foreign policy issues.

For example, in *My Life,* Clinton innocuously celebrates Boris Yeltsin's victory over the communists and the quasi-fascist candidate General Gennady Zyuganov, noting that the Russian president sought reelection using "American-style" campaign rallies and TV ads. What he doesn't mention is his own key role in running the Yeltsin campaign.

Ever since his inauguration, Clinton had decided that there was one key state in America (California) and one key nation besides America in the world: Russia. The electoral college math dictated the former, but it was former President Nixon's warning that history might ask "Who lost Russia?" that highlighted the latter. Nixon's comment was a haunting reminder of how Mao's communist takeover of China, and the consequent question "Who lost China?"—asked in large part by Nixon himself—undermined the popularity of President Harry Truman. Clinton was determined to provide Russia in general—and Yeltsin in particular—all the help he could. He was not about to allow Russia to be lost on his watch.

His advisers didn't feel the same way. They were worried about Yeltsin's dwindling popularity, and had largely given him up for dead. When Clinton returned from his meeting with the Russian leader at FDR's Hyde Park home, he told me he was amused that Yeltsin was optimistic about his reelection chances. "He's at nine percent approval and he thinks he can win," Clinton marveled.

"You're at thirty-eight percent and you think you can win," I sassed back.

But Clinton was determined to try to see Yeltsin through. I knew that the Russian leader's campaign had hired American political consultants, including George Gorton, Joe Shumate, and my former business partner Dick Dresner. I felt Dresner was—and is—the best political consultant still practicing in the United States, and happily reported to Clinton that Yeltsin was in good hands.

I suggested that I ask Dresner for the polling data on Yeltsin each week, and bring it to the White House for us to review in our meetings on foreign policy issues. Clinton loved the idea. "You know how Eisenhower used the CIA to overthrow governments he didn't like?" I said. "Now that we are a world of democracies, you're going to use your political skills to keep Yeltsin in office."

Each week, after the president and I discussed the latest results in Russia, he often passed Yeltsin his advice, once even phoning Yeltsin to urge him to agree to run a political ad prepared by Dresner et al., which proved to be particularly effective.

As Clinton prepared for his visit to Russia a few months before Yeltsin's election, he had me contact Dresner to get specific advice as to where he should go and what he should say. Dick and I communicated using code: our e-mails referred to Clinton as the "governor of California," and Yeltsin as the "governor of Texas." In one typical e-mail, Dresner coached Clinton, through me, about what Yeltsin wanted him to say about the "Mexican problem"—that is, Chechnya.

In Russia, Clinton let his itinerary be guided by Yeltsin's political needs, campaigning American style with Boris on his arm. Oddly, Clinton omits this colorful chapter from *My Life,* giving only a dry recitation of the agreements he concluded on the trip. Yet it was largely due to Clinton's help that Yeltsin was reelected, and communism—and fascist nationalism—did not come back into power in Russia. *Showtime* even produced a film, *Spinning Boris,* about the role of the American consultants and their connection to the White House.

But Clinton's trips to Russia were not always so pleasant. In May 1995, Clinton attended a celebration of the fiftieth anniversary of the end of World War II in Moscow. He notes, in *My Life,* that the trip was controversial because of international outrage against Russian tactics in suppressing the rebellion in Chechnya. But the real issue was the Russian sale of nuclear equipment to Iran. As Clinton writes, Yeltsin agreed not to ship any material to Iran that could be used to build a bomb.

But before Clinton left on his trip, he asked me to poll American opinion on the issue. I reported to him that voters were very concerned about Iran getting nuclear materials. But Clinton wanted to know what he could give Boris in return for ratcheting back the controversial but profitable dealings with Iran. And, more important, he wanted to find out how he could continue cooperation with Russia even if he didn't get a satisfactory answer on Iran.

"I don't want to hurt Yeltsin, and I need to know whether we can still give aid to Russia, politically, even with the Republicans attacking me over Iran," he told me during a private strategy meeting before his trip.

Clinton was relieved to find out that the poll revealed that Americans realized how important it was to help Yeltsin, and would approve of American aid to Russia regardless of Moscow's dealings with Iran. The poll also found that there was no particular rush, in the minds of American voters, for NATO to expand to include the former satellite nations in Eastern Europe. Voters understood that the extension of the NATO guarantees to these countries was an important step, and that we must take care not to do it in a way that offended Moscow.

After getting this poll briefing, Clinton decided to go slow on NATO expansion so as not to complicate Yeltsin's reelection chances the following year. In return, Yeltsin promised to acquiesce in NATO's growth after he was safely reelected.

President Clinton's forays into foreign political consulting were not always so successful. Committed to a peace settlement between Israel and the Palestinians, Clinton wanted the moderate Labor Party led by Shimon Peres to defeat the right wing Likud Party under Benjamin Netanyahu. Parallel with his work for Yeltsin, Clinton took advantage of the fact that his American pollster, Doug Schoen, was also working for the Labor Party to try to play the same role in the Peres campaign that he did on behalf of the Russian president.

Unlike Yeltsin, Peres lost. When Netanyahu began to run American-style negative ads, Clinton pleaded with Peres to answer the attacks and to hit back, but Peres wouldn't do it. In *My Life*, Clinton notes that Peres lost because he failed to respond to the pleas of his supporters to answer the attack ads aired on television by the Netanyahu campaign. By Peres's supporters, Clinton is really referring to himself!

The most glaring example of how Clinton tries to cover up his political life in *My Life* is his almost total silence on the subject that consumed a vast proportion of his waking hours: fund-raising. Apart from a few references to appearances at receptions designed to raise money for his campaign or party, and a brief discussion of the investigation of his fund-raising tactics and sources in the 1996 campaign, *My Life* has nothing to say about how the massive funding Clinton's political career required poured in during and between elections.

In 1996, a purple-faced Clinton exploded at me in the Oval Office, screaming that all he had time to do was raise funds. During the Clinton presidency, fund-raising consumed about a third of the president's public schedule when he was in the United States. Almost every night would include a trip to a fund-raiser; on travels around the country, there would often be several events on the same day. In scheduling the president, we looked first at his fund-raising schedule, building public and press events around the receptions, fitting them in between a fund-raising luncheon and the evening campaign finance events, so that Clinton could justify making the poor taxpayers—rather than the Democratic Party—pay for his travels.

At first, Clinton didn't think he'd be very good at fund-raising. In Arkansas, and in the 1992 and 1994 campaigns, money was hard to come by. Often, he had to make a last-minute trip to the bank to borrow money, on his personal credit, to finance the last week of television advertising.

When I came back to work for him at the White House after his 1994 loss of Congress, I urged him to begin massive national television advertising early in 1995, more than a year and a half before election day. "How will I raise the money?" he asked.

At the nadir of his political power, with the press calling him irrelevant, I told him: "About the only thing you can do these days is to raise money." Unconvinced, Clinton wondered if he would be able to raise the $40 million his preconvention advertising would eventually require. In fact, he raised many times that sum. A top finance official of the Clinton campaign in 1996 confided to me his estimate that the total cost of the president's reelection ran to over $300 million.

The prestige of the presidency, with its quasi-royal status, is so exalted that it is easy for a president to raise money, without even having to promise special favors or other consideration.

But the flip side of the bargain is that he must give of himself physically, posing for endless photos and shaking hand after hand after hand. Who can forget seeing Clinton standing up for hours on end, his feet aching, his back stiffening as he worked his way through the unending line of donors, one at a time, with a smile and kind word for each one? I frequently attended these fund-raisers in Washington; a few minutes of conversation with Clinton at the day's end was a welcome replacement for a late-night phone call when he finally returned to the White House. After hours of standing—and watching him standing—my entire body ached. The physical toll of fund-raising was extraordinary. I don't know how he did it.

In *My Life*, however—unlike in real life—money appears miraculously, without effort or exertion. Campaigns appear to finance themselves. For Clinton to avoid any mention of fund-raising during his presidency is like an athlete omitting any allusion to his training or physical conditioning, concentrating his memoir only on the glory of his exploits on the playing field. But for the athlete there would be no victory were it not for his grueling preparation, and for Clinton there would have been no reelection but for his exhausting fund-raising.

Not only does Clinton fail to address how he raised all the money he spent getting elected, reelected, and beating impeachment; except for one cursory reference, he also leaves out how he spent the money on political advertising throughout his term.

The centerpiece of Clinton's dramatic comeback in 1995–1996 was his massive use of television advertising eighteen months before the election. Yet, in *My Life,* the former president makes only scant mention of the ads, writing only that they began in June 1995 in targeted states and highlighted his administration's achievements.

But the ads were what kept him alive, moved him ahead, and let him stand firmly and successfully against the draconian Republican budget cuts Dole and Gingrich were pushing.

Clinton was anxious to conceal the advertising campaign from the very beginning. "I will be attacked in the media if I run ads now," he cautioned. "They'll say I'm so weak that I need to begin early."

"You are and you do," I replied.

"They'll accuse me of going over their heads and trying to circumvent the media."

I met his objections by saying that we would keep the advertising a secret.

"A secret?" he answered in disbelief. Laughing, he asked, "Just how do you plan to run an ad in half the country for two weeks and keep it a secret?"

"By not running the ads in New York or Washington," I replied brazenly. "That's where all the media live," I explained. "If we black out those markets, they'll never know we're on the air."

And that's exactly what we did. The ads ran throughout Ohio, Michigan, Illinois, Florida, California, Pennsylvania, upstate New York, Missouri, Kentucky, Louisiana, Arkansas, Tennessee, and other swing states, but not in New York City or Washington, D.C. Beyond an occasional reference in the media, nobody covered them. The press was so elitist and concentrated in those two cities they neither knew—nor much cared—what happened in the rest of the country.

When the extent and impact of the advertising campaign first came out in my book *Behind the Oval Office*, published in January 1997, Clinton told me he was concerned "that we'll have some vulnerability over the chapter on the TV advertising." Indeed, it was this evidence of massive early media spending that ignited the Republicans, leading to the probe of the sources of Clinton's early funding for the 1996 campaign. (Of course, I had no idea that he had sent out for Chinese food to pay for the ads.)

One tactic that Clinton naturally doesn't mention in *My Life*, was how we aimed the ads at the likely jury pool in Arkansas, which might have sat in judgment over Bill or Hillary if they were ever indicted by Kenneth Starr.

In early 1996, I met with Clinton in the White House residence and we discussed whether Starr would ever move to indict him or Hillary. "If he does," Clinton said, "he'll have a hard time getting a conviction from a Little Rock jury."

"Would he have to bring the action in Little Rock?" I asked.

"Or some part of Arkansas," he replied. "Or in D.C., which would be worse for him."

Clinton was alluding, of course, to the large number of African Americans who would sit on a jury in either location, who would be most unlikely ever to convict the popular president or his wife.

Taking his cue, I polled the attitudes of Arkansas African Americans toward Clinton and Starr. Based on these surveys, we cut ads that were aimed directly at African Americans in Arkansas. To dress it up, and help ensure that no one would figure out what we were doing, we also ran the commercials in Memphis, Jackson, and Baton Rouge. But the target was Arkansas.

The ads all featured the most liberal programs Clinton had passed—things like food stamps, child nutrition, day care, and job training, which were highly popular in the minority community. The advertisements all had the tag line: "Don't let them stop Clinton's program."

"Them," in the context of the ad, clearly meant Starr and the Republicans. After the ads began, I took regular tracking polls to measure the strength of Clinton's support among black voters in Arkansas, to see how the ads were doing in bolstering his standing. When his African American backing passed 100 percent, I stopped polling.

Clinton and I were the only ones who knew of the ad strategy we were using to help influence the Arkansas jury pool. I explained to the other consultants that the goal in running these ads only on African American–oriented programs in cities in or around Arkansas was to build up voter turnout in swing states.

But Clinton is silent even on more benign uses of polling in formulating his political appeal. Each year's State of the Union address is carefully chronicled in *My Life,* without any mention of the central way in which survey research governed its formulation. Clinton writes that each year he used the address "as an organizing tool" to stimulate the cabinet and staff to "come up with new policy ideas." But he does not mention that it was, in its essence and its specifics, a speech written by polls.

Months before the address—usually in early November—we would canvass the administration, just as Clinton says, for ideas that might be included in the address. Then we would take the mother of all polls, testing each idea to determine its political appeal.

In late 1994 and early 1995, we conducted a three-part, two-hundred-and-fifty-question survey, testing every single one of the budget cuts the Gingrich Congress was proposing. Based on the findings, we identified four major cuts on which to focus our fire: Medicare, Medicaid, education and the environment, a list Clinton repeats in *My Life,* verbatim, and which we referred to at the time as MMEE. (The original list was simply MME—Medicare, Medicaid and Education—but Al Gore insisted on adding the environment. This man, defeated by the voters who abandoned his ticket to support Nader and the Green Party, did more to hype the environment as an issue than any other politician I have ever met.)

We were particularly anxious to poll after the Oklahoma City bombing, to test the intensity of support for such anti-terror measures as expanding wiretap authority and requiring taggants in all explosive material to help law enforcement officials trace who had sold it and who bought it. Both of these proposals were important steps in fighting terrorism. Although the Republican Congress rejected them both, the expanded wiretap authority was one of the first things Bush asked for—and got—after 9/11.

But the ideas also had an underlying political purpose: to lead voters to identify the Oklahoma City bombing with the right wing. By making proposals we knew the Republicans would reject—in part because of opposition by the NRA—we could label them as soft on terror, and imply a connection with the extremism of the fanatics who bombed the Murrah Federal Building. Clinton still uses a page from this strategy in *My Life,* when he links the bombing to the anti-government atmosphere and intolerance created by his conservative critics on talk radio—a totally phony claim that only a nonlistener to these programs could believe.

Clinton's refusal to give an honest accounting of the role politics played in his administration shines through on virtually every page of *My Life.* In trying to make it appear that every decision was taken on its own merits, without regard for politics, Clinton leaves out a large part of each story. A few examples, to set the record straight:

- He writes of his decision to reform affirmative action rather than repeal it, characterizing it as an effort to help poor people get ahead. But affirmative action was Clinton's nightmare. When sentiment gathered in California for a ballot proposition repealing race-based and gender-based preferences, he smelled the political trouble far in advance. In one of our first meetings in late 1994, he cautioned that such a measure could be on the ballot in California two years hence, while he was running for reelection.

Clinton wanted to find a way to replace race and gender with objective criteria, like income or residence in a poor neighborhood, in awarding the government contracts and spots in colleges and universities set aside by affirmative action. "If I can figure out a way to take race and gender out of the equation, I will be able to use the change to convince people that I am really a new Democrat," he told me in one of our private weekly strategy meetings early in 1995.

But Clinton had a big, tall, and loud problem: Jesse Jackson. The civil rights leader had led him to believe that he would challenge the president in a Democratic primary if he fooled around with affirmative action. Clinton was terrified of a primary battle with Jackson. I tried to persuade him that such a contest would perfectly position him to win reelection in November, framing him for white voters as the dragon-slayer, but he wasn't buying it. The memory of how Ted Kennedy's challenge to Jimmy Carter had helped to elect Ronald Reagan in 1980 haunted him.

■ In describing his defeat in the 1980 governor's race in *My Life*, Clinton blames, in part, the demonstrations by Cuban immigrants held at Fort Chaffee, Arkansas. Sent to America by Castro, these Cubans included many inmates of prisons and mental hospitals, who were confined in such federal facilities while they could be screened and processed. More than 10,000 of the 120,000 were sent to Arkansas. Angry at their confinement, the refugees rioted and escaped, sowing fear in the surrounding area; after the riots, Clinton's prospects for reelection dimmed.

But what Clinton doesn't say in *My Life* is that he had agreed to take the refugees in the first place, to help Jimmy Carter beat Ted Kennedy in the Florida Democratic Primary in 1980. Voters in the Sunshine State were getting sick of the massive infusion of refugees. "I agreed to take the Cubans until the primary was over," Clinton told Eileen and me over dinner in 1981 as he looked back over his defeat. "He said he'd take them back before the election. He screwed me!" Clinton said, his voice rising.

- Clinton blandly relates his decision to propose a balanced budget in a national television address in June 1995. He recites all the familiar arguments for doing so, but omits the key fact: that his decision to give the speech and venture a presidential balanced budget was an enormous political gamble. His move to the center infuriated the liberals in the party, and the budget he proposed was rejected in the Senate by a vote of 99–0. Nobody stood with him. But Clinton courageously defied his own party, and insisted that the deficit be eliminated.

  Clinton's willingness to commit to the bottom line of a zero deficit marked the key point of departure from his party's left wing, and the key element of his move to the center, which saved him in the 1996 election.

  So why doesn't Clinton herald this brave act of apostasy? Because right now the Clintons' priority is helping Hillary court favor on the Democratic Party's left wing to stoke her own presidential ambitions. This is no time to remind the party faithful of that other, faithless, Clinton who once embraced the GOP orthodoxy in his commitment to a balanced budget.

- In recounting how he survived impeachment, Clinton makes no mention of the key political deal he consummated with the Democrats in the Senate. Holding his life in their hands as the jury that would sit in judgment on the House articles of impeachment, the Democratic senators forced Clinton to agree to make no deals with the Republicans for the balance of his term.

  Clinton was brimming with ideas for new negotiations to structure an across-the-board deal providing for national debt reduction, Social Security and Medicare stabilization, tax cuts, and a prescription drug benefit for the elderly. In 1997, we discussed plans to bring such an approach to my former client, Republican majority leader Trent Lott. Trent was willing, and we appeared to be headed for a broad-based settlement of the outstanding issues between the two parties.

The Senate Democrats knew something was up, though, and they realized that such a deal would leave them in the minority. (Of course it might have solved America's problems, too, but that was beside the point.) With the Senate Republicans and Clinton sharing the credit, the Democrats would be left out in the cold, robbed of the issue they would otherwise have used in winning back power.

To nip this bipartisan cooperation in the bud, the Senate Democrats overtly and covertly demanded a steep price for their support of Clinton in the impeachment: *Pass nothing,* they commanded, *and leave us the issues to use in winning the elections of 2000.* Clinton had no choice but to accede.

■ In *My Life,* Clinton's accounts of his own campaigns avoid any mention of his own negative advertising, or his attacks on his opponents. While meticulously cataloguing and recounting the barbs leveled at him, Clinton rarely discusses the shots he took at his political adversaries.

Yet Clinton's victory over Jerry Brown in the 1992 New York primary, which clinched the nomination, was far from a pretty affair. Brown, who had bested Clinton in the Connecticut primary the week before, entered the Empire State with momentum, and threatened the grip on the presidential nomination Clinton had appeared to secure after the withdrawal of his principal opponent, Senator Paul Tsongas, a few weeks before.

But then Brown made a big mistake. If he should win the nomination, he suggested, he might make Jesse Jackson his vice president. New York's Jews, still smarting from Jackson's description of their city as "Hymietown," turned away from Brown . . . and toward Clinton.

A few weeks after the New York primary, Los Angeles exploded in race riots after an all-white jury acquitted four white police officers of all charges in connection with the videotaped beating of Rodney King.

Two months after the Los Angeles riots, with race relations at the center of the political dialogue, Clinton played the race card overtly, denouncing rap star Sister Souljah for saying "If black people kill black people every day, why not have a week and kill white people?" His denunciation of the singer, however justified by the tenor of her remarks, sent a signal to white voters that Clinton was not going to pander to the African American community.

The former president spins the incident in *My Life,* pointing out that he would have looked bad if he hadn't attacked Souljah—and, as he always does, by blaming his staff for inducing him to make the comment. But both defenses are disingenuous. Clinton was reaching for a racial issue, as surely as Bush was in 1988 when he attacked Dukakis for pardoning convicted rapist and killer Willie Horton. He knew exactly what he was doing.

■ Nor is there any mention in *My Life,* of the pivotal role Clinton's use of the death penalty in Arkansas played in his 1992 election. He and I had often discussed how capital punishment had emerged as a litmus test issue for liberal politicians who were eager to convince blue-collar white voters that they shared their values. New York's mayor from 1977 to 1989, Edward I. Koch, had gotten elected by his strong support of capital punishment. As a Jewish liberal, Koch's position sent a message to white Catholic voters that he would stand up for them despite pressure from the minority community.

On December 17, 1991, two months before the New Hampshire primary, Governor Clinton set an execution date for Ricky Ray Rector, who had shot two men, including a police officer ten years before. After firing the fatal shots, Rector had attempted suicide, shooting himself in the head. Though he survived, the wound necessitated a prefrontal lobotomy, which severely impaired his mental capacities.

Nevertheless, Rector was found competent to stand trial, even though two outside experts said he had only a hazy memory of the shootings and "scant understanding of his surroundings." Rector reportedly "remained seated, stretched and yawned after the judge sentenced him to die."

Clinton set Rector's execution date for January 24, 1992, just twenty-five days before the New Hampshire primary. Rector, a black man, was one of four people (the other three were white males) whom Clinton allowed to be executed in the two years before the 1992 election. Before 1990, it had been twenty-six years since Arkansas had seen its last criminal put to death.

The left condemned the Rector execution; *Boston Globe* columnist Derrick Jackson called "the killing of human vegetables" an "exercise for brutes." But the signal to New Hampshire voters was unmistakable: Clinton was a new kind of Democrat, who wouldn't hesitate to use the death penalty to execute murderers of either race.

One month after the Los Angeles race riots, Clinton interrupted his campaign to return to Arkansas to deny clemency to Steven Douglas Hill. At the age of seventeen, Hill had shot and killed a state trooper as he attempted to hide following a prison escape. Despite pickets outside the Governor's Mansion, the execution proceeded.

Regardless of whether or not these executions were justified on the merits, Clinton was well aware of the political impact of a pro-death penalty stance in the 1992 presidential sweepstakes. In his years in the White House, Bill Clinton fairly earned a justified reputation as the president most sensitive to black aspirations in recent times. But his 1992 campaign was replete with signals that he would not be cowed by minority pressure.

■ In *My Life*, the former president meticulously catalogues his executive orders, dryly reciting what he signed on which day. But he never discusses his guiding strategy: that Clinton consciously chose to use these executive orders to permit presidential action, even though he was saddled with a Republican Congress that was implacably hostile to those of his proposals that required legislative approval.

Chief of Staff Leon Panetta was the architect of the executive-order strategy. Until 1995, Clinton had considered proposals for action simply in terms of legislation to submit to Congress. But with the Republicans in charge on Capitol Hill, he had to make adjustments.

The president has very broad authority to issue regulations governing the federal workforce. This power gave Clinton an ability to seem to be acting on issues, when in fact he wasn't doing very much at all.

For example, Clinton had repeatedly urged Congress to reduce the number of children killed or injured playing with their father's firearms by requiring trigger locks on all revolvers. Under NRA pressure, the GOP said no. So Clinton issued an executive order requiring all federal employees who carried pistols as part of their duties to install trigger locks. It was a way of putting the issue in play, within the confines of an executive-only decision.

We soon broadened the strategy to include giving speeches advocating policies over which the president had no power at all. By proposing teen curfews, uniforms for school, or free wireless cell phones for anti-crime community groups, for example, we harvested the political credit for good ideas, without having to issue either legislation or an executive order.

Would Clinton's image have melted if his readers had been told the truth—that he's a politician? Wouldn't our admiration for him increase as we savored his skills as a tactician no less than those as an elected official?

Clinton never used polling as a replacement for leadership. Rather, the surveys he commissioned, and the political calculus he constantly adjusted, simply *enabled* him to lead effectively. When he faced a difficult political situation, analyzing the polling told him how to do what he must—and to live to tell about it.

The catalog of unpopular positions Clinton took, and got away with, is very impressive. It was his political prowess that allowed him to survive, even as he took stands most people disagreed with—from opposing the balanced budget amendment to protecting partial birth abortion.

But Clinton's reluctance to talk politics in his memoir reflects his pride in figuring things out for himself. Just before he fired me in 1979, after I had helped him get elected governor, he looked me in the eye and said, "You are an assault on my vanity. You do better than I do the thing I do best in life: politics." A month later I was history.

Clinton never minded politics. He just didn't want anyone to know it.

Fear of Hillary

As we all know, in January 1998 President Clinton lied under oath in a deposition about his relationship with Monica Lewinsky, triggering the Starr investigation that led to his impeachment. But the only reason he was at a deposition in the first place was that he had refused to settle the Paula Jones lawsuit, which claimed that he had used his authority—as Arkansas governor and, in effect, Jones's employer—to summon her to his hotel room and make inappropriate demands.

Jones's lawyers had initially offered a very straightforward settlement proposal. They did not ask for money or even an acknowledgment of misconduct or an apology. They claimed that all they wanted was for Clinton to say that he met her at his hotel and that she did nothing immoral—that they just wanted to clear her name.

Let's be straight about this: These people were trying to get Clinton, to embarrass him, and to build up negative press about him as a womanizer. These folks weren't just crusaders for justice. That was a given.

So they presented what seemed to be a reasonable proposal. But if Clinton agreed to their demands, he would have been conceding that he had met with a state employee, during a state-sponsored event, in the middle of the day, in his hotel room, where she had no business being. And it would have gone a long way toward confirming Jones's allegation that it was a state trooper who brought her there, lending credence to the charge that Clinton used troopers to solicit women.

But so what? What was there in these admissions that was worth the risk of opening his personal misconduct to the scrutiny that court-ordered discovery and depositions would inevitably entail?

After all, Clinton had already virtually admitted adultery, conceding that he had had "problems" in his marriage and that he wasn't a "perfect" husband. So, we are compelled to ask, why did he put his presidency at risk, just to avoid allegations that he had done something he had already basically admitted to?

Clinton had always been able to get away with his woman problems. And he had no reason, at that point, to believe he couldn't do the same as president. So he probably hoped and thought that it would go away. And at that point no one would have ever believed that the troopers' story and the Jones lawsuit would lead to impeachment.

In refusing to agree to the lawyers' demands, Clinton was clearly trying to avoid a public backlash. But it was more than that. I believe he was even more fearful of the wrath of his wife. For months before the article about the troopers was originally published, top White House officials and even the president himself had apparently tried to stop the story. According to the *Washington Post,* Clinton himself spoke to the troopers, but "denied that he tried to pressure them not to speak to reporters."

In *My Life,* Clinton mentions that the trooper charges "hit Hillary hard." His fear of the issue was palpable. The year 1993 had not been a good one for Hillary. Her father had died, her friend Vince Foster had killed himself, her health care plan had been destroyed by her own party in Congress, and she had been implicated in the Travelgate scandal. By the end of the year, though, things were finally quieting down, and she was getting ready for a series of pre-Christmas soft interviews, when David Brock's story about the troopers appeared in the *American Spectator.* The story also mentioned that the troopers had brought a woman into the Governor's Mansion after Clinton was elected president.

Once the story broke, the Clintons faithfully played their usual roles: Bill quietly denied the story, while Hillary went out front to attack the accusers. In an interview picked up widely by the press, Hillary said: "I find it not an accident that every time he is on the verge of fulfilling his commitment to the American people and they respond . . . out comes a new round of terrible stories that people plant for political and financial purposes."

It was a repeat of the defense she'd mounted when the Gennifer Flowers story broke, and a warm-up for her reaction to the Lewinsky story. Once more, none of this was about anything Bill had done in his personal life. It was just another example of how those who were opposed to Clinton's policies, and jealous of his achievements, would do anything for money and power.

But if the story were actually true, it could have been very damaging. It was one thing for him to have been accused of involvement with other women. It was quite another for him to be accused of using state law enforcement officers to solicit young female state employees he had never met for a spontaneous sexual encounter in a hotel room.

The charges were first aired in Brock's article for the *American Spectator,* a right-wing magazine, at the end of 1993. The article quoted four troopers saying that they would solicit women Clinton wanted to meet as he toured Arkansas and the entire country while he served as governor. The more I saw how sensitive he was about the charges, the more I came to wonder whether they could be true.

The *Spectator* article included a charge by one of the troopers that Clinton had called him to offer a job on the federal payroll, with the implication that it was to buy his silence. Clinton claimed that he only called the trooper to get information on why people would be making up the story. In *My Life,* Clinton calls the troopers' stories "ridiculous." He reports that Brock later apologized to the Clintons in his book *Blinded by the Right.* In short, he does everything but deny them.

And a close reading of *Blinded by the Right* shows that even Brock is not prepared to say they the troopers' stories were untrue. Although

Brock apologized to Clinton, he could not identify anything in the story that was actually untrue. "I can't point to anything specific . . . that might be wrong," he told CNN. In fact, he said that when he wrote the story, he "was as sure of my story as a journalist can be." The troopers themselves have never recanted their stories.

I came to appreciate Clinton's hypersensitivity to the trooper issue when David Maraniss published *First in His Class,* which traced Clinton's prepresidential years. The book included a story I had told him about how Clinton and I had worked together to defeat Jim Guy Tucker and elect David Pryor, the former governor, in their 1978 race for senator from Arkansas.

After weighing a race for senator himself, Clinton had opted to take the path of least resistance and run, almost unopposed, for governor, leaving Pryor and Tucker to battle it out. But Clinton worried that Tucker, a charismatic, bright young congressman, might defeat Pryor. So, as Clinton explains in *My Life,* he recommended that Pryor hire me to help him in his campaign. Clinton says the reason he sent me to Pryor was that he liked the governor. But that wasn't it. Clinton told me that the last thing he wanted was another handsome politician vying for public attention on the narrow Arkansas stage. "Tucker is the only one who can really compete with me," he told me at our first meeting in 1977.

In my conversations with Maraniss, I revealed how Clinton and I had collaborated in writing the negative ads that brought Tucker down. Like two political consultants working together, I would come to see Clinton (then still Arkansas' attorney general) right after my meetings with Pryor, and together we would work on the ad scripts.

Clinton called me, furious, as soon as he read the advance manuscript of the Maraniss book. "What did you tell him about our work against Tucker for?" he demanded, screaming into the phone.

"What do you mean?" I answered, trying to keep my voice down in the Italian restaurant whose pay phone I was using to return the president's call. "You *ran* against Tucker!" (In 1982, four years after

Clinton and I had worked for Pryor, Tucker actually ran against Clinton for governor; we let him have it with a series of fierce attacks.)

"He knows all about 1982," Clinton screamed. "But he doesn't know we worked to beat him in '78!"

"What's the big deal?" I asked. "We did worse to him in '82 than '78 anyway."

"I know," Clinton answered. "But he forgave me for all that. He won't forgive me for 1978."

I was incredulous. "What the hell do you care if he forgives you or not? It happened fifteen years ago. You're president. He's just a governor."

Then Clinton revealed the real reason for his concern. Screaming into the phone, he mouthed the words distinctly, making sure I understood their meaning: *"He controls the state police!"*

His tone suggested that I was an idiot for not having foreseen the problem—as if it were obvious why he wouldn't want to antagonize a man who controlled the Arkansas State Police. But I felt like a dunce. I had no idea why he would care.

But the fear and panic in Clinton's voice remains with me still. He was a man terrified. *Of what?* I wondered. Even if the old *American Spectator* story acquired some new verisimilitude, so what? Clinton hadn't committed any crime; the issue would just die. No congressional committee would have jurisdiction to investigate it or hold hearings. It was all ancient history, dead and buried in his Arkansas past.

Yet Clinton was more scared than I had ever seen him. I hastened to call a mutual acquaintance, whom I frequently used as a conduit to Tucker, and asked him to find out if the governor was mad at Clinton. "Tucker just laughed," my friend reported back. "He says he knows all about what Clinton did with you in '78 and he's okay with it."

I reported the good news back to Clinton—but by then he had bigger problems on his mind.

As it turned out, Maraniss's book also contained a graphic account of how the satyr-governor had used state troopers to procure women. Most devastating, he gave as his source Betsey Wright, Clinton's Arkansas chief of staff and Hillary's close friend, as confirming the illegitimate use of troopers.

"For years, [Wright] told friends later, she had been covering up for [Clinton]. She was convinced that some state troopers were soliciting women for [Clinton] and he for them, she said. Sometimes when Clinton was on the road, Wright would call his room in the middle of the night and no one would answer. She hated that part of him, but felt that the other sides of him overshadowed his personal weaknesses."

Apparently, when Hillary read this paragraph in the Maraniss book, she completely flipped out—and Bill grew even more apoplectic than he had been over the Tucker story. After an initial period of animosity, Betsey and I had become very good friends, and I was always pushing her case with Clinton. Probably resentful of the tight leash she kept him on as his chief of staff during his gubernatorial years, the president shunted her aside and kept her out of the administration. I kept reminding Clinton of all that Betsey knew—she had been the point person in controlling "bimbo eruptions" in the campaign—and urging him to keep his relationship with her in good repair.

"She's finished," Clinton screamed at me in another phone call. "*Finished.* I don't care what she knows. I don't care what she'll say, I've had it with her. She's out. Out. *Out.*"

Trying to calm Clinton down, I asked what he was referring to. He told me what Betsey had said about the troopers. And not only was Hillary furious, he told me, but for the first time in all of his scandals Chelsea was mad at him, too. It was rare for Clinton to open up to me about his troubles on the domestic front. Clearly he was a man in pain, his marriage in turmoil.

It was obvious why Hillary took Betsey's statement so seriously: Betsey was her person. It was Hillary herself who brought Betsey back into Bill's life to run his comeback campaign for governor in 1982. Betsey was Hillary's eyes and ears on the governor's staff. If she said the trooper stories were true, Hillary must have realized they were.

Back then, the Clintons' marriage was not just an arrangement, a professional association in disguise. Bill's infidelities haunted Hillary. In the post-Monica era that may have changed, but in the mid-1990s, she ached with each new allegation of marital misconduct. (I had firsthand evidence of this: Once, as I've written elsewhere, she cried to me over the phone, sobbing that she just loved Bill and she didn't understand why people didn't believe her when she said she did.)

I flew down to Washington to help the president deal with the crisis he was expecting to erupt when the Maraniss book was released. It was clear from the president's reaction that Betsey's comments had stung very deeply in the Clinton household. The president was miserable. Brooding over the conflict in his domestic life, he appeared more worried about Hillary's reaction than about the public response.

Public opinion was my assignment, though, and I suggested a plan: Clinton should take some very public action during the weekend the book was published to assure that it was driven off the front pages. Clinton agreed, but distractedly. It wasn't the newspapers he was worried about. It was his wife.

That weekend, Clinton intervened in the strike that was then gripping major league baseball, and flexed his muscles threatening trade sanctions against China. The resulting publicity drowned out coverage of the offending book.

Even though the book got only limited exposure and did not kindle the national political crisis Clinton had feared, he was still determined to get a statement from Betsey denying that he had ever misused the troopers. When he first learned about her comments, Clinton had tried to track Betsey down at the Virginia hotel where she was staying. When I arrived at the White House, Clinton asked me to call Betsey—with him sitting silently beside me listening to my end of the call—and ask her to issue a retraction. Since Betsey was not actually quoted directly in the Maraniss book, she was willing to issue the statement Clinton wanted. But each time I would hang up with a draft statement from her in hand, the president would add new language that he wanted in the text. It took three or four calls before we finally agreed on the language.

Clinton wasn't worried about the story's impact in the press; he knew it would have no legs in the media, and indeed the press treated the charge as ancient history. It was Hillary, not the media, at whom Betsey's retraction was aimed.

(Betsey Wright did, indeed, know all about Clinton's foibles. Eileen and I spoke to her right after the 1992 campaign, and advised her to put her files on women Clinton had been involved with in a safe deposit box. "A safe deposit box?" Betsey howled with laughter. "A warehouse would be more like it!")

So we return to the initial question: Why didn't Clinton settle the Paula Jones lawsuit early on, when all she was asking for was a mild statement in which Clinton did not have to admit any guilt? Just as historians will eternally wonder what Nixon was trying to find when the burglars rifled the Watergate office of Democratic National Committee Chairman Larry O'Brien, one can only ask why Clinton didn't make the Jones suit go away when he could.

All Jones's lawyers were asking him to say was: "I do not deny meeting Paula Jones on May 8, 1991, in a room at the Excelsior Hotel. She did not engage in any improper or sexual conduct. I believe her to be a truthful person and moral person." That was it. No money. No admissions. No apology.

Why didn't Clinton jump at it? Because Hillary wouldn't let him.

Why did Hillary kill a settlement with such generous terms? In *Living History,* she writes that she "opposed the idea in principle, believing that it would set a terrible precedent for a president to pay money to rid himself of a nuisance suit." Since the proposed deal involved neither the payment of any money nor an admission of guilt, how would it have created any kind of precedent?

In retrospect, Hillary admits that it was "the second biggest tactical mistake" the Clintons made in handling the scandal allegations that swirled around them—second only to their agreement to have a special prosecutor.

And what did Hillary mean when she wrote in *Living History* that the "lawsuits would never end?" Did she really fear that the president of the United States was a target for frivolous lawsuits, or was she afraid of more and more embarrassment as the charges piled up?

When Jones offered to settle the litigation asking Clinton to give the statement her lawyers had written, Clinton's people countered with a version of their own:

"I have no recollection of meeting Paula Jones on May 8, 1991, at the Excelsior Hotel. It is entirely possible that I did meet with her on that date. If such a meeting occurred, neither she nor I did or said anything of a sexual nature. I regret the untrue assertions which may have been made about her."

The most important difference between his statement and the one she proposed is that Jones wanted Clinton to admit that she met him "in a room at the Excelsior Hotel." The president wouldn't do it—I suspect because Clinton did not want to admit that a state trooper had brought her upstairs.

And why was Clinton so fearful of the trooper scandal and of allegations of adultery? Because of the political damage it might cause? Not likely. Clinton's admissions during the 1992 campaign had defused the issue of adultery. The Jones allegations—like Flowers's charges before them—concerned his gubernatorial years, not his time in the White House. It would have been embarrassing, of course, but Clinton could have survived speculation about adultery.

Had Clinton ignored Hillary and settled the Jones case, he would never have been asked under oath about Monica Lewinsky. But Hillary could not see that a short-term admission of wrong-doing—or even a hint of it, as Jones's lawyers were proposing—would have been worth the sacrifice. In the past, they had skated by without making such admissions. Between their private detectives, who could dig up dirt on the women making the accusations, and the he said-she said nature of the charges, Hillary was confident that she could avoid embarrassment here, too. Her standard defense in cases where Bill was accused of personal misconduct was to say it never happened. There was no reason not to believe that this formula, so reliable over the years, would prove inadequate now. The discovery of DNA on a blue dress was far in the future.

In short, Hillary insisted that there be no settlement of the Paula Jones suit . . .

. . . because she could.

This was not the first time I recognized that the president was terrified of Hillary's reaction to the accounts of his infidelity.

As the Clintons prepared for their *60 Minutes* interview in 1992, during which they defended themselves against Gennifer Flowers's charges that Bill had conducted a twelve-year affair with her, Clinton called me for advice on what to say. I assumed Flowers's charge was true; Betsey had earlier told me that Bill generally only dated women who had as much to lose by disclosure as he did. "But there is one who was a real bimbo that I'm really worried about," she told Eileen and me over the phone. I assumed she had meant Gennifer.

I suggested to Clinton that he say that he had not always been faithful in his marriage, but that FDR had not been always faithful in his, nor had Eisenhower been in his marriage, nor had JFK been to Jackie, nor Johnson to Lady Bird, and that he hoped that he could overcome his failings and go on to be as great a president as these distinguished Americans turned out to have been.

"That'd be great," Clinton gushed, "but I'd have to find a new place to live."

This fear of Hillary's reprisals steered him wrong time after time. As the Jones lawsuit proceeded, and he was deposed, Clinton would plunge far deeper into trouble. Why did Clinton lie in the Jones deposition? Why not just admit to his affair with Lewinsky?

Clinton was too sophisticated a lawyer, and too good a politician, not to realize the legal troubles he was causing by his disingenuous answers. He knew that Lewinsky had somehow spilled the beans on his relationship with her. He didn't realize, as he gave the deposition, that the intern's conversations had been taped by Linda Tripp. But he knew that somehow the Jones lawyers had found out about the gifts he had given her, and that there was some reason they were zeroing in on this decidedly peripheral figure.

Clinton must have known they had something, and that he was putting his neck in a legal noose by lying under oath. The circumlocutions he went through in his deposition, giving misleading answers that could still be defended as truthful, were too cute by half.

It wasn't the first time Clinton had faced this kind of challenge. When the president was summoned to testify in the Whitewater trial of Susan and Jim McDougal and Governor Jim Guy Tucker, Clinton asked me: "What should I say if they ask about Susan McDougal?"

I assumed he was asking about whether he should reveal that they had had an affair. "If you have had a relationship with her, say so," I pleaded. "Don't lie. Don't lie under oath. If you tell the truth, you'll drop ten points in the polls, but you'll still be leading by seven, and we'll get the points back for you. But if you commit perjury, nobody can save you."

(He was never asked about an affair with Susan McDougal during the trial. McDougal has consistently denied that she had an affair with Clinton.)

Did Clinton lie during the Jones deposition because he wanted to avoid the political firestorm an admission of an affair would have likely triggered? Bill Clinton, the political master, must have realized that he could admit adultery and still survive politically. In fact, in the very same deposition he *did* admit to his affair with Gennifer Flowers, contradicting all his—and Hillary's—outraged (but crafty) denials during the 1992 campaign. Why would he fear Lewinsky but not Flowers? The fact that the Flowers affair had happened a long time ago in Arkansas, and the Lewinsky affair more recently in Washington, certainly made the latter more politically harmful. But Clinton was already in his second term; simply admitting to another affair would hardly be fatal.

Clinton must have known that the one thing that could cook him now was lying under oath. Out of the reach of an angry electorate, he had only legal proceedings to fear. So why not take the political hit and avoid the legal trouble?

He chose, instead, to lie. And I believe he did so for the same reason he couldn't settle the Jones suit, the same reason he had to conceal the trooper story: that he was deeply afraid of Hillary's reaction.

In *My Life,* he says so plainly: "In the deposition, I was trying to protect my family and myself from my selfish stupidity."

And so, out of fear of Hillary—not just concern over politics—Clinton planted a poisonous acorn, letting the Jones suit proceed until it became the full-blown scandal that nearly toppled his presidency.

Meanwhile, another acorn, also planted out of fear of Hillary, was also growing into a scandal tree—this one stemming from the Whitewater real estate deal.

When the *New York Times* broke the story of the Whitewater scandal during the 1992 presidential campaign, few people noticed. The details of the land deal were mind-numbing, and the intricacies of the dealings with the Madison Guaranty Savings and Loan Association seemed petty against the hundreds of billions at stake in the S&L scandal then making national headlines. Clinton's draft-dodging, and his relationship with Flowers, made infinitely better copy.

After Clinton took office, though, a number of related new charges emerged, and the media became skeptical of the Clintons' explanation that there was no fraud because they had lost money on the deal. That wasn't the point. The question was: Did McDougal's actions help them avoid a bigger loss—and did they constitute a bribe?

The facts were clear. The Clintons and the McDougals had agreed to buy property in the Ozark Mountains near the White River to subdivide and sell off as lots for vacation homes. They shared the down payment equally, and each couple owned half of the property. But the investment went bad as interest rates climbed in the early 1980s, and sales of second homes fell off sharply. And yet the mortgage bills kept coming each month.

At first Jim McDougal pestered the Clintons for the money to meet the debt service and to make the property saleable. But he soon realized that the Clintons were strapped financially and couldn't pay. They had bought the property expecting they would never have to pay, that sales of the early lots would take care of any ongoing obligation.

So McDougal began to pay the debt service himself; eventually he even repaid the Clintons for their down payment. All this would have been fine, had the governor and his wife signed over their half to McDougal. But Hillary wanted to have her cake and eat it too; when Susan McDougal suggested that Hillary allow her to buy out the Clintons' share, Hillary reportedly screamed at her: "No! Jim told me that this was going to pay for college for Chelsea. I still expect it to do that."

Having paid less than half of the debt service, and been refunded their entire down payment, the Clintons' continued ownership of half of the property smelled like a favor given for favors received.

When the *Washington Times* reported that Whitewater files had been removed from Vince Foster's office after his suicide, media interest in the scandal, long dormant, reawakened. The *Washington Post* demanded that the Clintons turn over all their Whitewater records, and faxed a list of inquiries to the White House about the deal.

George Stephanopoulos, the White House "ambassador" to the *Post*, reported that the paper's executive editor, Leonard Downie Jr., took a personal interest in the matter and that the paper's longtime White House correspondent, Ann Devroy, warned George that the newspaper would pursue the matter aggressively if they did not get the documents.

The *New York Times*, whose excellent investigative reporter Jeff Gerth had first broken the story in 1992, had suddenly fallen behind its Washington rival. In the friendly but brutal competition between the *Times* and the *Washington Post* for journalistic supremacy, once one newspaper broke a scandal, the other had to race to catch up.

It was clear to all who knew Washington that unless the Clinton administration assuaged the *Post*, the ensuing outcry would force

Clinton to agree to have his attorney general, Janet Reno, name an independent counsel to investigate Whitewater.

A fierce debate raged in the White House. As Stephanopoulos describes, Hillary resisted all suggestions that the first couple provide all of the Whitewater documents to the *Post*, even though President Clinton had no objection to doing so.

Just when George felt that he and journalist-turned-adviser David Gergen had finally succeeded in getting Clinton to send over the records, Clinton said he wanted to think about it some more (which often meant *clear it with Hillary*). Hillary "didn't want [the records] out—and she had a veto," George writes. "On this issue, Clinton wasn't commander in chief, just a husband beholden to his wife. Hillary was always the first to defend him on bimbo eruptions; now he had to do the same for her."

The former president essentially confirms Stephanopoulos's story in *My Life,* saying that he told his advisers that he had no objection to releasing the documents, but that he didn't want to have to appoint a special prosecutor. "My instincts were to release the records," he writes. But Hillary prevailed and the Clintons refused, saying they would give them to the Justice Department but not to the newspaper. Since a Clinton appointee ran Justice, this concession did nothing to mollify the *Post*.

Hillary writes in *Living History* that she worried that releasing an "inevitably incomplete set of personal documents" to the *Post* might only fan the desire for more disclosure. And why was the file "inevitably incomplete"?

Because she had shredded part of its contents!

Hillary told federal banking officials that, in 1998, she had sent some of the key documents about her work for Jim McDougal's bank, Madison Guaranty, to be shredded by the Rose Law Firm.

In her answers to written interrogatories, Hillary said that "While I have no personal recollection . . . I am informed that the Rose Law Firm . . . asked its members to review their old files to determine whether the firm could save money by reducing the number of closed, stored files. I cooperated with this effort and indicated that many of my closed client files, apparently including certain files relating to the firm's representation of Madison Guaranty, did not need to be retained."

And why was Hillary so worried about releasing the Whitewater records?

One clue comes from what did happen when the documents were released after they were given to the Justice Department, and leaked to the media from there: The documents included the Clintons' tax returns for 1978 and 1979, which contained the records of Hillary's massive winnings in the commodities market—which, until then, had never been exposed publicly.

Just as her husband was becoming governor, Hillary had invested $1,000 with a commodities broker recommended by her friend Jim Blair. Under Blair's guidance, the initial investment had multiplied to a gain of $100,000 in less than two years.

George Stephanopoulos concluded—and I agree with him—that the concealment of her commodities trading profits was Hillary's motive for talking Bill out of releasing the Whitewater records. This, he writes, was "a plausible theory as to why she had been so adamant about refusing to publicly release the Whitewater documents. The only real 'news' in the documents, which would have included the . . . tax returns, would have been Hillary's windfall."

The Clintons had tried to conceal the records once before, in 1982, when Bill was running to reclaim the governorship. When I raised the idea of releasing the records to shame incumbent Frank White, Clinton at first enthusiastically agreed, but then refused to release them for his years as governor—the very 1978 and 1979 returns that were part of the Whitewater documents Hillary refused to release. When the commodities trading information was published, exposing Hillary's trading profits, the president took me aside and whispered in my ear: "What are we going to do about

Hillary?" The revelation had shaken Clinton to the core. When we saw them together that night at a White House movie screening, it was clear why: The chill was on between them.

The rest is history. Janet Reno appointed Robert Fiske as independent counsel, which was bad enough for the Clintons. But the president stupidly agreed to sign a law allowing a special three-judge panel, appointed by right-wing Chief Justice Rehnquist, to review the counsel. The panel removed Fiske, putting Kenneth Starr in his place, and the investigations began in earnest.

Apart from the embarrassment of the revelation of the commodities trading profits, though, what was Hillary afraid of? Even if her commodities trading secret came out, what danger was she really in? The statute of limitations had long since lapsed on her trades; she could never be prosecuted. While fraudulent concealment of a transaction could prolong the statute, the Clintons were not actually required to release their tax returns, and other than that they had done nothing to hide their profits.

She was home free.

But Hillary has a perfectionist self-image. She couldn't handle the scrutiny, or the accusations that would come with the disclosure. She must have known that her claim—repeated in Bill's memoir—that she had traded based on her own research into the market would be dismissed out of hand. She realized that she would be ridiculed and reviled for the investment, and was determined to conceal it.

But Hillary must have known her mistake would come out, as eventually it did—not because the Clintons released it, but through a leak from the Justice Department. Rather than step up and take the hit, which she must have known was coming, she elected to postpone it for a few months by withholding the documents from the media. In doing so, she helped to force her husband's hand in naming an independent counsel, and brought no end of trouble on herself and Bill. All to buy a few extra months before the commodities market scandal would surface.

So both scandals—Jones-Lewinsky and Whitewater—had their roots in Hillary's fear (of humiliation in the former, embarrassment in the latter), and in Bill's fear of crossing the first lady. From these two acorns, huge trees of scandal grew; they would ultimately become entwined as Starr investigated the Lewinsky scandal, and the impeachment of a president was the result.

And yet in *My Life,* despite all of this, Clinton never blames Hillary.

I never really understood why he wasn't more angry with her. Every one of the nonsexual scandals that bedeviled his presidency was her fault:

- The Whitewater investment itself was Hillary's project. She was McDougal's lawyer and his primary contact on the issue.
- Vince Foster was Hillary's close friend at the Rose Law Firm. After his death it was her chief of staff, Maggie Williams, who was spotted removing documents from his office.
- The billing records at the Rose Law Firm concerned Hillary's time as an attorney.
- The commodities market scandal was entirely hers.
- She was the one who recommended hiring Craig Livingstone, the former bar bouncer who was found to have the FBI files on prominent Republicans on his desk.
- It was Hillary who decided to keep the sessions of the health care task force secret, triggering a successful lawsuit.
- It was Hillary who represented Jim McDougal as his attorney on the fraudulent Castle Grande real estate deal.
- Hillary was a partner in the Rose Law Firm when her husband funneled legal work to the firm.
- Hillary was the one who told David Watkins to fire the Travel Office staff.
- Webb Hubbell, at the epicenter of the Whitewater scandal, was Hillary's close associate and law partner. It was the "consulting fees" paid to him after the Rose scandal that drew fire during the Clinton years.

■ Hillary's brothers were the ones who pushed the pardon of a drug dealer and a con artist as her husband left the White House.

These scandals all led to Hillary. And even those that were Bill's doing—the troopers, Paula Jones, Monica Lewinsky—were prolonged because of Hillary's inclination to stonewall and hold firm, disclosing nothing, admitting nothing, settling nothing.

And yet, to read Clinton's memoirs, you would think Hillary was a candidate for canonization.

Clinton writes that all who knew Hillary felt she was "scrupulously honest" and "above reproach." He covers for her on her refusal to release the Whitewater records, implying that it was his decision, and even defends her transparently absurd claim to be named after Sir Edmund Hillary, who gained fame by climbing Mount Everest five years after her birth.

Bill Clinton may not always have been faithful, but he sure is loyal.

What kindles this blind faith on the one hand and the white fear of her anger on the other?

The key to understanding Bill's attitude is that his refusal to see any bad in Hillary is relatively recent. It dates back to the 1992 campaign, and Hillary's defense of Clinton during the Flowers scandal. Before that Bill was not above speaking ill of Hillary, and argued with her frequently. Any observer could see that their marriage was not very stable—not just from the stories of his adultery and her reaction to it, but from the interaction between them.

Throughout the 1970s and 1980s, their marriage was rocked by ups and downs. Indeed, before Clinton married Hillary, Betsey Wright heard him complaining "after a round of arguing with [Hillary] Rodham that he had tried to 'run Hillary off, but she just wouldn't go.'"

By all accounts—except their own—Bill and Hillary's relationship was fraught with conflict, rage, recrimination, and anger. Countless observers have witnessed and described numerous scenes of confrontation between the couple. One, the wife of a prominent United States senator, told me—off the record—of hearing the Clintons screaming at each other and Hillary cursing at Bill only minutes after he finished delivering his first inaugural address in 1993.

The Clintons were famous for their fights. Ron Addington, who worked for Clinton in his 1974 race for Congress in Arkansas, recalls a classic confrontation during the campaign: "Bill wanted to do one thing, [Hillary] wanted to do another. They started shouting at each other. I was driving. Bill was in the front seat, Hillary in the back. He was hitting the dashboard. She was hitting the seat. They were really going at it. We drove up a street near the headquarters and stopped at a light. Hillary said 'I'm getting out!' She got out and slammed the door. And Bill said, 'Go on' and drove away in a huff."

In the 1980s, Clinton often talked about leaving her. Maraniss recounts how Bill rocked the one-year old Chelsea to sleep in her cradle, singing so Hillary could hear, an improvised song: "I want a divor-or-or-orce. I want a divor-or-or-orce."

During the late 1980s, Clinton called me to say that he was actually considering a divorce, and asked what I felt the political fallout would be. (I told him he would be fine, and to do whatever he felt he had to do.)

Clinton had been "broaching the subject of divorce in conversations with some of his colleagues, governors from other states who had survived the collapse of their marriages," Maraniss reports. Hillary, for her part, told Betsey Wright that "she was unwilling to abandon the partnership [with Clinton]. She had invested too much in Bill Clinton and was determined to see it through."

But the divorce talk ratcheted up after Clinton decided not to run for president in 1988. Gail Sheehy writes of how Bill and Hillary "both believed that Clinton's political career was going nowhere." She writes that "the couple moved toward a momentous crossroads in their lives where it appeared their tracks were destined to separate."

In 1988–1989, according to Sheehy, Clinton was deeply involved with Marilyn Jo Denton Jenkins, a "tall, slim, blond, a striking divorcée in her early forties." A state trooper testified in his deposition in the Paula Jones case that Clinton, alluding to Marilyn, told him "It's tough to be in love with both your wife and another woman."

Their marriage was clearly on the rocks. But then Clinton began to see light at the end of the political tunnel. After Mike Dukakis failed in his bid for president in 1988, Clinton began to talk more and more about running for the office when the cycle came around again in four years.

It was that decision, set in stone by early 1990, that led him to reconcile with Hillary. Divorce was now out of the question for either of them. No longer did they feel the political content had been drained out of their marriage, leaving nothing behind. They were back in business.

Then came the event that totally altered their relationship: the Gennifer Flowers scandal.

In all of Clinton's Arkansas campaigns, his philandering went unmentioned in public. It was not covered in the media. Even his political opponents made no such accusations. It wasn't until 1990, just before his last Arkansas race, that a longtime enemy, Larry Nichols, aired the charges of womanizing against Clinton for the first time, publishing a list of women with whom he said the governor had been intimate. But nobody much cared at the time, and the story never became a factor in Clinton's last race for governor.

But when Gennifer Flowers came forward two months before the New Hampshire primary to accuse Clinton of a twelve-year affair, all that changed. Suddenly, the presidential candidate's political life was hanging by a thread—a thread Hillary could cut at any time. If she had walked out on him, he never would have been president. Even after the election, if subsequent allegations about his misuse of troopers (or even his being alone in a hotel room with Jones) had triggered Hillary's departure, he could probably have kissed his chances of re-election goodbye.

Hillary, in other words, had total control of Bill; she possessed life-and-death power over his political career. She was his get-out-of-jail-free card—the one person on earth he could not afford to alienate. So if Hillary demanded, as she must have, that Bill take risks to sustain her image as the perfect person, he had no choice but to give in.

But all was not well between them. Instead, during the first half of 1995, I had the impression that she wasn't even speaking to him because of the Maraniss book. And after the Lewinsky revelations came out, she admits that they weren't on speaking terms for months. The cold shoulder is Hillary's favorite weapon.

Bill knew it was tough to handle Hillary's sharpness when she was mad. And her grudges lasted for a long, long time. So it was inevitable that he should reject the settlement of the Jones lawsuit, for fear that it would so embarrass Hillary that she might leave.

And when Hillary demanded that he not release the Whitewater records because she couldn't handle the adverse publicity over her commodities trading, even if it meant that an independent counsel would eventuate, he had no choice but to give in.

And, finally, I believe it was Hillary—or a fear of Hillary—that dictated Clinton's last bit of self-destructiveness, his fatal misjudgment in lying to the Jones lawyers during his deposition.

Oddly, as Hillary's Senate candidacy approached, she went through a mirror-image of the experiences her husband had suffered at the start of his presidential race.

Just as Bill may have been planning to leave Hillary in the late 1980s, chafing at her demands and restive in the marriage, so the first lady may have planned to ditch Bill after her public humiliation during the Lewinsky scandal. But just as Bill's growing presidential ambitions in 1989 and 1990 led him to reverse his direction and bond with Hillary anew, so the first lady's Senate ambitions may have caused her to go back to him.

And now? They both need each other. Hillary needs Bill; he is her best cheerleader, fund-raiser, surrogate, liaison to the party, issue expert, political consultant, and chief adviser. She cannot reach the presidency without him.

And Bill needs Hillary. She is his ticket back to the White House, for what he must see as the third and fourth Clinton administrations.

10

She Said, He Said

And yet, with all the fealty Bill Clinton has obviously felt compelled to pay to Hillary through the years, the most curious thing about *My Life* is not the former president's tendency to canonize his scandal-plagued wife, but his virtual omission of any description of her role in the design, formulation, or implementation of public policy. It would be natural for Clinton to praise his wife's contributions extravagantly in his memoir. After all, she is the candidate now. One would have expected *My Life* to be filled with insights into Hillary's good ideas and brilliant initiatives. Instead she is treated almost offhandedly, as the person who accompanied him—usually with Chelsea mentioned in the same sentence—on his various foreign travels. Even when Hillary actually played a key role, her name is absent from the official account.

One wonders if Bill Clinton is exacting his own small measure of revenge against his wife, who got him into such hot water after she refused to let him settle the Jones suit or release the Whitewater files. Is he damning with faint praise this woman he must somehow resent because of all the scandals her behavior caused? Is there a more benign explanation—that he is so symbiotic with Hillary, for example, that he has lost the ability to see her as a separate person? Or is he truly so self-involved that he cannot recognize the contributions of anyone else, including his wife?

Whatever the reason, Hillary's virtual absence in Clinton's account of his presidency is striking—especially given the role she actually played in innumerable policy and political decisions.

For example, Hillary was pivotal in the process of assembling Clinton's cabinet. I recall constant discussions with her sizing up each possible nominee, measuring his or her strengths or weaknesses. As one White House aide later told the media, Hillary "had a huge cadre of friends and knows where she wants them in the administration." Her close associates and friends, including Rose Law Firm colleagues Vince Foster, Webb Hubbell, and William Kennedy III, were appointed to top positions. Bernie Nussbaum, her mentor on the Nixon Impeachment Committee, was named as Counsel to the President.

George Stephanopoulos also reports Hillary's central role in the decision to jettison attorney general nominee Zoe Baird after the revelation that she had not paid Social Security taxes on household workers she had hired.

And when the time came to interview Kimba Wood for the job, Barbara Olson reports that Hillary interviewed her "for ninety minutes, twice as long as the president did."

As Bob Woodward notes in *The Agenda,* his history of the early years of the Clinton presidency, Hillary was one of a select group—along with only future secretary of state and director of the transition Warren Christopher, Vice President Al Gore, and longtime confidante Bruce Lindsay—that played the key role in shaping the new administration.

It was no easy task to meet all the requirements for ethnic, racial, religious, geographic, ideological, and gender balance that Clinton set for his cabinet—and still appoint good people. Hillary's skill in helping him do so merited at least a mention in *My Life.* But she is entirely absent from his description of the process.

In *My Life's* account of his presidency, Clinton mentions Hillary one hundred and two times:

- Thirty-four times he simply describes trips the first couple took together. Most of these sections merely mention her name, usually along with Chelsea's. Clinton relates what happened during their visits to Arkansas, Martha's Vineyard, Australia, China, Moscow, Berlin, Northern Ireland, Russia, Kosovo, Cologne, Ghana, Latin America, Korea, Australia, Japan, Israel, Jordan, Turkey, Naples, Vietnam, Stamford, Paris, a New York state fair, Madrid, Rome, Pakistan, India, Nepal, Sri Lanka, and Bangladesh. Hillary trots along dutifully in these passages, rarely quoted or involved in any important meetings. Nor does he corroborate Mrs. Clinton's claim in *Living History* that she was involved in helping to get the Irish peace process back on track; he makes no mention of any involvement on her part.

- Twenty-six times, Clinton mentions Hillary in connection with Whitewater or other scandal investigations.

- Seventeen mentions relate to their relationship with one another, including touching avowals of love after the wearing days of the Lewinsky scandal.

- Eleven references praise Hillary's character, her integrity, references to her writing a book, her role in promoting American crafts, and so forth. These mentions are uniformly positive, but hardly substantive.

- Nine mentions describe her role in health care reform.

- And only five in the entire section on his presidency relate to any political or policy role his wife played, apart from her work on health care. He mentions her participation in a White House staff gathering at Camp David, her role in summoning me back to work for Clinton after the 1994 defeat, her speech in China defending women's rights, her campaign appearances in 1998 for Democratic candidates, and her role in promoting child protection legislation.

And that's it.

Even in discussing the health care reform proposal, Clinton's references to Hillary are little more than perfunctory. Apart from three routine mentions of her health care work, he makes only five significant comments about her work in that process. He notes how unusual it was for a first lady to play such a policy-making role. He notes that her task force meetings were criticized for being closed. He recalls that she sat next to the pediatrician Dr. T. Berry Brazelton and Dr. C. Everett Koop, the former surgeon general, as he announced the health care plan, and mentions her along with Ira Magaziner and Judy Feder as the authors of the program. Finally, he says that he and Hillary delivered the bill personally to Congress, and that his wife had been briefing members about the legislation.

In all, Clinton devotes fifty pages to health care reform, but includes only these five substantive mentions of Hillary in his account. Instead, he takes all the credit himself. Among the many references to his own role, he says:

- "I asked Congress" to cut medical cost inflation.
- "I spent the next two weeks" lobbying for the health care bill.
- "I decided" to delay health care until after the economic program had been considered by Congress.
- "I told Congress" that changing the health care system would be a challenge.
- "I suggested" to Dole that they negotiate a compromise.
- "I proposed" a system that would have had beneficial economic as well as social effects across the board.

I, I, I, I. Not much *she.*

Clinton never even mentions Hillary's trip up to Capitol Hill on his behalf on the morning of the impeachment vote in the House of Representatives, when she urged the Democrats to stay with her husband.

Perhaps not surprisingly, Hillary's chronicle of her White House years, in *Living History,* is considerably more generous in its description of her role in politics and policy. The contrast between what *she* writes and what *he* writes is striking:

- *She* writes that she supported the historic welfare reform bill: "I agreed that he should sign it and worked hard to round up votes for its passage." *He* makes no mention at all of Hillary in connection with welfare reform.

- *She* writes: "I worked hard to make after-school care more accessible," and notes that the administration introduced the 21st Century Community Learning Centers program to provide after-school and summer classes for 1.3 million children. *He* writes that "I reached" a budget deal with Congress that provided after-school programs for 1.3 million children. No mention of Hillary.

- *She* writes: "I had begun working inside the White House and with other Administration officials to save vital services and programs targeted by Gingrich and the Republicans." *He* writes: "I would never allow their budget to become law." No Hillary there.

- *She* writes: "I also spent two years helping . . . stave off cuts in legal services, the arts, education, Medicare and Medicaid." *He* writes: "I spent the entire month traveling the country campaigning against the Republicans' proposed cuts in Medicare and Medicaid." *He* makes no mention of any role Hillary might have played in the budget battle.

- *She* writes: "I had worked . . . to spearhead adoption reform," and says, "My hope was that through new legislation, we could speed up the process and remove arbitrary barriers that prevented" adoptions. *He* writes, with no mention of Hillary, how proud he was of his "sweeping reforms of our adoption laws."

- *She* writes that she was inspired by AIDS advocate Elizabeth Glaser to "begin working for better . . . drugs . . . to treat children with AIDS." *He* makes no mention of Hillary, noting that he appointed Patsy Fleming as his AIDS policy director and "outlined . . . new initiatives to combat AIDS." Clinton writes that he dedicated the announcement to "the guiding light of the AIDS fight, Elizabeth Glaser."

■ *She* writes: "I led the Administration's efforts to end the practice of 'drive through deliveries,' in which hospitals discharged new mothers twenty-four hours after a normal delivery." *He* writes that he signed a "bill that ended so-called drive-by deliveries, by guaranteeing a minimum of forty-eight hours of coverage to mothers and newborns." No Hillary.

■ *She* writes: "Bill and I wanted . . . tougher child support collection efforts." *He* writes that "I signed another of my priorities into law" when he approved the Child Support Performance and Incentive Act. No allusion to Hillary.

■ *She* writes: "Bill and I . . . convened White House strategy sessions on how to curb media violence directed at children." *He* writes that he agreed that children saw too much violence on television, and that this was why he was supporting "Al and Tipper Gore's drive to get V-chips into new TVs" which would permit parents to screen out offensive programs.

■ *She* writes: "I urged my staff to come up with ideas to improve" the Family Leave Law, and that "we worked . . . to modify family and medical leave so that federal workers could use up to twelve weeks of accrued paid sick leave to care for an ill family member." *He* writes: "I proposed . . . expanding the Family and Medical Leave Act," without mentioning her efforts.

■ *She* writes: "My staff continued to work closely with the President's . . . advisors to develop the groundbreaking policies Bill announced in his 1998 State of the Union Address." She cites improvements in child care, more access to day care for low-income working families, expansion of Head Start, and tax incentives for investment in child care. *He* writes that he proposed to expand child care for "one million more children." His only mention of Hillary is to thank her for preserving America's "treasures," including the original Star Spangled Banner, which led Francis Scott Key to write the poem that became the national anthem.

And not only does the former president exclude Hillary from any of the policy initiatives with which she claims to have been associated, but he totally leaves her out of any discussion of his political strategy as he confronted the Republicans before, during, and after the 1996 election.

So why no Hillary?

Is it because she didn't really play the role she says she did?

In my time in the White House, Hillary wasn't much involved in policy or in politics. Partly as a result of the 1994 election defeat and the health care debacle, the president and Hillary decided to reduce her visibility in the White House.

These days, we recall how many voters disliked Clinton because of his various scandals. But in 1994 and 1995, just as many voters were complaining about his perceived weakness. My polling had indicated that voters saw the first couple locked in a kind of zero sum game, in which any gain in her power meant an equal loss in his.

As a result, Hillary decided to absent herself from all White House political strategy meetings; media leaks suggesting that she was running things at the White House came to a stop.

Instead of trying to advance independent initiatives like health care, or attempting to provide management and direction to the often rudderless Clinton White House, Hillary embarked on her own strategy of foreign travel and issue advocacy. Again, our polls told us this was a good idea: We'd discovered that voters resented Hillary when her power was hidden, but welcomed her exercise of her position and stature for open, overt support for pro-family, pro-education, pro-feminist, pro-health care positions. In fact, the more she spoke out in public, the more they assumed that she wasn't spending time trying to run the country, a job to which nobody had elected her.

I was struck by how little input Hillary really had on issues, particularly as we formulated the annual State of the Union addresses, which constituted the president's to-do list and shaped his priorities for the ensuing year. As these critical speeches were being compiled, she was nowhere to be found.

But Bill Clinton excludes Hillary in areas where I know she played an important role. For example, he fails to mention her efforts at advancing child immunization, or at making sure vaccines and other drugs were safe for children. Hillary was also very involved in battling for veterans who suffered from Gulf War Syndrome as a result of the 1991 war. She pushed for annual mammograms under the Medicare law, as opposed to the biannual exams funded before her efforts. The first lady led efforts to include respite care funding for those who were trying to care for parents or other elderly people who suffered from debilitating diseases which required constant attention.

But the former president makes no mention—none at all—of Hillary's role in these initiatives. Indeed, in a book where he painstakingly details every one of his programs, he often omits mention of these issues entirely.

Is he dissing her?

It's hard to believe, after Hillary's unwavering support for her husband, that he would do so. After all, Clinton strongly supported Hillary's independent political career, making a Herculean effort to help her get elected to the Senate from New York. So it is hard to reconcile that with the idea that he would choose to cut her loose in his memoirs, by deliberately mentioning her only in supportive or traditional roles.

But it is impossible to escape the conclusion that Clinton goes out of his way to avoid giving Hillary credit, even when it is due.

Could this be a reflection of the tension in their marriage that surfaced in the 1980s, which was heightened in the aftermath of the Lewinsky-impeachment imbroglio? Is Bill Clinton declaring his independence?

Or is this just Clinton being Clinton? Self-absorbed and self-involved?

One thing is certain: In *My Life,* it's rare that Clinton gives *anyone* credit for anything except himself. Only when things go wrong, as we've seen, does he mention the involvement of other staff people or advisers or cabinet members, and then only to single them out for blame.

Is the book really a declaration of independence, or at least individuation, from a man who has been joined to his wife through so many difficult years in the public eye? Or is it his way of saying *MINE!!* as he recounts his achievements and initiatives, grouping Hillary in with so many others in his administration, cordoned off on the sidelines while Clinton stands alone in the spotlight one more time?

Like so much about the man, and his marriage, the truth may remain forever a secret.

11

Errata

Part of the mission of this book is to correct the historical record and set right the omissions, distortions, and self-serving interpretations that fill the pages of *My Life*. A presidential memoir is a work of history unlike any other, and falsehoods should not be permitted to stand without correction.

Here, then, is a partial list of the statements in *My Life* that require rectification.

GENNIFER FLOWERS

In Clinton's recital of the facts of the Gennifer Flowers scandal, he mentions that he helped to get his girlfriend a state job. But he leaves out a key element of the story: Only a few months before the 1992 New Hampshire primary, Clinton shunted aside a more qualified African American woman in favor of Flowers, overruling the unanimous finding of his own Grievance Review Committee to do so.

Flowers asked Clinton for a state job in early 1991, as the governor was gearing up for the presidential race. After one false start, Clinton's aide located a position as an administrative assistant at the State Board of Review. One Clara Clark, a unit supervisor at the board, was getting promoted, creating a vacancy. But there was a problem: Don K.

Barnes, chairman of the board, had already slated Charlette Perry, an African American board employee, to be promoted into Clark's job.

To bypass Perry and hire Flowers, the board changed the job description of Clark's position, emphasizing the need for someone with public relations experience—a bid to capitalize on Flowers' brief stint as a reporter for a local television station.

But Perry appealed to the Grievance Review Committee. The hearing on her case was held on October 9, 1991, just six days after Clinton announced his candidacy for president.

The committee ruled that Perry should get the job. "In the case at hand," they wrote, "the agency [which was to have hired Flowers] was unable to convince the Committee of any overriding need for an employee skilled in 'public relations' . . . to the extent that the maxim of internal hire should be breached."

Flowers was out, and the plaintiff was awarded back pay. But then Barnes, a Clinton political appointee, exercised his legal authority, overruled his committee, and kept Flowers in the job—a position she held for only a few months before she was fired for missing work after she spilled her story to the *Star*.

The key moment in the Flowers case came when she produced tapes of conversations with Clinton, which certainly substantiated a relationship, though its nature wasn't definitively settled by the recordings. In *My Life*, Clinton notes that a Los Angeles television station retained an expert who said that the tape was "selectively edited."

The expert, whom Clinton doesn't name, was the infamous private detective Anthony Pellicano, who has quite a background. Accused of using thuggish tactics on *Los Angeles Times* reporter Anita Busch to stop her from working on a story critical of one of his clients, Pellicano was arrested by the FBI for holding an arsenal of weapons including a drawer full of hand grenades and, in the words of one FBI agent, enough plastique to "take out a 747." The former president also does not mention that Flowers's tapes were submitted to the Truth Verification Labs, which found them to be authentic.

PAULA JONES

Clinton writes that Judge Susan Weber Wright dismissed all evidence in the Jones deposition relating to Monica Lewinsky because it was not essential to the core issue of sexual harassment in the lawsuit. The former president claims that this decision vitiated Kenneth Starr's contention that Clinton had committed perjury. Lying under oath, the former president writes, can only be a crime when it relates to a "material" matter, and the Wright ruling meant that the statements about his relationship with Lewinsky weren't material to the Jones case.

Here Clinton acts like the proverbial child who killed his mother and father and then pled for clemency because he was an orphan! The reason Judge Wright ruled that evidence pertaining to the Clinton-Lewinsky relationship wasn't pertinent was that Clinton had denied having an affair with the intern while she worked in the White House, so no sexual harassment could have been involved. But Clinton did indeed have an affair with Lewinsky while she worked for him as part of the White House staff; if Clinton had told the truth in his deposition, Wright would not have tossed out the evidence.

Clinton then goes on to point with pride to Judge Wright's summary judgment in the case, dismissing Jones's claims without a trial. He says that her action showed the "raw political" nature of Starr's inquiry. Starr, he said, was going after him for perjury in a deposition the judge had said was "not relevant," in a case she had dismissed as having "no merit."

Once again, the orphan asks for clemency. The Jones case was thrown out because there was no supporting evidence of a pattern of sexual harassment by Clinton—evidence that the Lewinsky relationship, had Clinton told the truth about it, might have provided.

Then Clinton says that he settled with Paula Jones, despite the fact that he had "won a clear victory" in the case, because he wanted to work for the American people and didn't want to spend "five minutes" more on the Jones case.

Hardly. Clinton would have likely lost on appeal, as he admits, because Wright's exclusion of Lewinsky as a possible witness was based on the president's lies under oath. The Clintons ended up paying $850,000 to settle the Jones suit, and were specifically barred from using their legal defense fund to pay the settlement. As Clinton admits, the settlement took half of his life savings.

There is no way Clinton would have settled if he'd ultimately expected to win the case. Hillary and Bill watched every last dime, and since most of their savings resulted from Rose Law Firm earnings, Hillary could not have been happy to lose the money because of her husband's indiscretions. He settled because he had to.

In a final sleight of hand, Clinton reports that Judge Wright sanctioned him for "violating her discovery orders." This is a euphemistic way of saying that she said he had lied under oath in the Jones deposition, and that this violated her order to testify truthfully. And the former president does not even mention that this sanction led the Arkansas Bar Association to suspend his law license for five years—a harsh penalty to mete out to a sitting president who had once served as the state's attorney general, its chief law enforcement officer.

WEBB HUBBELL

There is no dispute that Clinton's people worked overtime to get consulting jobs for Webb Hubbell after Bill and Hillary's longtime friend—and Mrs. Clinton's law partner—resigned from his position at the Justice Department in March 1994. In all, they succeeded in landing more than half a million dollars in consulting gigs for the Clinton crony.

The question for contemporaneous prosecutors and subsequent historians is: Were the contracts just ways of helping an old friend, or were they payoffs designed to keep Hubbell quiet about what he knew in the Whitewater scandal?

That Hubbell knew everything is not in dispute. Jim McDougal noted that Webb knew it all.

One key to grasping the motives of Clinton's friends in helping Hubbell is whether the Clintons knew that Hubbell had ripped off the Rose Law Firm—and by extension Hillary herself—through his overbilling, the offense for which he went to prison. If the first couple didn't know he was culpable, they would have had no reason not to help out an old friend. But if they realized that he had defrauded them, it's hard to believe that friendship could have been the motive for their zealous efforts to help Hubbell.

In *Living History* and in *My Life,* the Clintons both take the posture that they did not know. Hillary says that she "assumed that Webb was . . . being falsely accused."

As the *New York Times* has reported, though, they must have known the charges were true. The newspaper reported that Jim Blair, Hillary's erstwhile guide to the commodities market bonanza, was told that there was "strong proof" of Hubbell's overbilling, and that he needed to resign "as quickly as possible."

When the Clintons encouraged their friends and advisers—men like Small Business Administrator Erskine Bowles and Trade Representative Mickey Kantor—to come to Hubbell's aid, they both must have known that he had been stealing from Hillary's law firm for years.

CAMPAIGN FINANCE

Clinton writes, with outraged innocence, that the press was implying that he had been "selling" overnight stays in the White House for campaign contributions as he raised funds for the 1996 campaign.

He calls the allegations "ridiculous," and says he would never have used the White House "in that way."

He notes that a list of his first-term guests showed that 85 percent were relatives, friends of Chelsea's, dignitaries, or people the Clintons had known before he ran for president. But aren't these preexisting friends precisely the people Clinton would go to for campaign contributions?

Here is a partial list of contributions Clinton and the Democrats got from his overnight guests:

Donors Who Spent the Night at the White House and Gave More Than $100,000 to Clinton's 1996 Campaign and Other Democratic Committees

Name	Amount Contributed
Dirk Ziff	$436,000
Lew & Edith Wasseman	$301,088
William Rollnick	$279,000
Steven & Maureen Rattner	$265,000
David Geffen	$234,300
Peter W. May	$231,455
Paul L. Cejas	$265,775
Steven Spielberg	$225,000
Carl H. Lindner	$220,500
Carl Spielvogel & Barbaralee Diamonstein-Spielvogel	$218,500
Steven Grossman	$212,702
Bernard & Audre Rapoport	$208,750
Angelo Tsakopoulos	$194,000
Walter Kaye	$171,510
Eli Broad	$162,500
Steven P. Jobs	$150,000
Stanley S. Shuman	$139,500
Ron Burkle	$132,000
Roy L. Furman	$129,500
Lewis Rudin	$128,830
Merv Adelson	$117, 918

Together, these overnight guests alone contributed more than $4.4 million to Clinton's campaign and to other Democratic causes in the

1996 election cycle. Many more donors who gave less than $100,000 were also hosted overnight at the White House.

And during Hillary's 2000 Senate race, the *Washington Post* reported that one hundred overnight guests at the White House contributed a total of $624,000 to her campaign.

Continuing the charade, Clinton had also contended that the coffees he held at the White House were not fund raisers, just interesting discussions with people he was happy to meet anyway. (To have used the White House to hold fund raisers would have been illegal.) But *quelle chance!* It turns out that plenty of those who happened to turn up at the coffees gave generously to the Clinton campaign and other Democratic causes.

Big donors were called and especially invited to meet with the president at these special coffees in the White House. Nobody was crass enough to ask for a check then and there. But before they came, and after they left, they were solicited heavily.

Here's a list of attendees at these coffees who gave Clinton and other Democratic causes more than $100,000 in the 1996 election cycle:

Donors Who Attended White House Coffees and Gave More Than $100,000 to Clinton's 1996 Campaign and Other Democratic Committees

Name	Amount Contributed
Dirk Ziff	$436,000
Walter H. Shorenstein	$334,350
Haim & Cheryl Saban	$326,000
Gail Zappa	$292,650
William D. Rollnick	$279,000
Melvyn I. Weiss	$274,500
Dr. Richard Machado Gonzalez	$262,100
Jon S. Corzine	$251,750

Name	Amount Contributed
Julia E. Fishelson	$246,250
Peter W. May	$231,455
Craig & Kathryn Hall	$231,050
Paul L. Cejas	$226,775
Mark B. Dayton	$225,650
Carl H. Lindner	$220,500
Bernard & Audre Rapoport	$208,750
Angelo Tsakopoulos	$194,000
John E. Williams Jr.	$190,900
Paul Goldenberg	$186,475
David S. Steiner	$185,460
Frank & Debbie Branson	$175,304
Michael D. Palm	$166,400
J. Shelby Bryan	$165,400
Michael A. Caddell	$164,500
Lawrence F. O'Brien III	$163,650
Eli Broad	$162,500
David Bonderman	$157,750
Peter & Mary Beth Borre	$157,500
Stanley S. Shuman	$139,500
John P. Manning	$134,790
Diane Weiss	$132,200
Ron Burkle	$132,000
Barrie A. Wigmore	$131,500
Lewis Rudin	$128,830
Lionel I. Pincus	$127,500
Robert B. Menschel	$126,000
Stan L. McLelland	$123,700
Elaine Schuster	$121,210
Steven Roth	$115,500
James A. Harmon	$102,900
Raymond D. Nasher	$102,700

Donald Sussman	$102,000
William B. Dockser	$102,000
Peter Mathias	$100,000

Some of the names appear on both lists—because they had coffee in the White House *and* spent the night there!

Of course, many of the donors on both lists are well-known figures, who probably would have contributed even without such treatment. Two U.S. senators, for example, adorn the list: Jon Corzine of New Jersey and Mark Dayton of Minnesota. But the connection between the coffees and fund raising for most of the donors is quite clear. Together, these contributors gave more than $7 million to Clinton and other Democratic committees during the 1996 campaign cycle.

Clinton is almost totally silent on the accusations that the Chinese government funneled large sums of money into his reelection campaign in 1996, primarily through the auspices of his old friends the Riadys, the prominent Indonesian financiers. Indeed James Riady makes no appearance in *My Life,* despite his massive fund-raising for Clinton. Disingenuously, the former president makes only one reference to the scandal, which consumed vast amounts of media attention and has not yet been fully resolved. He notes that getting China admitted to the World Trade Organization (WTO) was made more difficult by a "spate of anti-China stories," in the media including allegations that Beijing had steered money into "the 1996 campaign." *Whose* 1996 campaign? He doesn't say. (While funds did flow from China into the coffers of several Democrats and Republicans candidates that year, the main story was the money that went into *Clinton's* campaign.)

The donations from China, all illegal, were quite overt and galling. Rich Lowry's book *Legacy: Paying the Price for the Clinton Years,* itemizes the contributions:

■ The head of Chinese military intelligence, General Ji Shengde, told Clinton fund-raiser Johnny Chung: "We like your president very much. We would like to see him reelected. I will give you $300,000. You can give it to the president and the Democratic Party." Chung gave $100,000 of this to the Democratic National Committee.

- Maria Hsia, identified by the Senate committee that investigated the scandal as "an agent of the Chinese government," organized a fund-raiser for Al Gore at Hsi Lai Temple and funneled about $150,000 into Democratic causes in the 1996 cycle.

- Ted Sioeng, whom the FBI called a "cultural agent" of the Chinese government, and his family gave $400,000 to the Democratic National Committee.

- Np Lap Seng, who the Senate Committee found was "a hotel tycoon in Macao with reputed links to organized crime who advises the Chinese government," gave $1.4 million to Clinton friend Charlie Trie to help fund his contributions to Clinton.

But what Lowry calls "the epicenter" of the fund raising from foreign sources was James Riady and the Lippo Group, an "enormous Indonesian business with ties to the Chinese government." Riady had given $750,000 in illegal contributions to the Democratic National Committee in 1992 and worked with John Huang to raise $1.6 million in illegal funding in 1996.

That wasn't the end of the services the Lippo Group extended to the Clintons. After Webb Hubbell resigned from the Justice Department, when the president's friends were scrambling around to find him work, the Lippo Group stepped up and signed a consulting contract with Clinton's old buddy. Later, after former Arkansas governor Jim Guy Tucker was indicted, convicted, and sentenced in connection with the Whitewater trial after prosecution by Kenneth Starr, the Lippo Group again stepped forward and concluded a financial deal to help the former governor.

Eventually, the Democratic National Committee had to return $2.8 million in illegal contributions to the 1996 campaigns.

Clinton also avoids any mention in his memoirs of his administration's highly controversial decision to allow U.S. satellite makers to do business with China, despite the possibility that American technology would be sent along with it. Loral Space and Communications and its chairman, Bernard Schwartz, profited immensely from the commercial deals that resulted. Schwartz was the biggest contributor to the Clinton campaign in 1996, and the largest donor to the Democrats in the 1998 midterm elections, giving a total of $1.1 million to the party from 1992 through 1998.

The flow of Chinese campaign contributions into Democratic (and some Republican) coffers is especially dangerous given China's propensity to use its contacts in the American aerospace community to acquire advanced technology, and its record of re-selling nuclear and missile information to Pakistan and other nations that are seeking to develop their arsenal—possibly including North Korea.

In *My Life,* the former president takes a benign view of the question, noting that his meeting with Chinese leaders in the summer of 1998 was "not free of controversy" because Republicans had attacked him for letting U.S. firms launch commercial satellites using Beijing's missiles—although, he writes, that satellite technology was "not accessible" to the Chinese.

But Bill Gertz, the defense and national security reporter for the *Washington Times,* begs to differ in his book *Betrayal: How the Clinton Administration Undermined American Security.*

Gertz reports that after the February 15, 1996, explosion of a Chinese rocket on its launch pad, "a team of scientists from Hughes [Electronics] and Loral [Space and Communications, Ltd.] was formed to find out what happened. Their conclusion: An electrical problem in the flight guidance system caused a malfunction." Helpfully, the two firms, "without informing the U.S. government . . . gave the results of its accident report to" China's missile developers. Gertz notes that the information "not only helped the Chinese company improve its commercial space launchers but also helped make China's nuclear-tipped missiles more reliable as ICBMs"—the type of rocket that can hit the United States!

Reporting on the incident, the Pentagon wrote in December 1998 that "the Chinese were provided with technical data and assistance from Hughes' failure investigation that enabled the Chinese launch manufacturer and launch service provider to make design and/or operational launch vehicle reliability."

The problems with technology transfers to the Chinese started in 1996, when "the export of advanced satellite communications technology was de-controlled by President Clinton when he removed the State and Defense Department oversight of high-tech 'dual use' items. The CEOs of Lockheed, Loral, and Hughes supported the Clinton executive order, and it allowed China to purchase sophisticated anti-jamming and encryption for its military satellite systems."

Clinton transferred control over export licenses for these high-tech products to the Department of Commerce, where strategic considerations were more likely to be sublimated to commercial concerns.

Clinton's claims that the technology had no military significance are belied by the fact that in 1998 Hughes "offered an advanced satellite . . . previously sold to China to the U.S. military for wartime communications."

As a result of this massive leaking of American technology, "Hughes was charged with no less than 123 violations of national security and Loral paid a record fine for its violations."

Clinton was also negligent in failing to crack down on China when it sold nuclear and missile technology to Pakistan and, possibly, to North Korea. As Gertz writes: "President Clinton ignored and covered up China's dangerous weapons and technology transfers," which other nations used to beef up their nuclear and missile delivery systems. "When the evidence of sanctionable activity could not be ignored, only the mildest sanctions were imposed, and even then they were quickly lifted."

In *My Life*, Clinton continues to make excuses for the Chinese. Defending his decision to admit China to the World Trade Organization without requiring progress on human rights issues in return, he notes that Secretary of State Warren Christopher sent him a report noting that China had resolved all its emigration cases, agreed to reform its prison labor practices, and agreed to adhere to the Universal Declaration of Human Rights. If Beijing has made any progress on granting democracy and human rights to its people, it will come as news to the one billion Chinese, who see little or no movement in that direction.

Why did Clinton play so fast and loose with our security? Gertz explains that "Clinton had promised American businesses not to punish weapons proliferators with sanctions so as not to interrupt trade with those nations."

President Clinton took office after the end of the Cold War, and he believed deeply that economics, trade, and job creation were the proper function of foreign policy. He tended to subordinate military and intelligence considerations to the economic requirements of a job-creating American economy. He felt that a focus on military rivalries with other nations was an antiquated and anachronistic throwback to an earlier age.

Politically, economically, and financially, he was very closely connected to the high-tech industries, particularly on the West Coast. With their strong support, he had carried all three coastal states and had added them to the Democratic Party base. It was his devout conviction that it was best to permit a relatively free flow of technology, in order to help America advance and prosper by strengthening the companies that bolstered the U.S. lead in these areas. If that required sales to foreign companies, he was proud to win the contracts for the United States and to shortcut efforts by the Europeans to horn in.

It wasn't that Clinton was a traitor, or was selling American security for campaign contributions. It was rather that, until 9/11, he failed to recognize how dangerous the world had become, and how easily technology could fall into the wrong hands. Whatever the innocence of his motivation, though, the fact remains: In the name of helping high tech companies in the United States, he severely compromised American security.

PARDONS

President Clinton's pardons at the end of his second term still rankle as some of the worst and most corrupt decisions of his presidency.

In *My Life*, he defends them by citing the fact that he pardoned only 456 people while Reagan had pardoned 406, Carter 566, and Ford 409. He states that the first President Bush pardoned only 77 people, but notes that they included those who were being prosecuted in the Iran-Contra scandal.

He defends his pardon to Marc Rich, the fugitive who denounced his U.S. citizenship and left the country rather than face justice at the hands of an American jury, and who has still refused to return to the United States. Why would the president pardon a man who gave up his American citizenship? Clinton blandly alludes to the fact that Rich's former wife, Denise, was "a supporter" of his.

"Supporter" hardly covers it. As CNN has reported, Denise Rich gave $450,000 to Clinton's Presidential Library Foundation, in three installments in 1998, 1999, and 2000. On a more personal level, she gave two coffee tables and chairs to the Clintons worth $7,375. She also gave $70,000 to Hillary Clinton's campaign, $10,000 to the Clintons' legal defense fund, and $1 million to the Democratic Party and Democratic candidates.

Contributions to the Clinton Library are really funds that the former president can use as he pleases, subject only to the oversight of a board he appoints and that serves at his pleasure.

In *My Life*, Clinton says that the key factor in his decision to grant a pardon to Rich was the intervention of Israeli prime minister Ehud Barak, who spoke of the millionaire's usefulness to the Jewish state. But neither Clinton nor Barak specify the nature of Rich's contributions to Israel, and why that should justify pardoning someone who no longer wished to be a U.S. citizen. In any event, one wonders why the president of the United States should feel inclined to pardon a fugitive because he is helpful to his adopted country. Clinton was far less obliging with Jonathan Pollard, the spy he refused to pardon despite the desperate entreaties of the American and Israeli Jewish communities.

While most attention focused on the Rich pardon, Clinton does nothing to defend his other pardons—many of which were, if anything, even more outrageous.

Incredibly, he says nothing about his pardons of the FALN Puerto Rican terrorists, of the New Square leaders, or of the clients of Hillary's brothers, particularly of the notorious drug trafficker Carlos Anabel Vignali.

The FALN (Fuerzas Armadas de Liberacion Nacional—the Armed Forces of National Liberation) is the Puerto Rican equivalent of the Irish Republican Army (IRA). Dedicated to achieving independence for Puerto Rico (despite the overwhelming rejection of that alternative in recent referenda on the island), they conducted 130 bombings in the United States from 1974 to 1983. Six people died in these attacks. One victim was the husband of a pregnant woman; another left two children, ages nine and eleven.

The pressure for these pardons came from New York's Puerto Rican politicians. New York Congressman José Serrano called them political prisoners and sent Clinton an open letter demanding their release. Despite the opposition of FBI Director Louis Freeh, the Justice Department, the FBI's assistant director of national security, and Carlos Romero-Barcelo, Puerto Rico's congressional delegate, Clinton offered sixteen FALN terrorists clemency in September 1999, just as Hillary was beginning her Senate campaign in New York.

Joseph Connor, whose father was killed in an FALN attack at Fraunces Tavern in New York City, writes: "The Clinton family traded the release of terrorists for votes; votes that were promised to be delivered by New York politicians to Hillary for Senate and Gore for president. That was clear."

It wasn't the only votes-for-pardon deal Clinton made. He also pardoned four leaders of the New Square Hasidic Jewish Community who had been convicted of defrauding the government of $40 million by billing for scholarships for 1,500 phantom students. Hillary visited New Square during her Senate campaign, and participated in an unusual White House meeting with New Square leaders on December 22, 2000, right after her election. The president pardoned all four of the imprisoned leaders. The New Square Community voted for Mrs. Clinton by 1,400 to 12, even though neighboring Hasidic districts went for her Republican opponent.

But the most outrageous pardon went to convicted drug dealer Carlos Vignali, who was convicted of shipping *half a ton* of cocaine to Minnesota and sentenced to fifteen years in prison. His father gave $160,000 to Democrats in the 2000 cycle, but also paid $200,000 to Hugh Rodham, Hillary's brother, to help secure a pardon for his wayward boy. Hillary denied any connection or knowledge of the pardon, and Clinton makes no mention of it in *My Life*. While Clinton says he pardoned "girlfriends" who were caught up in their boyfriends' drug dealing, often unknowingly, Vignali was no girlfriend: He was a flat-out drug trafficker.

(Hillary's brothers successfully promoted two other pardons-for-cash. One went to Almon Glenn Braswell, a con artist, who gave Hugh Rodham $200,000; the other went to Edward and Vonna Jo Gregory, carnival owners who were convicted of bank fraud, who gave brother Tony Rodham money to serve as their consultant while they pursued the pardon. The couple also gave $102,000 to Hillary and other Democrats.)

Clinton's abuse of his pardon power—the most absolute such power a president has—is, well, unpardonable. But perhaps even more shocking is that he felt able to spend so little time, in a book of almost a thousand pages, even attempting to defend any of these offensive decisions. He notes that the Justice Department routinely opposed granting pardons, which he attributes to a bureaucratic desire for self-protection, but he never provides any justification for overriding the advice of the professionals who were engaged to counsel him.

After a massive public storm, Hugh Rodham, at least, returned the money he was paid to secure pardons. But those on whose behalf he intervened are nevertheless free.

Why was Clinton so profligate with his pardons? Was it corruption, pure and simple? Of course the money that Denise Rich showered upon him—and any personal friendship they might have had—must have influenced his decision to pardon her ex-husband in response to her entreaties. And clearly Hillary's brothers must have played a role in his decision to pardon their clients as well.

But Clinton's library will cost upwards of $165 million. In that context, Denise Rich's $450,000 was really a pittance.

I believe that part of what motivated Clinton was that he was feeling bitter and alienated when he gave out his pardons. He used them to lash out at the judicial system, and felt a kinship with those who were its targets—whether deservedly or not. He lent a willing ear to those who shared stories with him of people who were unfairly prosecuted, each tale of woe likely reinforcing his own self-image as a victim rather than as a defendant who had lied under oath.

In *My Life,* he writes affectionately of Hillary's brothers, noting that they were "wonderfully supportive" during his impeachment ordeal. Both brothers spent large blocks of time with him in the White House during the process, doubtless bucking him up when he needed it. Clinton notes how Hugh Rodham flew up from Miami every week to talk sports, play cards, and joke with the embattled and isolated president. In this atmosphere of shared camaraderie and gallows humor, it is easy to see how the pardons of the brothers' clients were issued.

(What is less understandable is Hillary's ardent and repeated denial that she knew about the pardons of her brothers' clients. How likely is it that Clinton would have subjected his wife to the bitter press attacks that followed the revelation of the pardons—and the fees her brothers earned to obtain them—but not have told her about it in advance? When she was out there in public as the new senator from New York?)

The former president wins the chutzpah award when he criticizes the first President Bush for his pardon of former defense secretary Caspar Weinberger and five others who were indicted in Iran-Contra by special prosecutor Lawrence Walsh. The announcement that Walsh was about to indict Weinberger was made five days before the 1992 election, and may well have swung the result toward Bill Clinton. Tracking polls in the closing days of the 1992 election suggest that Bush was gaining quickly on Clinton and had about pulled even. But when Walsh announced he was going to indict Weinberger, the Bush momentum stopped and Clinton regained his former lead.

And why did Walsh feel free to spring this November surprise and announce the indictment days before the polls opened in the 1992 race? His partisanship in the timing of this announcement is far worse than any partisan intervention of Kenneth Starr. Starr never risked influencing an election by direct action hours before the voting. Walsh did.

And what does the former president say about his predecessor's pardons in *My Life*? He quotes with approval Walsh's comment that they demonstrate how "powerful people" can commit crimes without "consequence."

THE ROSE LAW FIRM

During the 1992 presidential race, one of Clinton's strongest opponents, former California governor Jerry Brown, criticized Hillary Clinton for receiving legal fees at the Rose Law Firm on state business sent to the firm by her husband, the state's governor. Clinton springs to Hillary's defense in *My Life*, noting that Hillary had these state fees deleted from the firm's income before her share of the prof-its was calculated, so she "did not receive any benefit" from business he had sent her.

What Clinton writes is technically true. But when I proposed to Hillary that she abstain from taking legal fees for state business while Bill was governor, she told me that she planned to increase her share of the draw on the remaining business the firm received to compensate for the loss of income from state business. Later, a well-known investigative reporter told me that he had seen an internal memo in the Rose Law Firm confirming that this practice had indeed been adopted.

Hillary's actions, then, disprove Bill's words: Indirectly, she made sure she *would* receive monetary benefit commensurate with the business her husband had sent the firm.

THE WHITE HOUSE TRAVEL OFFICE

The Travel Office firings never should have become a scandal. It was perfectly legal for the Clintons to fire the employees of the office, and except for some complaining by the media, it would have amounted to nothing—except that the Clintons tried to justify the firings by al-leging improprieties at the office. Hillary then made it into a full-fledged scandal by making, in the words of Special Prosecutor Robert Ray, "factually inaccurate" statements under oath about her role in the affair.

The Clintons didn't need to offer an explanation for the dis-missals. And they certainly shouldn't have attempted to besmirch the reputations of those who had staffed the office under Bush. They should simply have fired them.

In *My Life*, Clinton feels obliged to stick to the story that led to the scandal in the first place. He says that the firings took place after he had received the results of an audit by KPMG Peat Marwick, which found an "off-the-books ledger with $18,000 not properly ac-counted for."

But Clinton omits two points: First, the audit was completed after, not before, the Travel Office staff was fired. Second, the audit found no dishonesty. The funds were eventually fully accounted for, and Billy Dale, the head of the office for thirty-two years, was acquitted of all charges.

Why did the Clintons want to replace the Travel Office staff? Most likely because Harry Thomason, a key friend and supporter, had an interest in an air charter called TRM, and according to Barbara Olson he "was anxious to get a White House contract." It was Thomason who first raised a red flag about the Travel Office with the Clintons.

In *My Life*, the former president acts as though the firings of the Travel Office staff were initiated by Chief of Staff Mack McLarty and David Watkins, who was in charge of White House administration. In fact, Watkins noted that there was "pressure for action" from Mrs. Clinton.

I know what "pressure for action" from Hillary Clinton means. I have seen her when she's fixated on something, usually driven by a desire to pay back a friend or a donor for a favor. She nags and pushes until it gets done. Bill rarely cares one way or the other; in fact, he can be something of an ingrate when it comes to rewarding his friends. But Hillary is determined when she feels a loyal supporter has a good case. She was likely driven here by her feeling that the Travel Office staff, after so many years of Republican presidents (twenty years out of the previous twenty-four), was loyal to the GOP and could not be trusted. It was likely her fear of the partisanship of the Travel Office, coupled with her desire to reward Thomason, that prompted her to become such a bear on this issue.

But Hillary told the grand jury—and repeats in her book *Living History*—that it was just an "offhand comment" that sparked the vendetta against the Travel Office employees. But Watkins tells a different story. In a memo he wrote in January 1996, he said: "While I was in Memphis, [Vince] Foster told me that it was important that I speak directly with the First Lady that day. I called her that evening and she conveyed to me in clear terms her desire for swift and clear action to resolve the situation [i.e., firing the Travel Office staff]. She mentioned that [Harry] Thomason had explained how the Travel Office could be run after removing the current staff . . . and in light of that she thought immediate action was in order."

Watkins wrote to McLarty that "we both knew that there would be hell to pay if . . . we failed to take swift and decisive action in conformity with the First Lady's wishes."

But before the grand jury, Hillary denied playing the key role in the firings. Special Prosecutor Robert Ray—Starr's successor, who was generally kind to the Clintons—concluded that "Mrs. Clinton's input into the process was significant, if not the significant factor influencing the pace of events in the Travel Office firings and the ultimate decision to fire the employees."

So why was Hillary never indicted for perjury? As Fox News reported: "Prosecutors decided not to seek perjury charges because they said a key element, intent, would have been difficult to prove. The report said that when Mrs. Clinton testified she did not have a role, she might not have understood the impact of her conversations on White House staff."

Despite the harshness of the special prosecutor's report, and the narrowness of Hillary's escape, Clinton loyally reports that there was "no evidence of wrongdoing, conflicts of interest, or criminality" by anyone at the White House uncovered by any investigation of the Travel Office. Technically true—*just*.

MONICA LEWINSKY

Clinton discusses this scandal and the resulting impeachment at tedious length in *My Life*. But he never mentions the one pivotal fact upon which the entire process hinged: the DNA stain on Monica's famous blue dress. Telling the story of this sordid affair without acknowledging the forensic evidence that forced the president to tell the truth is like discussing Noah's Ark without mentioning the rain.

Yet in *My Life*, perhaps in a final attempt to fool history, the former president never explains his motivation for finally telling the world (or, if we believe his account, his wife) the truth about his affair with Lewinsky. He leaves it to us to guess why he confessed. We are left with the impression that it was his looming Grand Jury testimony that impelled the admission, as if lying under oath were something he would avoid at all costs.

But isn't it irrefutable that the evidence of the DNA forced the president to tell the truth about what went on behind closed doors? The stain took the scandal out of the realm of *he said–she said*, the land of ambiguity where he so often concealed his conduct, and put it into the realm of facts and evidence.

His failure to mention DNA, and Hillary's lack of candor in her book, make it doubly hard to believe that Hillary did not know about Lewinsky before Clinton told her, on the morning of his Grand Jury testimony, eight months after the relationship was publicly reported in the *Washington Post*.

Indeed, before that tearful confession, the following facts had appeared in the public press: that Lewinsky had been taped describing the affair in intimate detail; that she had frequently visited the White House long after she stopped working there; that Evelyn Lieberman—the deputy chief of staff and virtually a Hillary appointee—had moved to ship Lewinsky out of the White House for becoming too close to Clinton; that Bill had lied about his affair with Flowers to Hillary; that Lewinsky had told Vernon Jordan she had sex with Bill; and that the president had given her a copy of Walt Whitman's *Leaves of Grass*, the same book he gave Hillary after their second date.

Now, to find out that Starr had asked for a blood sample to match a stain on a blue dress Lewinsky had put back in her closet after a visit with Clinton—and still not know that the affair had taken place—is an act of either colossal blindness or total stupidity.

It's far more reasonable to believe Hillary knew all along.

Among the other facts Clinton omits from his description of the Lewinsky affair:

- That Vernon Jordan, his close confidante, had gotten Lewinsky to give him an affidavit denying an affair with Clinton.
- That he told the grand jury that his affair with Lewinsky took place after she left the White House, when it really happened while she worked there. The difference, of course, is whether the affair was relevant to a claim of sexual harassment such as Jones was making.
- Clinton writes about his visits with Lewinsky, but omits the more than one hundred times that Lewinsky claims they had intimate conversations over the phone.
- He never mentions his coaching sessions with his secretary Betty Currie, where he led her by saying things like "we [Monica and I] were never alone, right?"

Clinton also skirts the truth when he says that he "never asked [Monica Lewinsky] to lie." The fact is that he sent her to his friend, high-powered attorney Vernon Jordan, who persuaded her to give him an affidavit denying that she had an affair with the president. It was another technical truth that concealed the fundamental lie: Of course Clinton himself did not ask Monica to lie. But of course he was involved in Jordan's request that she do so.

Finally, throughout the description of the scandal and the impeachment that followed, Clinton regularly characterizes it as an attempt by the Republicans to reverse the course of an election and to force him out of power. He writes that "first, last, and always" his fight with the Republicans was about "power." He says that the Republicans thought that the people had made a mistake in electing him twice, and that they were determined to use "my personal mistakes" to oust him from office.

But it is worth remembering that a successful effort to remove Clinton from office would not have turned the nation over to

Gingrich and his ilk: In fact, it would have led to an Al Gore presidency. Clinton's policies would have been continued; only Clinton himself would have disappeared.

WHITEWATER AND KEN STARR

Clinton switches roles with Kenneth Starr in *My Life*. He becomes the prosecutor attacking the independent counsel, and Starr becomes the defendant. Condemning Starr's tactics, Clinton says that the Republicans and the special prosecutor pursued him so avidly in the hope that if they attacked him hard enough the media and the voters would come to blame Clinton for "their" bad conduct.

Casting the fight as a "struggle"—both legal and political—against people who "abused the criminal and civil laws and had seriously hurt many innocent people as they tried to destroy" his presidency, Clinton says he was determined not to let those he called "reactionaries" prevail.

In Bill Clinton's view of reality, the world is turned upside down: The hunted becomes the hunter, and vice versa.

Clinton's strategy in defeating the Starr investigation was akin to Czar Alexander's tactics in defeating Napoleon when the French emperor invaded Russia in 1812. The czar's troops lost every battle, as Napoleon's heretofore invincible armies marched deep into Russian territory. Fighting and retreating, battling and pulling back, they lured Napoleon deeper and deeper into Russia's heartland, stringing out his supply lines and trying his army's patience. By the time Bonaparte conquered Moscow—which the Russians burned as he marched in—he was demoralized and defeated by the length of his journey, even though he had won every battle. Then the Russian winter set in, and finished off the job the czar's army had begun.

In much the same way, Clinton lost the vast majority of his legal battles with Kenneth Starr. He sought to keep the Secret Service from testifying about his dalliances with Monica. His attorneys tried to quash Starr's subpoenas. His allies battled to acquit his Whitewater cronies, the McDougals and Tucker, after Starr indicted them. He went all the way to the Supreme Court to stop the Jones lawsuit from proceeding. And he lost at every turn.

But each defeat dragged out the Starr investigation, adding to the cost and further trying the public's patience. Like the scorched earth policy of the Russian army, where all towns, crops, and fodder were burned before Napoleon's army arrived, Starr met with stonewalling witnesses, shredded documents, and procedural delays at every turn.

Each delay meant another upward click of the meter in the cost of the inquiry, a statistic Clinton's defenders broadcast so frequently that it came to resemble McDonald's signs trumpeting its burger sales: "More than $52 Million Spent."

By the time Starr actually brought Congress his report, which led to Clinton's impeachment, he was like Napoleon arriving in Moscow to find the city in flames. Public discontent with his investigation had so metastasized that the prosecutor had a higher negative rating than the man he was investigating.

It was Clinton's genius to realize that Starr was, in effect, a candidate running against him, not a prosecutor probing him in a court of law. Each week we polled on Starr's favorable/unfavorable rating, celebrating any jump in his negatives as if we were facing another candidate in an election. In fact, in *My Life,* Clinton quotes the polls noting that only 26 percent felt that Starr was conducting an impartial investigation, while writing, on the same page, that his job approval was up to 72 percent.

To arrive at this distorted view of what the Starr investigation was really all about, Bill Clinton had to construct a structure of distortions, misinterpretations, omissions, and innuendo to build an entirely false and artificial idea of the prosecution and the independent counsel.

Returning from an interview with Starr's people in 1995 at the White House for a meeting with me, the president threw himself into his wing chair in his East Wing residence office. He leaned forward, animated with anger, and said that he was "so disgusted, so revolted, so sick at the slime of Starr's people"—his S's rolling off his lips—that he told me he had to take a shower after the ordeal. "I felt physically dirty to have been with these creepy, crawly people," he told me, his face crinkling with each *C*.

Given such an introduction, I was understandably hesitant when I arrived in late January 2001, one week after Bush's inauguration, for a cruise with the Dixie branch—the "rebel" chapter—of the Young President's Organization (YPO), only to find out that my co-speaker was none other than Kenneth Starr. Steeling myself, Eileen and I went over to his table and met the prosecutor and his wife, Alice. Expecting a stern, reactionary, bigoted prude, we found instead an engaging couple with a lively wit, a balanced perspective, and a deeply spiritual—but not doctrinaire—view of life.

As we rehashed old war stories, we became quite close and friendly; by journey's end, we were Alice and Ken, Eileen and Dick. (But the new camaraderie didn't stop me from opening my speech by noting that I'd only agreed to join Starr on a ship after my former boss had relinquished his control over the U.S. submarine fleet!)

Clinton's distortions of the Starr inquiry's record are truly a contortionist's attempt to bend the truth, satisfying his need for vindication by vilifying his enemy:

- The former president criticizes Kenneth Starr for indicting Clinton's old Arkansas friend Webb Hubbell after the former Justice Department official had served time for overbilling the Rose Law Firm. But he doesn't say that the indictment was for not paying taxes on the $700,000 in income Hubbell allegedly earned as a result of intervention on his behalf by Clinton operatives—money Starr said might have been hush money to silence Hubbell about Whitewater and other issues.

- Clinton says that Jim McDougal was under investigation to determine if he had made any illegal contributions to any politician. The former president then goes on to say that his campaign contributions were open for public inspection, and that neither he nor Hillary ever owed money to Madison Guaranty. Again, *technically* true. But Clinton did get lots of money for his gubernatorial campaigns from McDougal. The governor held a fund-raiser at Madison on April 4, 1985, to help him pay back a $50,000 personal loan Clinton had taken out (from another bank) for his 1984 campaign for reelection.

- Clinton complains that not only did he lose money in the Whitewater deal, but that he and Hillary didn't take the full tax deduction for their losses, to which he claims they were entitled. But the fact is that, as CNN reported: "The Clintons took tax deductions in 1984 and 1985 for loan payments that the McDougals actually had paid. The Clintons made up for the deductions in 1993, paying back taxes to the IRS." Even Hillary admitted that they had made an error on their returns.

- Clinton denies asking David Hale, who ran an investment company called Capital Management Services, Inc., to lend money to Susan McDougal, a key question that relates to his involvement in the Whitewater scandal. But in *Arkansas Mischief,* the book Jim McDougal wrote as he lay dying, Clinton's former business partner writes that the governor solicited the loan to help "pay off the last $25,000 note left over from Whitewater." McDougal writes that Clinton asked Hale, in his presence, "Did you discuss Susan's loan?" Hale replied, "That's been taken care of." Once again, Clinton's choice of words is quite specific, and intended to mislead. It is technically true that he did not ask for a loan. He only asked whether Hale and the McDougals had "discussed" the loan. But when the governor of the state inquires as to the status of a loan discussion, it is a universally recognized shorthand for: *I want that loan made.*

- No prosecutor seems to suit Clinton. He complains loudly not only about Kenneth Starr, but also about Robert Fiske, the independent counsel named by his own attorney general. He casts aspersions on Fiske's motivation by noting that during his period supervising the investigation, "a lot of people" developed a "vested interest" in finding wrongdoing in the Whitewater affair.

- Replying to accusations that Whitewater documents were shred- ded, Clinton writes that the Rose Law Firm only destroyed docu- ments that were not related to Whitewater, and that no one in the White House knew about the document destruction at the law firm. Well, nobody but Hillary: As noted above, she testified under oath to telling the Rose Law Firm that it could proceed with shredding documents related to the Madison Bank, since they were no longer needed.

- He characterizes the Senate investigations of Whitewater as an attempt by committee chairman Alfonse D'Amato to prove that Vince Foster's death was not a suicide. But the investigation only incidentally focused on the circumstances of Foster's demise; the main issue was the removal of Whitewater documents from his office shortly after his death.

- Clinton complains of how "unpleasant" D'Amato was to his and Hillary's close friend Susan Thomases. The former president neg- lects to mention one good reason D'Amato may have had to be perturbed with Thomases: her disconcerting memory lapses. Thomases answered that she did not remember key events in the Whitewater scandal 184 times during her testimony.

- Clinton repeats the hard-to-believe story that the Rose Law Firm billing records were lost inadvertently after they were found among Vince Foster's papers following his suicide, and he attacks Starr for summoning Hillary to testify before his grand jury, calling the decision a cheap publicity stunt. The billing records concerned legal work Hillary had done on a fraudulent real estate deal known alternatively as Castle Grande or IDC. McDougal, unable to do the deal in his own name, tried to de- ceive federal regulators by using Webb Hubbell's father as a straw man in his place. Hillary was the lawyer for the deal, and that fact presented her with a problem when she testified: If she had admitted doing the legal work, she might have been party to a fraud. If she denied it, that meant she had overbilled McDougal for sixty hours of legal work—the same offense that had landed Hubbell in jail. Asked about her legal work for the IDC at the grand jury session to which Clinton so strenuously objects, Hillary denied doing any work on the deal. She later explained, out of the hearing of the grand jury, that she had known the project only as Castle Grande.

I knew it by both names. It's inconceivable to me that she didn't know the same. But she got away with it.

- Clinton criticizes Starr for seeking to remove U.S. District Court Judge Harry Woods, a Jimmy Carter appointee, from hearing any Whitewater motions, saying he was the only judge in history to be removed from a case on the basis of press articles. The truth is more complicated. When Starr indicted Governor Jim Guy Tucker, the defendant moved to dismiss the charges, saying that the prosecutor lacked jurisdiction. Clinton's attorney general, Janet Reno, wrote to Woods saying she believed Starr indeed had jurisdiction. Furious, Tucker sent an emissary to me to threaten Clinton that he knew "all about the IDC" and would talk if Clinton "is going to play the game that way." After I told Clinton of the emissary's visit, the president called me later to say that he had "taken care of" the situation. Woods later dismissed the indictment. But a federal appeals court must have smelled a rat, overruled Woods, and removed him from the case. Woods had been a guest at the Lincoln bedroom and at Camp David during the Clinton years.

- He attributes Susan McDougal's refusal to answer Kenneth Starr's questions to a fear of prosecution for perjury unless she gave him the answers he sought. Clinton, of course, pardoned Susan McDougal for the crime of contempt of court. He could just as easily have pardoned her for perjury. Indeed, Jim McDougal flatly writes, in a book that appeared long before she was actually pardoned, that Clinton told him he would pardon Susan. And Susan must have known that she would get a pardon before Clinton left office, which doubtless reinforced her courage in choosing to go to jail rather than testify.

- Clinton characterizes his conduct in covering up his liaison with Lewinsky as an attempt to "spare oneself embarrassment over private misconduct." That was surely part of it, but hardly all of it. The core of the matter was that he lied under oath in the Paula Jones deposition. It was the crime of perjury for which he was being impeached, not his personal imbroglios.

- Clinton even misrepresents his own misrepresentations. In *My Life*, he writes that he told no one what he had done with Monica Lewinsky. Of course, he had to stick to this story; it's the only way he could cover Hillary and let her continue to pretend that she was actually being deceived by him when she was blaming the charges on the right wing. Indeed, Clinton writes that when he saw his wife charge that a "vast right wing conspiracy" was behind the Lewinsky charges, he was "ashamed" about what he had done. But Clinton told me the truth and has admitted doing so. And former Dukakis campaign manager Susan Estrich told a national television audience on the Fox News Channel show *Hannity & Colmes* that Clinton had also admitted the affair to her.

- Clinton says that he felt badly that his friend Vernon Jordan was caught up in the Lewinsky scandal. Yet it was he who sent Monica to Jordan in the first place, hoping that she would absolve him of blame by signing a phony affidavit claiming that they had not had any intimate relationship. Clinton was also the one who asked Jordan to get her a job—as part of an effort to keep her placated and cooperative.

- Then, yet again, Clinton besmirches the reputation of poor Kathleen Willey. Unlike Flowers and Lewinsky, Willey did not say yes to Clinton. Nor did she make money from her charges against him, as they did. All she did was go into the Oval Office one day and ask Clinton to give her a job. While there, she claims that Clinton groped and propositioned her. She didn't even tell her story voluntarily but did so only after she was dragged before a grand jury and compelled to tell the truth. She says that she only went on the television show *60 Minutes* to tell her story to defend herself after Clinton's people had smeared her reputation.

- Clinton belittles the Starr investigation by saying that the entire investigation boiled down to "parsing" how one defines sex. Again, one senses the world turning upside down: It was Clinton, after all, who began the absurd attempt to define away sex, by claiming that what he did with Monica Lewinsky was not "sexual relations."

- Clinton charges that Starr had a conflict of interest because he says he volunteered to prepare a friend-of-the-court brief on behalf of Paula Jones. Not exactly true. Well before he became independent counsel, Starr volunteered to an independent group of conservative women supporting Jones to do a brief on the narrow issue of whether a president could be subject to a civil lawsuit while he was in office. He did not propose to comment on the merits of the Jones suit. (He never wrote the brief.)

- Clinton says that Starr went on television to defend Paula Jones. Again, not true. All he did was to say on television—before he became independent counsel—that a president could be sued in a civil action while serving in office.

- Clinton says that former U.S. attorney Jay Stephens investigated the RTC case against Madison and the Clintons, and recommended that the investigation be terminated since there was no wrongdoing. What he doesn't say is that Stephens's recommendation was made before Hillary's billing records were found, and before a check was found from Madison, endorsed by Susan McDougal, with the notation "Repayment, Clinton Loan." Clinton denied, under oath, getting any such loan.

- Clinton says that Monica Lewinsky was held against her will for hours. But in an interview for this book Starr's deputy confirmed that Monica was always free to go, and did in fact leave in the middle of the interrogation for roughly an hour, during which time she visited a nearby mall and made several phone calls (including, it was later learned, an attempt to reach the president). The reason her questioning took hours was that Lewinsky insisted on her mother's presence, and her mom would only come by train and would not fly.

Finally, he comes full circle and accuses Starr of "unconscionable conduct." He says that the prosecutor tried to attack him so that the public would fall in line, blaming the president not only for his own misconduct, but for the tiresome spectacle of Starr's investigation as well. In his formulation, he is the victim at last, Starr the offender.

The real result, however, was quite different. By the time the impeachment went to the Senate for trial, in fact, Starr himself was radioactive. Voters blamed him, not Clinton, for bringing the investigation's graphic account of the president's private life to the attention of the nation and its children. The president's misconduct was largely overlooked, and the Republicans' zeal in dragging him through impeachment was widely condemned.

I have never believed that Bill Clinton should have been removed from office. In my view, although he may not have told the truth, his conduct was not sufficiently serious to warrant overturning the results of a national election. But I *do* think that he should have been prosecuted by the Bush administration after he left office, like anyone else who may have committed perjury. If he were convicted, a civil fine would have been the appropriate punishment. Only banana republics imprison their former presidents.

THE DETECTIVES

In *My Life,* Clinton regularly cites information derogatory to his opponents. What's mysteriously missing is any account of how it came to be unearthed. The former president writes as if he were entirely unconnected to the process. But in fact the Clintons maintained a rolodex of private detectives, paid at first by their political campaign committees and later by their lawyers, to do their dirty digging for them.

These operatives, who included Terry Lenzner and Jack Palladino, worked to investigate both the Clintons' political adversaries, and women who had been objects of his private philandering.

For example, in trying to undermine the credibility of the state troopers who said they had procured women for him while he was governor, Clinton notes that several of them had been investigated for insurance fraud connected with a state police car that was destroyed in a crash in 1990. How did the story come out? Who dug it up? Who planted it in the media? *My Life* offers no answers: Clinton just repeats the charges, and leaves us to wonder.

And right in the middle of the impeachment, the incoming speaker of the House, Congressman Bob Livingston of Louisiana, was forced to resign because of a personal scandal. At about the same time, scandals also emerged concerning the private lives of other leading Republicans, including House Judiciary Committee Chairman Henry Hyde and House Government Reform Committee Chairman Dan Burton, two leading Clinton accusers. *My Life* is silent on how details of the personal lives of each of these top Republicans were unearthed just as they began to move to impeach Bill Clinton. But it seems hardly a coincidence that in each of these situations the backgrounds of Clinton's accusers suddenly surfaced on their own accord, just when they were gunning for the president.

But at least Livingston, Hyde, and Burton were politicians, and thus semi-legitimate targets for political counterattack. More often, the Clintons' detective squad has been focused on the women with whom Clinton has been linked. Whether they said yes or no to his advances, they have always been at risk of seeing their lives dragged through the media if they talked and told the truth.

Nowhere is Clinton's disingenuousness more unattractive than when he laments the damage the Starr investigation did to innocent people.

Innocent people? The road behind Clinton's ascension to the White House and his continued tenure there is littered—figuratively— with the corpses of dozens of them, all innocent people caught up in his dark world of lying and private misconduct. Here are some truly innocent people who were smeared with mud:

- Former Clinton girlfriend Sally Perdue, who told the *London Telegraph* that a "Democratic operative" told her he "couldn't guarantee the safety of her pretty little legs" if she admitted having an affair with Clinton.
- Kathleen Willey, whose tires were punctured with nails and whose cat was stolen. Later, a strange jogger approached her in a park, mentioning the names of her children and alluding to the car and the cat, saying, "Don't you get the message?"
- Elizabeth Ward Gracen, a former Miss America, whose hotel room was ransacked (though $2,000 she had there was left untouched) in what she suspected was an effort to find incriminating tapes of her relationship with Clinton. She claimed that future Clinton Secretary of Commerce Mickey Kantor offered to find her acting jobs in exchange for denying that she'd had an encounter with Clinton.
- Dolly Kyle Browning, whom Clinton campaign operatives threatened to "destroy" if she came forward to confirm her affair with the governor.
- Juanita Broaddrick, whose story of rape by Governor Clinton was covered on network television.
- Linda Tripp, who was indicted, and then acquitted, for taping her conversations with Monica Lewinsky, and whose confidential personnel file was leaked to the media by the Pentagon.
- And Monica Lewinsky, who was called a "stalker," and whose former boyfriend, unearthed by Clinton detectives, said she had bragged of bringing her "presidential kneepads" to Washington.

These women, compromised by Clinton's private detectives, were the true innocents victimized by the president. The conduct of the Clintons and their house detectives smacks of Richard Nixon and

J. Edgar Hoover at their terrible, temperamental worst. The fact that such snooping was done by private detectives, not a White House "plumbers unit" or FBI agents, makes little difference. What it all adds up to is an unmistakable history of intimidation of women, by a governor and then by a president, that is the sorriest chapter in Bill Clinton's political career.

12

Clinton's Legacy

The Transitional President

How on earth did Bill Clinton ever get to be president? How did he manage to stay there for eight years?

And how should history judge his performance?

The obstacles between Clinton and a successful presidency were daunting, and mostly of his own making. He dodged the draft, using every means at his disposal, and admitted as much in writing. His longtime affair with Gennifer Flowers became public knowledge. He paid almost $1 million to settle a case in which Paula Jones, a state employee, charged that he made graphic, inappropriate, and obscene demands on her while he was governor. His Whitewater investments were subject to massive scrutiny during the campaign and throughout his presidency. He received millions in illegal campaign contributions directly traced to the Chinese government. Just when it seemed he had nearly overcome his obstacles, he was caught lying in a court-ordered deposition about his affair with a young White House intern. Even as he was leaving office, he pardoned a major crack-cocaine dealer, an infamous money launderer, and a fugitive from justice whose wife gave Clinton's library almost half a million dollars.

And yet Bill Clinton left office with more than a 60 percent approval rating and high personal popularity.

How did he do it?

One key to his success was the distinction he drew between his private conduct and his public advocacy, which helped ensure his political viability. Once again implicitly invoking the concept of parallel lives, Clinton effectively told voters to elect him or defeat him based not on what kind of a man he was, but on what he could do for them.

In public, he was an opponent of sexual harassment. In private, he was guilty of it.

Publicly, he promoted personal responsibility. Privately, he constantly evaded it.

Before the cameras, he asked for a spirit of community and national service. But he did all he could to avoid serving his country in Vietnam.

His political program included curfews for teenagers, school uniforms, V Chips to help parents screen out sexual programs, and databases to identify child care workers with past sexual offenses. But behind closed doors, he had an affair with an intern only slightly older than his daughter.

How did he get away with it all? Because, in the narrow window during which he governed, Bill Clinton demonstrated an uncanny knack for grasping what America needed—and what the American voter wanted.

Clinton knew he was serving during a transitional time in American history, helping us move from one era to the next. He often compared his role with that of Teddy Roosevelt, who served near the turn of the last century and managed the transition between the unfettered capitalism of the late-nineteenth-century robber barons and the Progressive Era of social reform that opened the twentieth century. But if Teddy helped America through a social transition, Bill saw his role as guiding Americans through an economic transformation: from the industrial to the information age, from the domination of nation-state economics to the emergence of the global marketplace. His emphasis on education was intended to help ensure that Americans would always command jobs at the top of the global pecking order. His efforts to drive down trade barriers were designed to help the United States profit in the new worldwide economy.

Rather than trying to stave off these sweeping changes, Clinton focused on economic strength to help his country prepare for them. Like a governor of the United States, rather than its president, he toured the world pushing for American products and promoting U.S. companies. He took measures to give our technology sector an advantage in competing with other countries, and kept his eye firmly fixed on policies that led to job creation at home.

For all his talk about such broader trends, though, Clinton was ultimately a details man. As we've seen, he was always drawn away from broad themes and toward specific problems. He understood that, in the absence of some galvanizing national issue, voters can always be counted on to vote their pocketbooks. And in this, he recognized, lay the key to his success as a politician.

In *My Life,* Clinton asks rather frankly: How did Americans bring themselves to choose him as their president, when he was "carrying more baggage than an ocean liner?" And the answer he gives is critical: During the 1990s, as he rightly notes, the economy was the biggest issue on the voters' minds, followed by the deficit and health care. These issues, he says, left the "character issue trailing."

That insight led Bill Clinton to settle on the strategy that would preserve him throughout his presidency. The one way he could get voters to discount his character, he realized, was to get them to focus on his programs.

Even as early as the 1992 primary season, Clinton had formulated this take on "the character issue." Addressing voters in Dover, New Hampshire, shortly before the primary, he said:

> It has been absolutely fascinating to me to go through the last few
> weeks and see these so-called character issues raised, conveniently,

after I zoomed to the top by talking about your problems and your future and your lives.

Well, character is an important issue in a presidential election. . . . I'll tell you what the character issue is: Who really cares about you? Who's really trying to say what he would do specifically if he were elected president? . . . Who is determined to change your life rather than to just get or keep power?

Then he went on the offensive:

I'll tell you what I think the character issue in this election is: How can you have the power of the presidency and never use it to help people improve their lives till your life needs saving in an election. That's a character issue. . . .

In other words, it doesn't matter what you think of me. It matters what I can do for you.

The key to pursuing this strategy fell into place through the polling I did for the president, when we discovered in 1996 that it was older voters and younger ones who held Clinton's character problems against him. To voters under thirty-five and over fifty, the way Clinton had lived his personal life was offensive, contrary to the values the former were trying to implant in their children and the latter had followed all their lives. Those in the middle, on the other hand—the baby boomers—didn't hold his personal morality against him. Having come of age in an era of loose standards and changing values, they adopted a live-and-let-live attitude toward their political leaders.

Moreover, while the younger and older voting groups both disapproved of his morality, each did so for different reasons. The voters over fifty disapproved of Clinton for moral or religious reasons, but those under thirty-five just thought he had acted like a jerk. In one survey, I gave voters two ways to describe how they felt about moral and ethical issues, and asked them to choose the one that mirrored their views.

The first paragraph read:

(A) I believe in a strict code of morality and right and wrong which comes from God's word and the Bible. I try to live by it. Drugs and illicit sex are wrong so I don't engage in them. To do so would violate my personal moral and religious beliefs.

The second posited a contrasting view:

(B) My conduct is governed more by common sense and practicality than by an abstract morality. It is more factors like the danger of AIDS, the possibility of pregnancy, and the importance of a good marriage than morality or religion that stop me from illicit sex. The bad experiences people have had with drugs and the way I have seen it mess up lives is the reason I abstain from them, not some moral judgment that drugs are wrong.

The results were fascinating. Those over fifty chose statement A by 54 to 32; voters under thirty-five opted for B by 45 to 40. The younger voters were guided by their life experiences, not their religious beliefs. To them, Clinton wasn't evil or immoral; he was just reckless and irresponsible. Our conclusion: The over-fifty voters wouldn't forgive Clinton, but the younger voters would.

And younger voters needed a president to help them live good lives—in Clinton's phrase, to have "better stories." They had children to raise and families to sustain. To them, the social and economic policies that were initiated in the White House were critical. Many Americans don't really need a president until danger from abroad threatens. The middle-aged and prosperous, who aren't dependent on any federal program, whose children are no longer in school, have little use for the government. But for many younger voters, government attention to their needs is indispensable. Parents with children at home need a president to help ensure them of good schools, job opportunities, retraining to upgrade their skills, medical care for their children, and to enforce curbs on the drugs, violence, sex, guns, alcohol, and cigarettes to which their kids are exposed.

So Clinton played the best card he had, using his efforts to improve people's lives to negate their condemnation of his personal character. I referred to this strategy as "public values defeat private scandal."

Once again, the polls showed us how to tap into this reservoir of forgiveness among the young. We asked voters what was more important to them—the economy or social values issues like health care, education, and crime. The elderly felt the economy was more important, by three points. Baby boomers agreed that the economy was paramount by eight points. But the Generation X voters wanted a focus on social values over the economy—by nineteen points! So social values it was. (In lighter moments, I kidded Clinton that he was winning the support of young parents, who hoped to raise their children to be better people than they felt their president was!)

By deluging America with proposals to help young parents, Clinton secured their votes and their lasting support. The proposals aimed at these voters rolled off the assembly line at the White House; soon Clinton was proposing a different measure each day:

- Raise national education standards.
- Give parents a choice of public schools.
- Connect all schools to the Internet.
- Increase investment in job-creating technologies.
- Convert more defense industries to civilian uses.
- Ensure the safety of drinking water.
- Expand clean air programs.
- Clean up toxic waste sites.
- Reclaim polluted urban brownfields.
- Expand the Earned Income Tax Credit.
- Make health care benefits portable from job to job.
- Provide health coverage for all uninsured children.
- Issue work requirements and time limits for welfare recipients.

- Expand day care for welfare-to-work mothers.
- Give incentives to hire welfare mothers.
- Increase the minimum wage.
- Have AmeriCorps offer scholarships in return for national service.
- Issue tax credits equaling free tuition at two-year community colleges.
- Ban assault rifles.
- Enact waiting periods for handgun purchases.
- Offer family leave for childbirth, adoption, or care of a sick relative.
- Hire 100,000 more police officers.
- Hire 100,000 more teachers.
- Promote charter schools.
- Install V chips in televisions to screen out sex and violence.
- Persuade networks to issue ratings of their television shows.
- Promote school uniforms.
- Promote increased anti-truancy programs.
- Promote teenage curfews.
- Issue a ban on advertising tobacco to teenagers.
- Offer incentives to increase adoption.
- Call for a big increase in school construction and renovation.
- Improve school bus safety.
- Require screening of child care workers for past sexual offenses.
- Launch a national program to track firearms.
- Raise funding for AIDS research and care.
- Offer tax credits for job retraining for adults.
- Encourage character education in schools.
- Cut class sizes to a maximum of eighteen in the first three grades.
- Call for an end to social promotion in schools.
- Expand Medicare to fifty-five to sixty-five-year-olds who buy in.
- Fund major increases in research on diseases.
- Issue report cards for schools.
- Offer family leave for doctors' visits and parent-teacher conferences.

- Require trigger locks on guns.
- Reduce interest and increased repayment of student loans.
- Raise standards for security of private pension plans.

Every day, President Clinton would make a public appearance promoting one or more of these proposals; once a year he would enumerate them all in his marathon State of the Union speeches, which were watched by more than 60 percent of American voters. These speeches were like the towers of a suspension bridge holding Clinton's ratings aloft: Though Clinton's ratings were often dipping a bit early in the year, the speech never failed to buck them up again. After all, if you can't find a program that affects you on the list of his proposals, you'd have to be living in a hermetically sealed biosphere.

By reaching out to the people with specific policy initiatives to improve their everyday lives, Clinton helped overcome the doubts about his character. As I used to tell him, no one really cares about the personal character of their mayor. They just want their garbage collected on time.

Clinton was roundly criticized for these initiatives, which many said trivialized the presidency. In *My Life*, Clinton comments on those who called his proposals "small bore," noting that he was also pushing large, omnibus programs in areas like education and crime. Yet Clinton's was also the perfect approach for a president who saw policies not in broad patterns, but as responses to individual stories—and who needed to reach as many individuals as he could, in order to keep his negatives from dragging down his presidency.

Most of Clinton's proposals cost almost nothing and didn't require congressional action. Indeed, many of them didn't even fall within the purview of presidential powers. When Clinton wanted to instigate reform within the educational system, which is controlled by states and local boards, he used the presidential bully pulpit to call for school uniforms, teen curfews, anti-truancy programs, character education, and the like—all presidential proposals that became locally adopted policies. When he wanted the television networks to start rating their programs for sexual and violent content, he invited their leaders to a White House conference and shamed them into agreeing. When he wanted to encourage community groups to report crimes in progress, he persuaded cell phone companies to donate instruments to community groups, and to pay for any calls to 911.

After years of this daily pounding of proposals, Clinton's popularity with voters under thirty-five—dubbed "soccer moms" by the media—was deeper and broader than ever. When the Republicans tried to impeach and oust Clinton, they were counting on the support of over-fifty voters and parents under thirty-five who shared their point of view. But they were only half right. The older voters may have lined up against Clinton, but the Generation X voters rallied to his cause. Clinton was *their* president, helping them lead *their* lives. He was the first president who seemed to know the challenges they faced and who was willing to lend a hand, to be relevant and helpful. They needed him in office, and they were determined to keep him there, no matter how big an idiot they felt he had been in his private conduct.

The soccer moms never left Clinton. Their support and loyalty sustained him during each of his scandals, and represent a base of support he still enjoys today. Since few of these Gen Xers are yet in pivotal positions in the media, the establishment does not understand the reasons for Clinton's sustained popularity. But the Gen Xers know very well why this president, despite his prodigious baggage, managed to stay in office: because he catered to them. And ultimately—though, as we've seen, he may not even recognize it himself—the tidal wave of small solutions enacted during the Clinton years added up to more than the sum of their parts. Clinton cleaned up a set of problems that had bedeviled America since the 1960s; he brought to solution the challenges that had fueled domestic political debate since John F. Kennedy was president.

Ever since Lyndon Johnson refused to raise taxes to fund the Vietnam War, the federal deficit had preoccupied presidents and partisans alike. As the United States competed with the Soviet Union in the Cold War by increasing defense spending on one hand and cutting taxes to stimulate the economy on the other, we had piled up deficits and debt at a stunning rate. Just as FDR borrowed lavishly to finance World War II, so Reagan ran gigantic deficits to fund his competition with the Soviets. The result was a victory in the Cold War, but by the time George H. W. Bush and then Clinton took office, the bills had come due, and the huge ongoing debt was clogging the arteries of economic growth.

In a singular act of political courage, the elder George Bush sacrificed his presidency to reduce the deficit. Breaking his famous vow, "Read my lips: No new taxes," he raised levies to cut the deficit and paved the way for the reforms that dominated the 1990s. Clinton, too, sacrificed courageously on the altar of deficit reduction, losing Congress largely as a result of his 1993 tax increases, which cut the deficit further and brought about its eventual elimination. (One wonders whether either Bush or Clinton would have been so brave had they realized the likely outcomes of their courage.)

After LBJ's War on Poverty, America was left with an intractable welfare problem. Generations were being born, growing up, living, aging, and dying on the dole, only to be followed by equally dependent and despondent children and grandchildren. In 1937, when FDR addressed the nation in his second inaugural speech, he said that he saw "one third" of America "ill-clothed, ill-housed, and ill-fed." He may have seen the problem, but he didn't solve it. For all of the efforts of Roosevelt's New Deal, Truman's Fair Deal, and Kennedy's New Frontier, the poverty rate remained high until Johnson took office. LBJ's Great Society brought down the poverty rate to about one-sixth or one-seventh of the nation.

But the 1970s, and even the Reagan prosperity of the 1980s, did little to lower the poverty rate.

The welfare burden kindled a strong middle-class resentment against the poor, which overtook the compassion that had predominated during the 1960s. Fed up with welfare mothers and worried about their own jobs, blue-collar Americans switched in protest from union Democrats to Reagan Republicans.

By adopting Republican work requirements and time limits for welfare, and combining them with the other elements of the welfare reform mosaic, Clinton reduced the poverty rate by about one third— the first real progress in thirty years.

For this magnificent achievement, he must share the credit with Senator Trent Lott of Mississippi. The majority leader led his Republicans away from confrontation with Clinton over welfare reforms, and eliminated the poison pills in the legislation that would have guaranteed a presidential veto. Realizing that he had a Congress and a president genuinely willing to make welfare recipients work for their benefits, Lott pruned the bill of its veto bait, and passed a version Clinton could and did sign.

Ever since the days of Richard Nixon's presidency, crime had been a festering sore in American political dialogue, kindling racial resentments among both white and black. For decades, Republicans had used the law and order issue to win elections, blaming liberal Supreme Court judges for handcuffing the police and letting violent criminals go free.

While the right wing complained about crime, Clinton, in coalition with the Republicans in Congress, actually did something about it, with common-sense measures that generally got bipartisan support.

While the federal criminal justice system had dictated harsh sentences ever since tough reforms were passed with strong bipartisan backing in the late 1980s, state inmates accounted for 90 percent of America's prisoners. And state justice systems were porous: Criminals got light sentences, made lighter still by paroles, probation, and furloughs. Clinton realized that the problem was not so much liberal judges as crowded prisons, and he provided for massive federal subsidies for state prison construction in his 1994 Crime Bill, which passed with support from both parties. (In order to get the aid, states had to toughen their sentencing and parole policies.) Clinton's Justice Department beefed up federal prosecutions, particularly of teenage gangs; over Republican objections, Clinton also increased the number of police officers by about 14 percent, with federal subsidies paying much of the bill. Combined, these measures almost doubled prison population during the 1990s, and brought about a fifty percent reduction in violent crime, which has continued into the new century.

With crime and welfare on the wane, and jobs on the rise, racism and friction dropped too—another lasting legacy of the Clinton years.

At the time, these achievements seemed enormous. The quartet of problems—deficits, welfare and poverty, crime, and jobs—that had occupied our attention as a body politic for decades were winding their way down to resolution. (Today, the budget deficit is back, but it seems likely to drop of its own accord when the economy cycles back to full growth and expenditures for homeland security and the war in Iraq go back to normal. The structural deficit, I believe, has been eliminated.)

In that narrow sliver of time between the disappearance of the Soviet threat and the emergence of America's new enemy, empathy and specificity ruled. And so did Bill Clinton.

For a moment, it looked as though the Clinton-era focus on social and economic issues would carry on indefinitely. Terrorism was never mentioned as an issue in the 2000 election: In the style of the Clinton White House, the debate between Bush and Gore focused on the specifics of a proposed prescription drug benefit for Medicare patients, how to apportion tax cuts, and the long-term health of Social Security.

And then on September 11, 2001, everything changed—including the nature of politics, and the concerns of the American voter Clinton had worked so hard to understand. The small-bore proposals of the Clinton years seemed to pale in the face of falling Twin Towers and the threat of weapons of mass destruction. Suddenly character mattered more than the issues. It was not as important what was in a candidate's platform, but what was in his soul and guts—whether or not he had the strength, integrity, and resolution to protect us.

It was only after 9/11 that Clinton—along with the rest of us—really came to understand the true nature of the turn-of-the-century transition. The moves from the industrial to the information age and from nationalism to global economics were, of course, part of the process, but they were dwarfed by the larger challenges we only came to appreciate on that dark day.

Perhaps Clinton was more like Grover Cleveland than Theodore Roosevelt, serving as the end of the old era rather than the herald of the new one. Just as Cleveland was the last president to focus almost entirely on domestic issues—before his successor, William McKinley, led us into the Spanish-American War and a legacy of global involvement—Clinton may have been the last chief executive who could occupy himself with smaller domestic problems rather than facing the specter of global terrorism and other new technologically rooted challenges.

Clinton is now open to reevaluation as an interwar president, who ruled in the time of peace that came between the end of the Cold War and the start of the War on Terror. His tenure bridged the gap between the threat of global annihilation, held in check by deterrence—and the reality of a global terrorist jihad, unmitigated by any fear of retaliation. We went from a world that could destroy itself but wouldn't, to one where random acts of violence became the norm.

But the true nature of the Clinton transition will likely only become apparent after several decades have passed. It may well be that Clinton was the last president to rule in "normal" times before the more acute, sweeping, and complex problems of the twenty-first century seized our attention.

After 9/11, the old domestic problems overnight came to seem like quaint anachronisms, as reminiscent of a bygone era as Cleveland's concerns about the tariff and hard currency. Daunting as it once seemed, a problem like the welfare burden seemed almost minor compared with the prospect of terrorists armed with nuclear, biological, chemical, or radioactive weapons. The Soviet nuclear arsenal of yesteryear appears tame, and the Communist leaders look like wise stewards, when we consider the increasing chances that North Korea or the ayatollahs of Iran might be similarly armed.

As Clinton neared the end of his second term, he must have been haunted by the question of whether he would be remembered as the man who balanced the budget, created a full-employment economy, cut welfare in half, and slashed violent crime, or as the man who disgraced his office and became one of only two American presidents to be impeached. It is the bitter irony of his administration that the true threat to his legacy did not emerge until nine months after he had left office. As with Calvin Coolidge, we did not appreciate Clinton's defects and deficiencies until he left the White House and things went to hell.

Now it seems that the legacy of unpreparedness, so painfully sketched by the 9/11 Commission, will be the leading scar on his tenure in office. Despite his numerous achievements—and his comparable number of scandals, lies, omissions, dodges, and investigations—it is what Bill Clinton did *not* do that will haunt his place in history.

The truth is that we don't yet know the full dimensions of what Clinton didn't do:

- Will North Korea unleash a nuclear attack on the South or on Japan, using the bombs it developed right under Clinton's nose to destroy millions of people?
- Will Iran—empowered by technology Clinton allowed it to get from Russia, and funded by the investments in its oil industry Clinton allowed by waiving sanctions—lend terrorism a dreadful new dimension? Will there be an Iranian nuclear bomb to

strengthen that vicious regime in its demented rush back into the middle ages?

- Will Pakistan use the missiles it received from China—as Clinton looked the other way—in a full-scale nuclear war with India?
- Will Clinton's failure to negotiate a deal protecting Social Security and Medicare lead to the bankruptcy of these systems? Through his failure to act in times of plenty, did he squander an irreplaceable opportunity to repair these programs?

It will be many years before we can assess what Clinton's inaction on these fronts has or will cost us.

But what Clinton has left us is, perhaps, a deeper understanding of what kind of character we want in the White House.

On one level, his empathy for his fellow citizens is a trait we will surely seek in his successors. His ability to recognize, and respond to, the challenges of people in America (and around the world) is a characteristic for which we should take care to screen candidates in the future.

On another level, though, our experience with Clinton demonstrates that we must scrutinize future candidates for the signs of mendacity and untruthfulness that Clinton showed early in his days on the national stage. After the fall of Richard Nixon, we learned to beware of politicians who began their careers as negative attack dogs, only to present themselves later as "new," more positive candidates. Since Nixon's time, we have elected only presidents who were largely, and genuinely, positive in their outlook and their political speech. Those who appeared to be wolves in sheep's clothing—Bob Dole among them—never made it to the White House.

But the Bill Clinton story has taught us a new and different lesson: that we must learn to attend carefully to the scandals and controversies that arise during a person's pursuit of the presidency, for they are likely to provide clues we need to understand what kind of a president he or she will be. If we had paid more attention to the convolutions

Clinton went through to escape blame for the trifecta of early scandals—over the draft, Gennifer Flowers, and Whitewater—we might have chosen another man for the job.

In doing so, what would we have lost—a president who solved domestic problems that had dogged America for generations, or one who fiddled while the storm clouds of international hostility grew on the horizon?

Would we have been served better, or worse, by giving the job to a more honest but less effective leader?

In the long run, it's a question only the voters—and the candidates they choose—can answer.

Notes

Chapter 1: Cracking the Clinton Code

1   "A riddle wrapped": Winston Churchill, Russian Enigma Speech, BBC Broadcast, October 1, 1939, http://www.churchill-society-london. org.uk/RussnEnig.html.

4   "clear story line": Bill Clinton, *My Life* (New York: Knopf, 2004), p. 489.

6   "give people a chance": Ibid., p. 15.

12   "I think that I did something": *60 Minutes,* Dan Rather interview with Bill Clinton, June 20, 2004.

12   "I think that's about the most": Ibid.

Chapter 2: Running on Empathy

16   "becomes absorbed with": Helen Palmer, *The Enneagram in Love and Work* (San Francisco: HarperSanFrancisco, 1995), p. 223.

16   "can see all sides": Ibid.

17   1975 which he spent: Bill Clinton, *My Life* (New York: Knopf, 2004), p. 229.

19   he writes of how difficult: Ibid., p. 8.

20   "born in a log cabin": Ibid., p. 22.

21   "luxurious bus": Ibid., p. 38.

21   In 1961, for $30,000: Ibid., p. 50.

21   Clinton's relatives: Ibid., p. 33.

24   "full of anger": Ibid., p. 10.

24   When his mother returned: Ibid., p. 20.

24   "disturbing" part of life: Ibid., p. 51.

25   "perhaps most important": Ibid., p. 15.

25   Her father confided: Ibid., p. 490.

27   "overwhelmed with input": Helen Palmer, *The Enneagram in Love and Work* (San Francisco: HarperSanFrancisco, 1995), p. 232.

27   story of Ron and Rhoda: Bill Clinton, *My Life* (New York: Knopf, 2004), p. 417.

28   25 million people: Ibid., p. 723.

32   Clinton extended the EITC: Ibid., p. 494.

38   he dutifully records that he promised: Ibid., p. 685.

40   He notes that tobacco: Ibid., p. 661.

Chapter 3: Timidity, Passivity, and Blame: The Negative Consequences of Clinton's Empathy

47   "if you merge": Helen Palmer, *The Enneagram in Love and Work* (San Francisco: HarperSanFrancisco, 1995), p. 228.

47   "want to hear": Bill Clinton, *My Life* (New York: Knopf, 2004), p. 258.

52   "tired of waiting": Ibid., p. 498.

53   "hold out": Ibid.

53   "furious . . . for agreeing to": Ibid., p. 499.

53   "I gave in to the people": "Clinton Felt Personally Responsible for Waco," Reuters, July 25, 2000.

53   "I went through it": "Reno Recalls Waco Chat," *Associated Press*, July 27, 2000.

53   "the plan included": Remarks by President Clinton in Question and Answer Session with the Press: 1:36 P.M. EDT, April 20, 1993.

54   "under no circumstances": Ibid.

54   Clinton had no extensive: Bill Clinton, *My Life* (New York: Knopf, 2004), p. 491.

55 "dumping responsibility": "In Defense of Janet Reno," *Wall Street Journal* (Eastern edition), April 21, 1993, p. A1.

55 "the flip side is": "The President and Waco Editorial," *Washington Post,* April 21, 1993, p. A18.

55 "It is not possible": "Mr. Clinton Takes a Stand," *Atlanta Journal and Constitution,* April 21, 1993, p. A16.

55 "gut" argued against: Bill Clinton, *My Life* (New York: Knopf, 2004), pp. 498–499.

56 "negatives are worse": Jude Wanniski, "Memo To: Brit Hume, FoxNews Networks, Re: No Fault Government," *Polyconomics.com,* http:/www.polyconomics.com/searchbase/08-30-99.html.

58 "because some religious fanatics": "Mr. Clinton Takes a Stand," *Atlanta Journal and Constitution,* April 21, 1993, p. A16.

58 "after Waco": Bill Clinton, *My Life* (New York: Knopf, 2004), p. 499.

58 "approved" of the operation: Ibid., p 552.

58 "did not envision": Ibid., pp. 552–553.

58 "any parameters": Ibid., p. 553.

59 was much more careful: Ibid., p. 554.

59 period of "transition": Ibid., p. 552.

59 "finish the job": Ibid.

60 "The youth were surprised": John Miller, "Greetings America. My Name Is Usama bin Laden. Now That I Have Your Attention . . . ," *Esquire,* vol. 131, no. 2, February 1999.

61 Clinton agreed . . . respect for the United Nations: Bill Clinton, *My Life* (New York: Knopf, 2004), p. 513.

61 When Serb outrages: Ibid., p. 512.

61 "was bound to fail": Ibid., p. 513.

61 he disapproved . . . dual key approach: Ibid., p. 534.

64 a few thousand troops: Ibid., p. 593.

64 The former president blames: Ibid.

64 "we would have been": Ibid., p. 526.

68   "thirty-year-old-bond traders": Ibid., pp. 493–494.

69   The senator forced: Ibid., p. 460.

69   he admits, led voters: Ibid., p. 483.

70   "dominated by the politically": Michael Kelly, White House Memo: "President's Early Troubles Rooted in Party's Old Strains," *New York Times*, February 2, 1993, p. A1.

70   he broke his commitment: Bill Clinton, *My Life* (New York: Knopf, 2004), p. 493.

70   the venerable Senator: Ibid., p. 500.

71   Clinton admits that his critics: Ibid., p. 555.

71   He was the one: Ibid., p. 547.

71   He did it . . . ruled out compromise: Ibid., p. 577.

72   Clinton well understood . . . doomed the bill: Ibid., p. 601.

72   Someone high up: Ibid., p. 481.

72   according to Clinton, the press was at fault: Ibid., p. 516.

72   Clinton swears . . . The firings: Ibid., p. 519.

72   "factually inaccurate": "Counsel Blasts Hillary's Testimony," *Associated Press*, October 18, 2000.

73   The reporters, he writes: Bill Clinton, *My Life* (New York: Knopf, 2004), p. 520.

73   They told him twice: Ibid., p. 518.

73   It was the fault of the Republicans: Ibid., p. 521.

74   he heard from a friend: Ibid., p. 530.

75   he even apologized: Ibid., p. 942.

75   "too tired and keyed up": Ibid., p. 441.

75   Tony Lake said: Ibid., p. 504.

75   Ron Brown's fault: Ibid., p. 415.

75   "I guess I would": Max Boot, "Kerry's Commanding Position on the Fence," *Los Angles Times*, January 29, 2004.

76   Clinton felt he couldn't: Bill Clinton, *My Life* (New York: Knopf, 2004), p. 435.

76   "to release the records": Ibid., p. 573.

76   Turns out George: Ibid.

76   Pat Griffin and Counsel: Ibid., p. 607.

76   "venomous" language: Ibid., p. 651.

76   Clinton wanted to intervene: Ibid., p. 807.

77   It was the fault of: Ibid., p. 831.

77   Jones' lawyers made him: Ibid., p. 773.

77   "reluctantly" went before: Ibid., p. 776.

77   "titanic" battle with Congress: Ibid., p. 811.

78   "surprised" that he was scheduled: Ibid., p. 628.

78   "the children who got me elected": Ibid., p. 521.

79   "not to blame others": Ibid., p. 634.

81   "He [Morris] did me a lot of good": Ibid., p. 258.

Chapter 4: Anger Without Management

85   "primitive, primordial, [version of] Stockholm Syndrome": Interview with a prominent social worker who wishes to remain anonymous, July 31, 2004.

85   "made me feel": Bill Clinton, *My Life* (New York: Knopf, 2004), pp. 9–10.

87   "There were so many": Ibid., p. 19.

89   "tornado": George Stephanopoulos, *All Too Human* (New York: Little, Brown & Co., 1999), p. 96.

89   "tirades": Ibid.

89   "screaming": Ibid., p. 217.

89   "silent scream": Ibid., p. 288.

89   "morning roar": Ibid., p. 286.

90   "slow boil": Ibid., p. 287.

90   "nightcap": Ibid.

90   "the show": Ibid., p. 288.

90   "last gasp": Ibid.

91   "out of control" . . . "constant anger": Bill Clinton, *My Life* (New York: Knopf, 2004), p. 42.

91   "didn't handle it well": Ibid., p. 519.

91   "irritated" . . . when Mack McLarty: Ibid., p. 531.

91   "angry" at Vince Foster: Ibid., p. 531.

91   "furious" at himself: Ibid., p. 409.

91   "internal life": Ibid., p. 149.

91   "angry" about Whitewater: Ibid., p. 693.

91   "fumed" over policy criticisms: Ibid., p. 380.

91   Jerry Brown "angered": Ibid., p. 425.

91   "anger" over the Starr investigation: Ibid., p. 589.

91   "normally sunny disposition": Ibid.

91   "burned up": Ibid., p. 830.

91   "griped too much in the morning": Ibid., p. 830.

92   still too "angry": Ibid., p. 803.

92   "Wagging his finger": BBC.co.uk/broadbandspecial_news_consolestm?3831000/3831465.

92   "Let me just say this": Ibid.

92   "Nobody in your line of work": BBC.co.uk/broadbandspecial_news_consolestm?3831000/3831465.

Chapter 5: AWOL on Terror: Clinton's Disastrous Passive Mode

96   "cabinet-level officials": *The 9/11 Commission Report* (New York: Norton, 2004), p. 114.

97   "danger of snatching": Ibid., p. 113.

97   "use force": Ibid., p. 126.

97   "no capture plan": Ibid., p. 114.

97   signed several Memoranda: Bill Clinton, *My Life* (New York: Knopf, 2004), p. 804.

98   "the strike": Ibid., p. 116.

98   "Since the missiles": Ibid., p. 117.

98   "a few minutes": Bill Clinton, *My Life* (New York: Knopf, 2004), p. 799.

98   "had a cumulative effect": *The 9/11 Commission Report* (New York: Norton, 2004), p. 118.

98   "President Clinton and Berger": Ibid., p. 120.

99   "two senior State Department": Ibid., p. 125.

99   "CIA assets in Afghanistan": Ibid., p. 140.

99   "when the decision came": Ibid.

100   American officials gun-shy: *The 9/11 Commission Report* (New York: Norton, 2004), pp. 140–141.

100   Clinton blames the cancellation: Bill Clinton, *My Life* (New York: Knopf, 2004), p. 925.

103   he knew how Kennedy felt: Ibid., p. 552.

104   "terror" or "terrorism": Ibid., pp. 656, 717.

104   September 1996 UN speech: Ibid., p. 675.

104   crash of TWA 800: Ibid., p. 718.

104   he laments Congress's delay: Ibid., p. 703.

104   "Terrorism was not": David Johnston and Douglas Jehl, "Report Cites Lapses Across Government and 2 Presidencies," *New York Times,* July 23, 2004, p. 1.

106   Clinton devotes only on paragraph: Bill Clinton, *My Life* (New York: Knopf, 2004), p. 497.

106   "no opening": John W. Mashek, "White House Feeling Tremors from Bombing," *Boston Globe,* March 2, 1993, p. 1.

106   "overreact" to the bombing: Ralph Blumenthal, "Crisis at the Twin Towers: The Overview; Inquiry is Pressed on Cause of Blast at Trade Center," *New York Times,* March 2, 1993, p. 1.

106   "It wasn't the kind of thing": Judith Miller, "A Nation Challenged: The Response; Planning for Terror but Failing to Act," *New York Times,* January 30, 2002, p. 1.

107   just its "financier": *The 9/11 Commission Report* (New York: Norton, 2004), p. 109.

108   "when Bin Laden": Ibid., pp. 109–110.

108   "had no legal basis": Ibid., p. 110.

108   "on their own separate": Ibid., p. 110.

108   "has claimed that Sudan": Ibid.

109   Woolsey said: David Horowitz interview with David Corn, *Hannity & Colmes,* Fox News Channel, August 12, 2002.

109   CIA director is mentioned: Bill Clinton, *My Life* (New York: Knopf, 2004), p. 455.

109   "paper tiger": John Miller, "Greetings America. My Name is Usama bin Laden. Now That I Have Your Attention . . . ," *Esquire Magazine,* vol. 131, no. 2, February 1999.

109   "infiltrate such [terrorist] organizations": Neil Lewis, "Clinton Plan Would Broaden F.B.I. Powers," *New York Times,* April 25, 1995.

110   he would not loosen: John Harris, "President Expands Proposal for Countering Terrorism; 1,000 New Jobs, Tagging Explosives, Military Included," *Washington Post,* p. A1.

110   what was on Moussaoui's computer: Michael Isikoff and Daniel Klaidman, "Access Denied," *Newsweek Web Exclusive,* October 1, 2001.

110   warned off it by George: George Stephanopoulos, *All Too Human* (New York: Back Bay Books, 2000), p. 40.

111   Mohammed Atta was stopped: Jim Yardley, "Mohamed Atta in Close Call in Incident at Miami Airport," *New York Times,* October 17, 2001, p. B1.

111   Two other 9/11 hijackers: "Okla. Trooper Cited Hijacker for Speeding Last April," *Washington Post,* January 21, 2002, p. A2.

111   he responded to the crash: Bill Clinton, *My Life* (New York: Knopf, 2004), p. 719.

112   "at the time, CAPPS": Matthew Wald, "Threats and Responses: Responsibilities; Looking Back and Looking Ahead, Panel Assesses the Opportunities for Prevention," *New York Times,* July 23, 2004.

112   "hav[ing] one's checked baggage": *The 9/11 Commission Report* (New York: Norton, 2004), p. 84.

112   "primarily because of concern": Ibid.

112   "this policy change": Ibid., p. 83.

112   did not address: Al Gore, "White House Commission on Aviation Safety and Security: Final Report to President Clinton," February 12, 1997.

113   nineteen hijackers as "suspicious": Matthew Wald, "Threats and Responses: Responsibilities; Looking Back and Looking Ahead, Panel Assesses the Opportunities for Prevention," *New York Times,* July 23, 2004.

113   "was selected by . . . CAPPS": *The 9/11 Commission Report* (New York: Norton, 2004), p. 84.

113   "under security rules": Ibid., p. 1.

113   "selected by extra scrutiny": Ibid., p. 84.

113   "the only consequence": Ibid., p. 3.

113   the Gore Commission left: Ibid., pp. 4–10.

113   "While the FAA rules": Ibid., p. 84.

114   "a proposal to ban": Ibid.

114   "on the FBI and CIA": Ibid., pp. 83–84.

115   "We will improve airport": Bill Clinton acceptance speech at Democratic National Convention, August 29, 1996.

115   "Bin Laden Preparing to Hijack": Andy Stolis, "Clinton Received Red Flag on Hijackings in '98," *New York Post,* p. 7.

116   the eventual Saudi execution: Bill Clinton, *My Life* (New York: Knopf, 2004), p. 717.

117   "We are working": Bill Clinton acceptance speech at the Democratic National Convention, August 29, 1996.

118   Clinton waived the sanctions: Thomas Lippman, "U.S. Aides Still Divided over Sanctions on Foreign Investors in Iran," *Washington Post,* March 6, 1998, p. A33.

119   Clinton catalogues the four-day bombing: Bill Clinton, *My Life* (New York: Knopf, 2004), p. 833.

119   Clinton's irresponsibility: Daniel Williams, "U.S. Bid to Build Coalition on North Korea is Resisted: China, Japan Opposing Sanctions Approach," *Washington Post,* June 10, 1994, p. A1.

120   With Japan and South Korea: Ibid.

120   "very positive step": R. Jeffrey Smith and Ann Devroy, "Carter's Call from N. Korea Offered Option: Administration Seized on New Chance at Diplomacy," *Washington Post,* June 26, 1994, p. A1.

121   North Korea was cheating: David Sanger, "North Korea Site an A-Bomb Plant, U.S. Agencies Say," *New York Times,* August 17, 1998, p. A1.

121   further information about the violations: Dana Priest, "Activity Suggests N. Koreans Building Secret Nuclear Site," *Washington Post,* August 18, 1998, p. A1.

Chapter 6: Ducking the Draft

126   "might have made different": Bill Clinton, *My Life* (New York: Knopf, 2004), p. 161.

127   "Failing to serve": George Stephanopoulos, *All Too Human* (New York: Little, Brown & Co., 1999), p. 70.

127   classified as 2S: Dan Balz, "Clinton and the Draft: Anatomy of a Controversy," *Washington Post,* September 13, 1992, p. A1.

128   "sympathetic to the zeitgeist": Bill Clinton, *My Life* (New York: Knopf, 2004), p. 117.

128   except those in medical school: "Clinton and the Draft: Anatomy of a Controversy," *Washington Post,* September 13, 1992, p. A1.

128   from an aide to Sen. Fulbright: William C. Rempel, "Induction of Clinton Seen Delayed by Effort," *Los Angeles Times,* September 2, 1992.

128   "We've got to give him time": Ibid.

129   his poor hearing: Ibid.

129   Clinton was the only: Ibid.

129   After he eventually passed: Bill Clinton, *My Life* (New York: Knopf, 2004), p. 152.

129   He tried the National Guard: Ibid., p. 164.

129   "looked into the air force": Ibid., p. 154.

129   on July 17, 1969: Ibid., p. 155.

130   "had the authority": William C. Rempel, "Induction of Clinton Seen Delayed by Effort," *Los Angeles Times,* September 2, 1992.

131   "put himself back in the draft": Roberto Suro, "Clinton Asked Senators Help on Draft, His Aides Confirm," *New York Times,* September 19, 1992.

131   "I don't believe in deferments": Bill Clinton, *My Life* (New York: Knopf, 2004), p. 159.

132   thanking him for "saving": Bill Clinton's letter to Colonel Holmes, December 3, 1969, quoted in David Maraniss, *First in His Class* (New York: Simon & Shuster, 1995), pp. 199–205.

132   "came to believe": Ibid.

133   "loathed the military": Ibid.

133   "subject himself to the draft": David Maraniss, *First in His Class* (New York: Simon & Shuster, 1995), p. 191.

134   it was a "fluke": George Stephanopoulos, *All Too Human* (New York: Little, Brown & Co., 1999), p. 70.

134   "You would have thought": Ibid., p. 71.

135   "There's the imminent danger": Affidavit of Colonel Holmes, February 5, 1992.

135   "I believe that he [Clinton]": Jeffrey Birnbaum, "Clinton Bid to Avoid Vietnam May Prompt Fresh Scrutiny," *Wall Street Journal,* February 8, 1992.

135   "then made the necessary": Ibid.

135 "never *knowingly* received": Dan Balz, "Clinton Disputes Draft Evasion Suggestions," *Washington Post,* February 7, 1992.

136 "if he ever received": Gwen Ifill, "Vietnam War Draft Status Becomes An Issue For Clinton," *New York Times,* February 7, 1992.

136 "That's it. We're done.": George Stephanopoulos, *All Too Human* (New York: Little, Brown & Co., 1999), p. 74.

136 "I was dropping": Bill Clinton, *My Life* (New York: Knopf, 2004), p. 389.

138 "What I didn't know": George Stephanopoulos, *All Too Human* (New York: Little, Brown & Co., 1999), p. 69.

137 "I gladly would have": Michael Kelly, "Days After 'Final Word' on the Draft, Clinton Faces Renewed Questions: The Democrats," *New York Times,* September 5, 1992.

138 "standard enlisted man's": William C. Rempel, "Induction of Clinton Seen Delayed by Effort," *Los Angeles Times,* September 2, 1992.

138 "It's all news to me": Michael Kelly, "Days After 'Final Word' on the Draft, Clinton Faces Renewed Questions: The Democrats," *New York Times,* September 3, 1992.

138 "Meyers said that Clinton's": Michael Kelly, "Clinton Said He Was Told of Draft Aid," *New York Times,* September 5, 1992.

139 "limited to advice": Robert Suro, "Clinton Asked for Senator's Help on Draft, His Aides Confirm: Candidate's Record," *LA Times,* September 19, 1992.

140 "lashed out against the press": Glen Ifill, "Clinton Accuses Press of Bias," *New York Times,* September 8, 1992.

140 "assorted enemies": Michael Kelly, "Clinton Readies Answer to Bush in Draft Issue: The 1992 Campaign," *New York Times,* September 15, 1992.

140 "unprepared" for the issue: Bill Clinton, *My Life* (New York: Knopf, 2004), p. 388.

141 he kept a detailed diary: Ibid., p. 141.

141 "that I had not been a draft resister": Ibid., p. 152.

Chapter 7: The Politician and the Boy Scout: Bill Clinton's Parallel Lives

143   "parallel lives": Bill Clinton, *My Life* (New York: Knopf, 2004), p. 775.

147   "in a hurry": Ibid., p. 263.

147   "do too many things": Ibid., p. 521.

148   Clinton decided to help: Ibid., p. 264.

148   He proposed predicating: Ibid., p. 265.

149   Some of these farmers: Ibid., p. 265.

149   "a policy success": Ibid., p. 263.

150   "thirty-year-old bond traders": Ibid., p. 460.

152   How he had his economists: Ibid., p. 535.

153   he points to the tax increases: Ibid., pp. 630–631.

154   "He's cantankerous": Todd S. Purdum, "The Newest Moynihan," *New York Times,* August 7, 1994, Section 6, p. 25.

154   Far from being rolled over: Ibid.

155   good-faith negotiations: Bill Clinton, *My Life* (New York: Knopf, 2004), p. 611.

156   When the initiative failed: Ibid., pp. 602, 620.

158   "effective national counter message": Ibid., p. 631.

161   He was not interested: Ibid., p. 456.

161   He was present: Ibid., p. 802.

161   He urged Democratic: Ibid., p. 826.

161   She attended a retreat: Ibid., p. 488.

161   He and his wife stayed: Ibid., p. 500.

161   It was at his urging: Ibid., p. 776.

161   He was present in the solarium: Ibid., p. 802.

161   He and his wife produced: Ibid., p. 918.

161   He was on Air Force One: Ibid.

161   He came to the administration: Ibid., pp. 491–492.

162   He agreed with Laura Tyson: Ibid., p. 494.

162   He was present in the solarium: Ibid., p. 802.

162   He announced that he was leaving: Ibid., p. 804.

162   He attended a staff retreat: Ibid., p. 488.

162   He . . . conducted a 1998 survey: Ibid., p. 824.

Chapter 8: Politics Is Not Spoken Here

168   "wanted to politicize": Bill Clinton, *My Life* (New York: Knopf, 2004), p. 660.

169   the meetings became larger: Ibid.

170   "American-style" campaign rallies: Ibid., p. 718.

171   giving only a dry recitation: Ibid., p. 708.

171   the trip was controversial: Ibid., p. 654.

172   Yeltsin agreed not to ship: Ibid., p. 655.

173   Clinton notes that Peres: Ibid., p. 714.

175   except for one cursory reference: Ibid., p. 682.

177   "as an organizing tool": Ibid., p. 695.

177   Based on the findings: Ibid., p. 681.

178   Clinton still uses: Ibid., p. 651.

178   He writes of his decision: Ibid., p. 662.

182   "If black people": Ibid., p. 411.

183   "scant understanding of": Charles F. Allen and Jonathan Portis, *The Comeback Kid: The Life and Career of Bill Clinton* (New York: Birch Lane Press, 1992), p. 183.

183   "the killing of human": Ibid.

Chapter 9: Fear of Hillary

188   "denied that he tried": Michael Isikoff and Ruth Marcus, "Clinton Tries to Derail Trooper Allegations," *Washington Post*, December 21, 1993.

188   "hit Hillary hard": Bill Clinton, *My Life* (New York: Knopf, 2004), p. 565.

189   "I find it not an accident": Ruth Marcus, "First Lady Lashes Out at Allegations," *Washington Post,* December 22, 2004.

189   troopers' stories "ridiculous": Bill Clinton, *My Life* (New York: Knopf, 2004), p. 565.

189   Brock later apologized: Ibid.

190   "I can't point to": CNN's Jonathan Karl and the *Associated Press,* March 10, 1998, http://www.cnn.com/ALLPOLITICS/1998/03/10/brocks.remorse.

190   Clinton says the reason: Bill Clinton, *My Life* (New York: Knopf, 2004), p. 565.

192   "For years, [Wright] told": David Maraniss, *First in His Class* (New York: Simon & Schuster, 1995), p. 440.

194   "opposed the idea": Hillary Clinton, *Living History* (New York: Simon & Schuster, 1995), p. 440.

194   "the second biggest tactical mistake": Ibid.

195   "I have no recollection": George Stephanopoulos, *All Too Human* (New York: Little, Brown & Co., 1999), p. 272.

198   "In the deposition": Bill Clinton, *My Life* (New York: Knopf, 2004), p. 774.

199   "No! Jim told me": James Stewart, *Blood Sport: The President and His Adversaries* (New York: Simon & Schuster, 1996), p. 133.

199   The *Washington Post* demanded: George Stephanopoulos, *All Too Human* (New York: Little, Brown & Co., 1999), pp. 225–226.

199   Ann Devroy, warned George: Ibid., p. 226.

200   "didn't want [the records]": Ibid., p. 228.

200   "My instincts were": Bill Clinton, *My Life* (New York: Knopf, 2004), p. 573.

200   "inevitably incomplete set": Hillary Clinton, *Living History* (New York: Simon & Schuster, 1995), p. 206.

200   "While I have no": Marilyn Rauber, "Hillary Admits Filing Records in the Shredder," *New York Post,* January 20, 1996.

201   "a plausible theory": George Stephanopoulos, *All Too Human* (New York: Little, Brown & Co., 1999), p. 245.

204   "scrupulously honest": Bill Clinton, *My Life* (New York: Knopf, 2004), p. 396.

204   "above reproach": Ibid., p. 589.

204   He covers for her: Ibid., p. 573.

204   named after Sir Edmund Hillary: Ibid., p. 870.

204   "after a round": David Maraniss, *First in His Class* (New York: Simon & Schuster, 1995), p. 342.

205   "Bill wanted to": Ibid., p. 335.

205   "I want a diver-or-or-orce.": Ibid., p. 394.

205   "broaching the subject": Ibid., p. 450.

205   "both believed that Clinton's": Gail Sheehy, *Hillary's Choice* (New York: Random House, 1999), p. 180.

206   "tall, slim, blond": Ibid., p. 182.

206   "It's tough to be": Ibid., p. 185.

Chapter 10: She Said, He Said

210   "had a huge cadre": *U.S. News & World Report,* quoted in Barbara Olson, *Hell to Pay* (Washington, D.C.: Regnery, 1999), p. 246.

210   Hillary's central role: George Stephanopoulos, *All Too Human* (New York: Little, Brown & Co., 1999), p. 109.

212   "I asked Congress": Bill Clinton, *My Life* (New York: Knopf, 2004), p. 555.

212   "I spent the next two weeks": Ibid., p. 582.

212   "I decided" to delay: Ibid., p. 492.

212   "I told Congress": Ibid., p. 577.

212   "I suggested" to Dole: Ibid.

212   "I proposed" a system: Ibid., p. 549.

213   "I agreed that he": Hillary Clinton, *Living History* (New York: Simon & Schuster, 1995), p. 368.

213   "I worked hard": Ibid., p. 385.

213   "I had begun working": Ibid., p. 383.

213   "I would never allow": Bill Clinton, *My Life* (New York: Knopf, 2004), p. 662.

213   "I also spent two years": Hillary Clinton, *Living History* (New York: Simon & Schuster, 1995), p. 380.

213   "I spent the entire month": Bill Clinton, *My Life* (New York: Knopf, 2004), p. 673.

213   "I had worked": Hillary Clinton, *Living History* (New York: Simon & Schuster, 1995), p. 385.

213   "sweeping reforms": Bill Clinton, *My Life* (New York: Knopf, 2004), p. 770.

213   "begin working for better": Hillary Clinton, *Living History* (New York: Simon & Schuster, 1995), p. 385.

214   "the guiding light": Bill Clinton, *My Life* (New York: Knopf, 2004), p. 633.

214   "I led the Administration's": Hillary Clinton, *Living History* (New York: Simon & Schuster, 1995), p. 385.

214   "bill that ended": Bill Clinton, *My Life* (New York: Knopf, 2004), p. 729.

214   "Bill and I wanted": Hillary Clinton, *Living History* (New York: Simon & Schuster, 1995), p. 367.

214   "I signed another": Bill Clinton, *My Life* (New York: Knopf, 2004), p. 795.

214   "Bill and I . . . convened": Hillary Clinton, *Living History* (New York: Simon & Schuster, 1995), p. 383.

214   supporting "Al and Tipper": Bill Clinton, *My Life* (New York: Knopf, 2004), p. 854.

214   "I urged my staff": Hillary Clinton, *Living History* (New York: Simon & Schuster, 1995), p. 381.

214   "I proposed . . . expanding": Bill Clinton, *My Life* (New York: Knopf, 2004), p. 777.

214   "my staff continued": Hillary Clinton, *Living History* (New York: Simon & Schuster, 1995), pp. 382–383.

214   preserving America's "treasures": Bill Clinton, *My Life* (New York: Knopf, 2004), p. 777.

Chapter 11: Errata

220   "In the case at hand": George Carpozi Jr., *Clinton Confidential: The Climb to Power* (Del Mar, CA: Emery Dalton Books, 1995), pp. 321–327.

220   "selectively edited": Bill Clinton, *My Life* (New York: Knopf, 2004), p. 387.

220   "take out a 747": Carl Limbacher, "Pellicano Tapes Could Spell Trouble for Bill and Hillary," *Newsmax.com*, November 12, 2003.

221   "material" matter: Bill Clinton, *My Life* (New York: Knopf, 2004), p. 778.

221   "raw political" nature: Ibid., p. 784.

221   "won a clear victory": Ibid., p. 830.

222   The Clintons ended up paying: Dan Froomkin, "Case Closed," *Washington Post.com*, December 3, 1998, http://www.washingtonpost.com/wp-srv/politics/special/pjones/pjones.htm.

222   As Clinton admits, the settlement: Ibid.

222   "violating her discovery orders": Bill Clinton, *My Life* (New York: Knopf, 2004), p. 830.

223   "Jim McDougal notes": Jim McDougal quoted in Ann Coulter, *High Crimes and Misdemeanors: The Case Against Bill Clinton* (Washington, D.C.: Regnery, 1998), p. 197.

223   "assumed that Webb was": Hillary Clinton, *Living History* (New York: Simon & Schuster, 1995), pp. 221–222.

223   there was "strong proof": Stephen Labaton, "Advisors Knew of Hubbell Plight," *New York Times*, May 5, 1997, p. A1.

223 "selling" overnight stays: Bill Clinton, *My Life* (New York: Knopf, 2004), p. 746.

223 "ridiculous" . . . "in that way": Ibid., p. 747.

224 Donors Who Spent: *MotherJones.com* list of 400 top donors to Clinton 1996 campaign: http://www.motherjones.com/news/special_reports/coinop_congress/97mojo_400/mojo_400.html.

225 And during Hillary's 2000: Michael Kelly, "Dumb v. Dishonest," *Washington Post,* September 27, 2000, p. A23.

225 Donors Who Attended: *MotherJones.com* list of 400 top donors to Clinton 1996 campaign: http://www.motherjones.com/news/special_reports/coinop_congress/97mojo_400/mojo_400.html.

227 "spate of anti-China stories": Bill Clinton, *My Life* (New York: Knopf, 2004), p. 852.

227 "We like your president": Rich Lowry, *Legacy: Paying the Price for the Clinton Years* (Washington, D.C.: Regnery, 2003), p. 141.

228 "an agent of the Chinese government": Ibid.

228 "cultural agent": Ibid.

228 "a hotel tycoon": Ibid.

228 "the epicenter": Ibid.

228 After Webb Hubbell resigned: Webb Hubbell, *Friends in High Places* (New York: Morrow, 1997), p. 324.

228 after former Arkansas Governor: Press Conference by Judicial Watch, March 19, 2001, http://www.judicialwatch.org/archive/2001/875.shtml.

228 the Democratic National Committee: Ibid.

228 Schwartz was the biggest: Rich Lowry, *Legacy: Paying the Price for the Clinton Years* (Washington, D.C.: Regnery, 2003), p. 230.

229 "not free of controversy" . . . "not accessible": Bill Clinton, *My Life* (New York: Knopf, 2004), p. 792.

229 "not only helped the Chinese": Bill Gertz, *Betrayal: How the Clinton Administration Undermined American Security* (Washington, D.C.: Regnery, 1999), p. 85.

230   "the Chinese were provided": Ibid.

230   "the export of advanced": Charles R. Smith, "Military Technology for Sale, Dangerous Exports to the Chinese Army," *NewsMax*, May 6, 2004, http://www.newsmax.com/archives/articles/2004/5/6/93304.shtml.

230   "offered an advanced satellite": Ibid.

230   "Hughes was charged": Ibid.

230   "When the evidence": Bill Gertz, *Betrayal: How the Clinton Administration Undermined American Security* (Washington, D.C.: Regnery, 1999), p. 135.

231   "Clinton continues to make excuses": Bill Clinton, *My Life* (New York: Knopf, 2004), p. 598.

231   "Clinton had promised": Ibid.

232   defends them by citing: Ibid., p. 939.

232   "a supporter" of his: Ibid., p. 941.

232    $450,000 to Clinton's: Ted Barrett, "Dems Say Denise Rich Helped Fund Clinton Library," *CNN*, February 9, 2001, http://www.cnn.com/2001/ALLPOLITICS/02/09/pardon.probe.

232   she gave two coffee tables: Barbara Olson, *Final Days: The Last Desperate Abuses of Power by the Clinton White House* (Washington, D.C.: Regnery, 2001), p. 66.

232   She also gave $70,000: Andrew Goldstein, "Countdown to Pardon," *CNN.com*, February 19, 2001, http://www.cnn.com/ALLPOLITICS/time/2001/02/26/countdown.html.

233   Six people died: Barbara Olson, *Final Days: The Last Desperate Abuses of Power by the Clinton White House* (Washington, D.C.: Regnery, 2001), pp. 16–17.

233   The pressure for these pardons: Dan Morgan, "First Lady Opposes Puerto Rican Clemency Offer," *Washington Post*, September 5, 1999, p. A1.

233   "the Clinton family traded": E-mail from Joseph Connor to the author, March 21, 2004.

233   The New Square Community: Barbara Olson, *Final Days: The Last Desperate Abuses of Power by the Clinton White House* (Washington, D.C.: Regnery, 2001), pp. 143–144.

234   His father gave $160,000: Ibid., p. 151.

234   he pardoned "girlfriends": Bill Clinton, *My Life* (New York: Knopf, 2004), p. 940.

234   Hillary's brothers successfully: Barbara Olson, *Final Days: The Last Desperate Abuses of Power by the Clinton White House* (Washington, D.C.: Regnery, 2001), pp. 151–153.

234   He notes that the Justice: Bill Clinton, *My Life* (New York: Knopf, 2004), p. 940.

235   But Clinton's library: Betsy Schiffman, "Long Live the Presidential Library," *Forbes.com,* June 6, 2004, http://www.forbes.com/realestate/2004/06/11/cx_bs_0611home.html.

235   "wonderfully supportive": Bill Clinton, *My Life* (New York: Knopf, 2004), p. 846.

236   "powerful people" . . . "consequence": Ibid., p. 457.

237   "did not receive any benefit": Ibid., p. 396.

238   But Clinton omits: Barbara Olson, *Hell to Pay* (Washington, D.C.: Regnery, 1999), p. 243.

238   "was anxious to get": Ibid., p. 242.

238   the former president acts: Bill Clinton, *My Life* (New York: Knopf, 2004), pp. 519–520.

238   "pressure for action": Barbara Olson, *Hell to Pay* (Washington, D.C.: Regnery, 1999), p. 242.

238   "offhand comment": Hillary Clinton, *Living History* (New York: Simon & Schuster, 1995), p. 172.

239   "we both knew that": Barbara Olson, *Hell to Pay* (Washington, D.C.: Regnery, 1999), p. 244.

239   "Mrs. Clinton's input": Media Research Center Cyber Alert, October 19, 2000, https://secure.mediaresearch.org/news/cyberalert/2000/cyb20001019.asp.

239   "Prosecutors decided not to seek": Ibid.

239   "no evidence of wrongdoing": Bill Clinton, *My Life* (New York: Knopf, 2004), p. 520.

241   That Vernon Jordan: Ann Coulter, *High Crimes and Misdemeanors: The Case Against Bill Clinton* (Washington, D.C.: Regnery, 1998), p. 33.

241   "we [Monica and I]": Ibid., p. 46.

241   "never asked [Monica Lewinsky]": Bill Clinton, *My Life* (New York: Knopf, 2004), p. 829.

241   "first, last, and always": Ibid., p. 862.

242   "their" bad conduct: Ibid., p. 837.

242   "struggle" . . . "abused the criminal": Ibid., p. 776.

243   Clinton quotes the polls: Ibid., p. 778.

244   The former president criticizes: Bill Clinton, *My Life* (New York: Knopf, 2004), p. 836.

244   But he doesn't say: Susan Schmidt, "Indictment Claims Hubbells Lived Lavishly," *Washington Post,* May 1, 1998, p. A1.

244   Clinton says that Jim McDougal: Ibid., p. 564.

245   The governor held a fund-raiser: George Carpozi Jr., *Clinton Confidential: The Climb to Power* (California: Emery Dalton Books, 1995), p. 207.

245   Clinton complains that: Bill Clinton, *My Life* (New York: Knopf, 2004), p. 571.

245   "the Clinton's took tax": "Whitewater Started as Sweetheart Deal," *CNN,* May 6, 1996, http://www.cnn.com/US/9604/13/whitewater.background.

245   Clinton denies asking David Hale: Bill Clinton, *My Life* (New York: Knopf, 2004), p. 571.

245   "Did you discuss Susan's loan?": Jim McDougal and Curtis Wilkie, *Arkansas Mischief: The Birth of a National Scandal* (New York: Holt, 1998), pp. 220–221.

245   "vested interest" in finding: Bill Clinton, *My Life* (New York: Knopf, 2004), p. 584.

246   Replying to accusations: Ibid., p. 587.

246   she testified under oath: Marilyn Rauber, "Hillary Admits Filing Records in the Shredder," *New York Post,* January 20, 1996, p. 2.

246   He characterizes the Senate: Bill Clinton, *My Life* (New York: Knopf, 2004), p. 670.

246   "unpleasant" D'Amato: Ibid.

246   Clinton repeats the hard-to-believe: "The Senate Hearings," *CNN.com,* Updated April 7, 1997, http://www.cnn.com/ALLPOLITICS/1997/gen/resources/infocus/whitewater/senate.hearings.html.

247   Asked about her legal work: Barbara Walters interview with Hillary Clinton, *ABC,* January 19, 1996.

247   Clinton criticizes Starr: Bill Clinton, *My Life* (New York: Knopf, 2004), p. 710.

247   "all about the IDC": Dick Morris with Eileen McGann, *Rewriting History* (New York: ReganBooks, 2004), p. 163.

247   He attributes Susan McDougal's: Ibid., p. 726.

247   Jim McDougal flatly writes: Jim McDougal, *Arkansas Mischief* (Holt, 1998), p. 284.

248   "spare oneself embarrassment": Bill Clinton, *My Life* (New York: Knopf, 2004), p. 839.

248   he writes that he told no one: Bill Clinton, *My Life* (New York: Knopf, 2004), p. 775.

248   "vast right wing conspiracy": Ibid., p. 776.

248   Susan Estrich told: Sean Hannity, Susan Estrich, and Dick Morris, "Analysis with Dick Morris," *Hannity & Colmes,* Fox News, June 4, 2003.

248   Clinton says that he felt badly: Bill Clinton, *My Life* (New York: Knopf, 2004), p. 779.

248   Clinton besmirches the reputation: Ibid., p. 780.

249   "parsing" how one defines: Ibid., p. 802.

249   Starr had a conflict of interest: Bill Clinton, *My Life* (New York: Knopf, 2004), p. 613.

249   Well before he became independent: Interview with Jackie Bennett, deputy to Kenneth Starr, August 16, 2004.

249   Starr went on television: Bill Clinton, *My Life* (New York: Knopf, 2004), p. 613.

249   All he did was to say: Interview with Jackie Bennett, deputy to Kenneth Starr, August 16, 2004.

249   the U.S. attorney for Arkansas: Bill Clinton, *My Life* (New York: Knopf, 2004), p. 670.

249   the comment concerned sending: Interview with Jackie Bennett, deputy to Kenneth Starr, August 16, 2004.

249   former U.S. attorney Jay Stephens: Bill Clinton, *My Life* (New York: Knopf, 2004), p. 691.

250   Stephen's recommendation was made: Interview with Jackie Bennett, deputy to Kenneth Starr, August 16, 2004.

250   Monica Lewinsky was held: Bill Clinton, *My Life* (New York: Knopf, 2004), p. 775.

250   Monica was always free: Interview with Jackie Bennett, deputy to Kenneth Starr, August 16, 2004.

250   "unconscionable conduct": Bill Clinton, *My Life* (New York: Knopf, 2004), p. 837.

251   several of them had been investigated: Ibid., p. 565.

251   And right in the middle: Ibid., p. 834.

252   he laments the damage: Ibid., p. 776.

252   Former Clinton girlfriend Sally Perdue: Carl Limbacher, "Hillary's Private Eye Arrested in Reporter Intimidation Case," *Newsmax.com*, November 23, 2002.

252   Kathleen Willey, whose tires: Brian Bloomquist, "More Mystery; As Sex Files Continue; Starr Probes Weird Willey Warnings," *New York Post*, October 4, 1998, p. 12.

252   Elizabeth Ward Grayson: Joyce Milton, *The First Partner: Hillary Rodham Clinton* (New York: Morrow, 1999), p. 226; Steve Dunleavy,

"I Was Victim of Clinton Reign of Terror," *New York Post,* September 27, 1998, p. 10.

252   Dolly Kyle Browing: Joyce Milton, *The First Partner: Hillary Rodham Clinton* (New York: Morrow, 1999), p. 225.

253   Juanita Broaddrick: Bruce Gottlieb, "What's in the Evidence Room?" *Slate Magazine,* December 30, 1998, http://slate.msn.com/id/1002010.

253   Linda Tripp: "Tripp Wiretap Case Collapses," *BBC,* May 24, 2000, http://news.bbc.co.uk/1/hi/world/americas/762661.stm.

253   "stalker": *BBC,* February 8, 1999, http://news.bbc.co.uk/1/hi/events/clinton_under_fire/latest_news/274792.stm.

253   "presidential kneepads": Carl Limbacher, "Hillary's Private Eye Arrested in Reporter Intimidation Case," *Newsmax.com,* November 23, 2002.

Chapter 12: Clinton's Legacy: The Transitional President

257   "carrying more baggage": Bill Clinton, *My Life* (New York: Knopf, 2004), p. 445.

257   "It has been absolutely fascinating": Ibid., p. 391.

Index